Christian and Muslim Dialogues

Gorgias Eastern Christian Studies

29

Series Editors

George Anton Kiraz
István Perczel
Lorenzo Perrone
Samuel Rubenson

Gorgias Eastern Christian Studies brings to the scholarly world the underrepresented field of Christianity as it developed in the Eastern hemisphere. This series consists of monographs, collections of essays, texts and translations of the documents of Eastern Christianity, and studies of topics relevant to the unique world of historic Orthodoxy and early Christianity.

Christian and Muslim Dialogues

The Religious Uses of a Literary Form in the
Early Islamic Middle East

David Bertaina

Gorgias Press LLC, 954 River Road, Piscataway, NJ, 08854, USA

www.gorgiaspress.com

Copyright © 2011 by Gorgias Press LLC

All rights reserved under International and Pan-American Copyright Conventions. No part of this publication may be reproduced, stored in a retrieval system or transmitted in any form or by any means, electronic, mechanical, photocopying, recording, scanning or otherwise without the prior written permission of Gorgias Press LLC.

2011

ISBN 978-1-61719-941-7   ISSN 1539-1507

Printed in the United States of America

Table of Contents

Table of Contents v
List of Illustrations vii
Preface ix
Acknowledgments xi
Introduction 1
    Theoretical Problems and Definitions of Dialogue 1
    The Historiographical Problem and the Lived Experience
        of Dialogue 5
    The Literary Form 8
    Book Structure 12

1   Dialogue as Christological Debate 19
    Origins 19
    Dialogue and Christology in the Bible 23
    The Melkites, Jacobites, and Church of the East 30
    Dialogue and Christology in Late Antiquity 36
    Conclusion 41

2   Dialogue as Divine Exegesis: The Case of the Qur'an 45
    Reading the Qur'an as Dialogue 45
    The Qur'an's Use of Dialogue 51
    The Qur'an's Christian Audience 53
    Dialogues with Christians in the Qur'an 61
    Conclusion 69

3   Dialogue as Conquest and Conversion 73
    Conditions for Christian Dialogue in the Aftermath of the
        Islamic Conquest 74
    Conditions for Early Muslim Dialogue with Christians 83
    John of Sedra and the Muslim Emir 87
    'Ali and the Byzantine Monk 94
    'Ali and the Patriarch 99
    'Ali and the Bishop of Najran 104

	Conclusion	106
4	Dialogue as Competing Historiographies	109
	Muhammad and the Christians of Najran	115
	The Islamic Bahira and Muhammad	120
	The Christian Sergius-Bahira and Muhammad	124
	Conclusion	130
5	Dialogue as Theological Education and Dialectic	133
	A Christian Monk of Bet Hale and an Arab Notable	138
	Patriarch Timothy and Caliph al-Mahdi	145
	Imam al-Rida and The Arab Christians	159
	Conclusion	165
6	Dialogue as Hagiography	167
	Wasil of Damascus and The Byzantine leaders	169
	Hisham ibn al-Hakam and the Patriarch Bariha	175
	Imam Musa al-Kazim and the Monk and Nun of Najran	179
	Theodore Abu Qurra Against the Outsiders	182
	Conclusion	190
7	Dialogue as Scriptural Reinterpretation	193
	Imam al-Rida and The Patriarch	195
	Abraham of Tiberias and 'Abd al-Rahman al-Hashimi	199
	Theodore Abu Qurra and Caliph al-Ma'mun	212
	Conclusion	228
8	The End of Dialogue?	231
	Elias of Nisibis and George the Monk	231
	Significant Themes of Christian Dialogues	236
	Significant Themes of Muslim Dialogues	241
	From Creation to Collation	245
Bibliography		249
Index		276

LIST OF ILLUSTRATIONS

Figure 1. Map of the Medieval Islamic World. viii
Figure 2. Theodore Abu Qurra and al-Ma'mun. Illustrated by the Rt. Rev. Mark Melone. xii
Figure 3. A Hagiographical Portrait of Theodore Abu Qurra. Illustrated by the Rt. Rev. Mark Melone. 192

Figure 1. Map of the Medieval Islamic World.

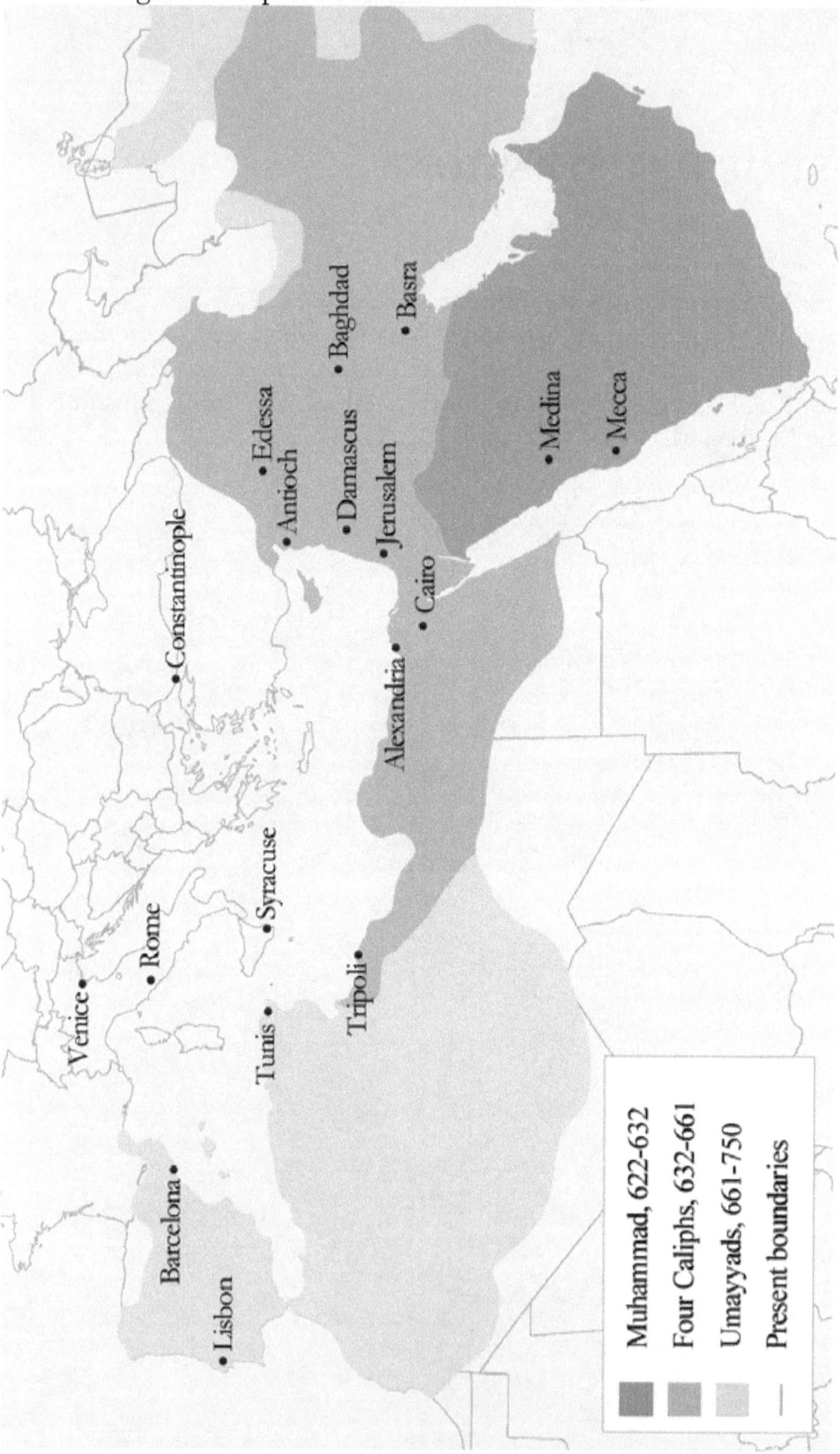

PREFACE

This book is the product of several years of research and teaching about the history of Christian-Muslim encounters. When acquaintances hear about my specialty, they are much more interested in the question of its relevance for contemporary affairs. My hope is that past events and our historical interpretations have intrinsic worth for the reader. I also hope that the reader finds value in understanding the origins, development, and continuity (or discontinuity) between pre-modern and modern forms of dialogue.

Since the intended readership for this book includes both the specialist and non-specialist, I have chosen to leave out diacritical marks, typically used to transliterate Arabic, from the body of the text. The presence of macrons and dots on the page, while correct transliteration, distracts the eye and can be detrimental to reading comprehension. Moreover, those who read Arabic will have no trouble in understanding the words without the diacritical marks. My concern for clarity on behalf of the uninitiated served as my primary guide in this decision. For quotations from the Qur'an, I have based my translations upon my own reading of the Arabic and the translations done by Majid Fakhry in *An Interpretation of the Qur'an*. For quotations from the Bible, I have used the Revised Standard Version.

David Bertaina

Acknowledgments

It is with great satisfaction that I would like to acknowledge the institutions and people who made the completion of this book possible. Sidney Griffith was the guiding force behind this topic, and it could not have been written without his advice and contributions to the field of Christian Arabic studies. I am also grateful to The Catholic University of America and the use of their Semitics ICOR library. Shawqi Talia, Monica Blanchard, and Michael O'Connor were all helpful in the early stages of writing the manuscript. The Bibliotheca Apostolica Vaticana graciously provided me with me with a copy of one of their manuscripts. The University of Illinois Springfield was also generous in giving me a course reduction to allow time to edit this work. I would like to thank the librarians who procured books and articles for me during the latter half of my research. Father Mark Melone created beautiful iconography for the book as well.

A number of friends and colleagues were instrumental in improving the text by offering comments and suggestions on the manuscript, including Aaron Berkowitz, Wendy Bignami, James Bockmier, Sebastian Carnazzo, John Lamoreaux, Gabriel Said Reynolds, and Peter Shapinksy. Their contributions helped me clarify a number of issues and avoid several mistakes in the process of completing the book; any remaining ones are solely my responsibility. I would also like to thank Andrew Bertaina and Vicki Bertaina, who helped me clarify my ideas to non-specialists. My students and colleagues at the University of Illinois Springfield were also supportive in helping me revise the work. Katie Stott at Gorgias Press helped me prepare and format the text. Most of all, I offer gracious thanks to my wife Cheryl and our children Joseph and Anna, who gave me love, support, insights, and stability during my time writing, editing and revising the book. To them I present my love and gratitude.

Figure 2. Theodore Abu Qurra and al-Ma'mun. Illustrated by the Rt. Rev. Mark Melone.

Introduction

Theoretical Problems and Definitions of Dialogue

Most supporters of religious dialogue today are not fond of the early history of Muslim and Christian encounters. According to the common narrative, the legacies of Jihad and Crusade are products of the past that must be overcome through dialogue which eschews rhetorical and physical confrontation. Even the textual history of dialogue encounters, when relegated to the genre of disputation, is depicted as an embarrassing past that offers no insight for contemporary dialogue. However, I wish to challenge the contemporary historiography of religious dialogue, which is an Enlightenment creation, in which dialogue functions as an elaboration of liberal tolerance and ecumenical mutual understanding. The Enlightenment attempt to divorce pre-modern and modern forms of dialogue fails to show that contemporary dialogue has its own forms of religious conflict and ways of accommodating and resisting dialogue. I would argue, rather, that the notion of religious dialogue is part of a long history stretching back to Platonic philosophical usage, Aristotelian dialectic, Middle Eastern poetry, and medieval religious debate. In problematizing the theory of dialogue as a modern creation, we can recover the potential for understanding the organic connection of modern dialogue with medieval apologetics, polemics, and disputations. These methods are also legitimate forms of religious dialogue.

My purpose is not to project liberal assumptions of dialogue back into the seventh century in an attempt to rehabilitate pre-modern Christian-Muslim encounters. Rather, I argue that beneath our contemporary assumptions of tolerance, there are forms of continuity between early medieval Christian and Muslim dialogue and contemporary discourses. For instance, pre-modern and modern forms of dialogue recognize the reality of religious pluralism.

Both dialogues provide examples of polite, theological, and respectful discussions. Both forms of dialogue are likewise apologetic and polemical. The primary difference is that pre-modern forms of dialogue tend to make this agenda explicit, whereas many contemporary forms of dialogue, despite claims of neutrality and tolerance, have their own subtle polemics, partisan assumptions, and ideologies. The reality of power relations, patronage, and asymmetrical relationships in modern religious dialogues are minimized or often ignored. There is continuity between pre-modern and contemporary forms of Christian-Muslim dialogue because each group accepts the necessity of dialogue while insisting on religious difference. However, there can be no such thing as a successful religious dialogue based on liberal preconceptions of tolerance and respect. Christians and Muslims do not hold to a unified doctrine or practice, but are individuals in communities committed to fundamentally different truth claims about how God has entered history and irrevocably communicated his signs of divine authority and knowledge. This is why contemporary dialogue tends to focus not on matters of faith, but on matters of liberal reason promoted as common moral issues. This type of dialogue has produced important collaborations between groups on social issues, moral values, economic development, and the promotion of peace. But in another sense, liberal dialogue attempts to make meaningful things seem insignificant, such as religious truth claims, while it emphasizes things which tolerant liberalism finds meaningful, or at least innocuous to the power of the secular nation-state.

One considerable point of discontinuity between pre-modern and modern forms of dialogue is the end (*telos*) of dialogue. For pre-modern believers, dialogue required an alliance of faith and reason in partnership. Dialogue was meant to encourage ways of thinking that incorporated the traditions of rational thinking found in Christianity or Islam, without a relativist perception to mitigate their universal claims. The purpose of dialogue, for them, was that their beliefs would prevail. According to this view, dialogue only failed when the discussion partners missed the point of a truth communicated to them. On the other hand, the teleological end of modern liberal dialogue is not persuasion, but the dialogue itself. In the realm of modern dialogue, competing religious views are guaranteed equal access but likewise prohibited from making claims to being more reasonable or truthful. Thus, under the guise of being neutral and tolerant, modern dialogue acts in a partisan and exclusionary fashion. From this perspective, dialogue is a creedal faith commitment. It functions as a therapy meant to redeem religious groups from their commitments to objective truth and persuasion. In other words, liberal dialogue emphasizes not the content of what is expressed but rather the form of dialogue itself. From this viewpoint, the action of expressing oneself is meaningful, rather than the content of that expression.

While pre-modern and modern forms of dialogue differ in their assumptions, there is one striking similarity between pre-modern forms of dialogue and some critics of liberal dialogue. The continuity lies in their mutual distrust of another institution (the policies of the caliphate, or the state policies of secular liberalism) serving as the sole adjudicator of dialogue based upon its notions of tolerance and neutrality. Many Christians living under Islamic law and Muslims living under secular liberal states have found these forms of "neutrality" and "tolerance" to be oppressive. If these matters are to be taken seriously, we must assess the past forms of dialogue and how they might inform contemporary understandings of dialogue. Dialogue that does not take seriously the truth claims of its participants in matters of faith and reason becomes simply another ideology (dialogue as an end in itself), rather than a means to fulfill epistemic commitments such as that of Christians to evangelization and Muslims to mission (*da'wa*). Religious dialogue depends upon intellectual differences, differing goals, and openness to conversion. For these reasons, the study of the religious uses of dialogue in the early Islamic Middle East is a worthwhile endeavor.

A second theoretical problem this book challenges is the concept of an impermeable boundary between real interreligious conversations during the early Islamic Middle East and the actual dialogues that survive in texts. While it is true that discussions have a spontaneous characteristic in contrast to the crafted literary form of dialogue, I argue that this model creates an unnecessary bifurcation of intellectual production and lived practice. These two qualities informed one another in the spiritual writings of Muslim and Christian authors who shared in the dialogical exchanges of texts and readings through participation in the literary world of the medieval Middle East. The literary dialogues were a product of those experiences of time and place, and they merit due consideration, within proper historical contexts, as dialogues in their own right.

The process of dialogue in the medieval period, and the dialogue texts representing this process, can be read as part of a religious polyphony that mutually shaped Christians and Muslims. The event of dialogue itself speaks to the complementary and crosspollinating relationship between Christian and Muslim communities. Dialogue texts are not only intellectual abstractions written down on paper. They are embodied words belonging to the writer, readers, listeners, and interpreters who participated in dynamic and living exchanges from one person to another.

The concept of shared exchange contrasts with models that argue for the dualistic "self/other" in reconstructing Christian and Islamic identities during the early medieval period. For these authors, Christians and Muslims erected theoretical and real boundaries to separate and isolate each group from the other. They argue that each group developed primarily in antithesis to the other, and interactions were limited to polemical clashes, misunderstandings, or cultural constructions. Claiming that there was an immediate parting of the ways between the communities, they assert that dialogues are imaginary fabrications that supported the internal cohesion of a single community and reflect no real engagement. According to this theory, historians will only find value in Christian-Muslim encounters insofar as they signify self-definition and difference.

The arguments for self-identity and differentiation are certainly valuable. However, explaining difference is not always a clear matter, but it is dependent upon such factors as time and place. Rather than advocating a model dependent on the language of boundary and partition, I propose that we can narrate more fruitfully with models that acknowledge dialogue as an inherent part of Christian and Muslim identity. Christian and Muslim texts, beliefs, and practices continued to be relevant to one another from the seventh century well into the medieval period. The relationships between Muslims and Christians did not diverge quickly or clearly: the confessional communities embodied real connections with one another at the levels of written and oral communication. For instance, Arab Christians had a nuanced relation with Arab Muslims based upon their shared ethnic, social, linguistic, and cultural ideals. Sometimes these individuals and communities identified more closely with their Arab colleagues than their western Christian counterparts. These realities facilitated dialogues that were multiple and incongruous discourses that projected outward while internalizing the religious other. In short, the history presented here discloses how Muslim and Christian communal identities were contingent upon dialogue and interaction from the Qur'an to the time leading up to the Crusades.

THE HISTORIOGRAPHICAL PROBLEM AND THE LIVED EXPERIENCE OF DIALOGUE

Contemporary historians have become increasingly aware of the challenges in interpreting the historical and cultural context of formative Islam due to the many competing methods that seek to account for its development. Scholars of Islamic origins remain at odds over the interpretation of the earliest centuries of the Islamic communities, largely because they cannot agree on the authority of the sources that claim to document the rise of Islam in the seventh century. Recently, some scholars have described the early Islamic Believers' movement through a process of differentiation. Instead of using a normative model of divinely-inspired history, they employ a model where early Islamic Believers exhibited growing self-awareness through their encounters with the ideas and practices of other monotheistic believers.[1] While some paradigms assume that Islamic communities developed as a result of a reformulated system in light of the pre-Islamic Arabian social milieu, or that Islam was the product of a unique (and divinely-inspired) history, other models posit that nascent Islamic thought and practice gradually developed in response to religious conversations with Christian (Orthodox Melkite, West-Syrian Jacobite, and East-Syrian Church of the East), Jewish, and pagan communities. The study of dialogue literature in this book avoids Islamic exceptionalism, which argues that Islam emerged as a fully-elaborated system by the death of Muhammad, hermetically sealed from its historical context in the Mid-

---

[1] On the developing historical awareness of Islamic communities, see Fred Donner, *Muhammad and the Believers: At the Origins of Islam* (Cambridge, MA: The Belknap Press of Harvard University Press, 2010); and Fred Donner, *Narratives of Islamic Origins: The Beginnings of Islamic Historical Writing* (Princeton, NJ: Darwin Press, 1998).

dle East.² Recognizing the realities of historical development and using literary dialogues as a guide, we learn that Muslims and Christians did not go through an immediate parting of ways intellectually or socially. Instead, Muslim and Christian individuals were often ambivalent and unsure of their relation to one another and were willing to adopt or share in common ideas and practices of other believers. In this context, a clear understanding of the intellectual, social, and political history of the early Islamic Middle East is required for understanding dialogue literature. Examining how Muslims and Christians employed the literary genre reveals the development of their own doctrines in tandem – together they challenged each other's ideas and their historical and truth claims. Dialogues are therefore a fruitful area for understanding the early history of Islamic communities in the religiously plural Middle East.

I also argue that Christian-Muslim dialogue was a significant feature in the construction of early Islamic and Christian social identities, since they shared a common worldview of divinely-inspired Scripture (in the widest sense of the term), and they both appropriated biblical and qur'anic models for elaborating faith and practice.³ For instance, Middle Eastern Christians and Muslims interacted in a contact zone through their interpretations of dialogue texts. As different Christian and Muslim writers shared in the practice of constructing dialogues, their works intersected and overlapped one another in their use of familiar sources, languages, and theologies. Authors engaged in the complex and unregulated

---

² On approaches to Islamic history, see Chase Robinson, "Reconstructing Early Islam: Truth and Consequences," in *Method and Theory in the Study of Islamic Origins*, ed. Herbert Berg (Leiden: Brill, 2003), 101-134. On the topic of exceptionalism, see especially 128-134. For a survey of controversial issues in the academic field, see Adam Silverstein, *Islamic History: A Very Short Introduction* (Oxford: Oxford University Press, 2010), 80-107.

³ See for instance the work of Uri Rubin, *Between Bible and Qur'an: The Children of Israel and the Islamic Self-Image* (Princeton: Darwin Press, 1999); Uri Rubin, *The Eye of the Beholder: The Life of Muhammad as viewed by the Early Muslims* (Princeton, NJ: Darwin Press, 1995); and Uri Rubin, "Prophets and Caliphs: The Biblical Foundations of the Umayyad Authority," 73-99.

process of engaging other individuals, communities, texts, concepts, and practices through the literary form with shared assumptions about the ways in which dialogue communicated their worldview and place in history.

The present work examines the history of encounters between Christians and Muslims through two levels of dialogue. On a literary level, the dialogue form is dependent upon the skills of the composer, the receptivity of its readers, and the influence of ideas on the wider culture. We can study these texts, their readers, and their interpretations to learn about the ways in which Christians and Muslims constructed figures and concepts using dialogues. In most cases, the audience belonged to the author's community. Some Christian authors used popular discourse to depict witty heroes responding to provocative questions that reflected an imagined discussion partner. On a historical level, the dialogue form can be used as a tool for comprehending the social implications of religious interaction between Muslims and Christians in the early medieval Middle East. Christians and Muslims wrote dialogues because they reflected part of their personal experience. At the literary level, the dialogue form may not have demonstrated significant or real engagement. In historical terms, the fact that Christians and Muslims took the time and effort to recall interreligious encounters reveals an authentic concern, even mutual dependence, on making sense of one's community in tandem with other communities.[4]

The themes outlined in this book are not meant to form a complete or comprehensive model for the uses of dialogue. The study of medieval Christian and Muslim dialogues reveals the political, socio-cultural, and religious particulars that shaped encounters between individuals of diverse social standing, communal identity, and geographical location. Encounters through shared sociocultural environments indicate that there were many ambiguities between communities. Recognizing the diversity of groups among Christians (Melkites, Jacobites, Church of the East) and Muslims

---

[4] See also Sidney Griffith, *The Church in the Shadow of the Mosque: Christians and Muslims in the World of Islam* (Princeton: Princeton University Press, 2008), 39, 100-103.

(proto-Sunni and Shi'ite groups), this book explores a wide range of textual encounters at various points of intersection and sites of conversation, while analyzing the dynamism of this dialogue and the resulting crosspollinations.[5]

THE LITERARY FORM

The literary form of dialogue used by Muslims and Christians in the Islamic Middle East repeated longstanding traditions that had their origins in the earliest periods of Christianity and Islam. In the formation of communal discourse, early Christians sought to distinguish their faith and practices according to their belief in Jesus Christ as the Messiah as well as to verify Christianity as the fulfillment of messianic expectation. They sought to attain their goals through discussions with rival Jewish groups and Hellenistic pagans while seeking to supplant their ways of life.[6] By the time that Islam arose in the seventh century, Eastern Christians had developed an established structure for religious discussions that utilized models found in the Old Testament, New Testament, and patristic theological reflection. In the same fashion, early Muslims sought to differentiate their submission to God and the uniqueness of their prophet Muhammad from the beliefs and observances of the Jews and Christians in Arabia and the Meccan polytheists by way of apologetic and polemical discourses. These discourses acknowledged and employed some of the ideas of other religious communities. Many verses of the Qur'an are products of these conversations which acclaimed the superiority of the one God within a religious-

---

[5] For resources on these topics, see David Thomas and Barbara Roggema, eds., *Christian-Muslim Relations: A Bibliographical History, Volume One (600-900)* (Leiden: Brill, 2009); and Georg Graf, *Geschichte der Christlichen Arabischen Literatur*, 5 vols. (Vatican City: Biblioteca apostolica vaticana, 1944-1953).

[6] See Leonard Rutgers, *Making Myths: Jews in Early Christian Identity Formation* (Leuven: Peeters, 2009). Rutgers argues that while Jewish scriptural thinking was co-opted by Christian biblical interpretation in the literary realm, Christians were also converting synagogues into churches in the material realm.

ly-competitive context. By the beginning of the Abbasid period (750-1258), Muslim intellectuals made use of conventional patterns of debate established in the Qur'an and early Islamic traditions as a source for interreligious dialogue and interpreting confessional identities. This process of dialogue represents a crucial understanding of how Christians and Muslims lived, thought, and acted. The dialogues in Christian and Muslim scriptures were foundational components for subsequent religious literature and for forming identity in relationship to others.[7]

During the formative period of Islam, authors attempted to construct logical and revelatory models for commending the truth of their religion to other communities. To do this, Muslim and Christian writers experimented with various methods of composition. Many religious intellectuals selected the literary genre of dialogue as a means of communicating the fundamental concepts of their respective religions.[8] They wrote dialogues that functioned on two levels: first, as systematic, philosophical and theological discussions, or second, as popular, apologetic and entertaining debates. Some texts functioned on both levels. Muslim and Christian writers considered the dialogue form vital for several reasons: to acclaim the truth of their positions, reinforce orthodoxy, provide rhetorical entertainment and instruction, protect the integrity of their scriptures, beliefs, and practices, and to criticize the veracity of religious

---

[7] See Fred Donner, "From Believers to Muslims: Confessional Self-Identity in the Early Islamic Community," *Al-Abhath* 50-51 (2002-2003): 9-53.

[8] The terms "dialogue," "literary dialogue," and "dialogue text" are used interchangeably throughout this text since religious authors of the medieval period used the same form regardless of the content of their compositions. One reason for avoiding the use of the term "disputation" is that some texts are free of polemical rancor. More importantly, the term moves the reader away from the Enlightenment concept that dialogue is a modern tolerant construct while pre-modern discourse is an inherently polemical endeavor.

opponents' arguments. Through dialogue texts, they transformed and determined the patterns of interreligious conversation.[9]

Many writers depicted religious conversations in an authentic fashion to add verisimilitude to the discussion. Dialogues were literary examples of the real debates that took place between various intellectuals on matters of interest to the communities. Historically, these conversations are part of the well-known tradition of medieval Islamic culture. Muslim leaders patronized such dialogues because they added to their prestige while providing entertainment for the court. Within this culture of dialogue, the speakers would address one another in front of the audience. They followed a detailed form of conduct for debate and for determining the victor. One speaker would serve as the questioner while the other discussion partner would serve as the respondent. Since the initiator could ask leading questions, they were considered to have the advantage in the dialogue. The respondent would have the privilege of more time to speak and offer evidence. Victory was dependent upon responding to the questioner, or being reduced to silence. The prominence of courtly debate culture in literary dialogues is another indicator of their connection to the lived experience of the medieval Middle East.

Christian and Muslim authors wrote within this framework with similar intents and purposes. While the formal construction of literary dialogues was similar, the content varied depending upon the needs of the author. Formally, writers employed dialogues as a means by which they could extol or criticize particular matters, without the hazard of speaking publicly in an adversarial atmosphere. Dialogues also conveyed authors' theological perspectives and objectives to the reader. For instance, composers of debate texts employed scriptural reasoning in order to communicate their principles to their audience. Scriptural reasoning means three different methods of engagement: using the Bible or Qur'an as a

---

[9] For a historical survey of Christian-Muslim dialogue and authors, see Jean-Marie Gaudeul, *Encounters & Clashes: Islam and Christianity in History*, 2 vols. (Rome: Pontificio istituto di studi arabi e d'islamistica, 2000).

model for argumentation, using the Bible or Qur'an as a starting point for a dialectical argument, or using the Bible or Qur'an as evidence to support rational claims. Dialectic, which is the use of philosophical and logical argumentation in a conversation between a questioner and a respondent, was another important instrument for interreligious discussion. Dialectical reasoning complemented the authority of Scripture and tradition in discerning the true religion and served to point out poor arguments.[10] Dialogue texts functioned simultaneously as a religious and socio-political discourse that focused on defeating the opponent. Through dialogue, the authors intellectually validated and defended their positions while critiquing their opponent's worldview.

The literary form served as a vehicle for memory-making among the Christian and Islamic communities of the medieval Middle East. The reminiscence of an intellectual conquest was a testimony and means of empowerment for the community. Christian encounters with Muslims prompted a new form of minority historiography: literary debates produced narratives of hagiographical heroes who bore witness to future hope.[11] Depictions of historical figures offered examples of power in contrast to the communi-

---

[10] Dialectic signifies the art of philosophical and logical conversation while debating an issue. Christian-Muslim literary dialogues utilized dialectic as a method of scrutinizing broad abstract ideas derived from the analysis of particulars. Not all Christian-Muslim literary dialogues used dialectic. Some authors exploited the methods of sophistical logic or inductive reasoning to achieve their ends. For a broader description of this method, see Jan Beckmann, "Dialektik," in *Lexicon für Theologie und Kirche*, ed. Michael Buchberger and Walter Kasper (Breisgau: Herder, 1995), 3:188-189.

[11] Georg Graf made this point in his article on early Christian Arabic works. See Georg Graf, "Christliche Polemik gegen den Islam," *Gelbe Heft: Historisch und Politische Blätter für das Katholische Deutschland* 2 (1926): 825-842. More recent work has called attention to the language of memory as a sociological device for culture making, such as in the work of Elizabeth Castelli, *Martyrdom and Memory: Early Christian Culture Making* (New York: Columbia University Press, 2004).

ty's perceived impotence. The texts sought to develop a relationship between the victorious debater and the sympathetic reader.

Contemporary interpretive models of dialogue emphasize how such literature might be understood meaningfully in terms of Christian-Muslim relations. Christian and Muslim authors commended their theological positions through dialogic techniques that provided their own worldview within the context of their religious interlocutors' language. For instance, Christian authors utilized dialogues to define themselves and their communities within the Islamic cultural environment and within the context of the Arabic Qur'an. They shared literary forms as well as scriptural and philosophical presuppositions with their Muslim conversation partners.[12] Thus, identity was not only tied up in confessional circles so much as in the dynamic discourse itself, the back-and-forth that occurred between individuals and communities in this process of crosspollination and mutual discovery.[13]

BOOK STRUCTURE

There are a number of dialogues commemorating early medieval encounters between Christian and Muslim groups. More than twenty texts written in Arabic and Syriac (Christian Aramaic) from the seventh century to the eleventh century have been preserved, with the likely possibility that more are yet to be discovered.[14] This

---

[12] For an introduction this context, see Sidney Griffith, *The Church in the Shadow of the Mosque*, 129-155.

[13] For more on the concept of relational crosspollination between Islam and Christianity from a historiographical and theoretical viewpoint, see the article by James M. Montgomery, "Islamic Crosspollinations," in *Islamic Crosspollinations: Interactions in the Medieval Middle East*, ed. Anna Akasoy, James E. Montgomery, and Peter Pormann (Exeter: Gibb Memorial Trust, 2007), 148-193.

[14] For a complete list of Christian-Muslim dialogues see David Thomas and Barbara Roggema, eds., *Christian-Muslim Relations*. See also Robert Caspar, et al, "Bibliographie du dialogue islamo-chrétien," *Islamochristiana* 1 (1975): 125-181; 2 (1976): 187-249; 3 (1977): 255-286; 4 (1978): 247-267; 5 (1979): 299-317; 6 (1980): 259-299; 7 (1981): 299-307.

book provides a survey of this material and analyzes the religious uses of the literary form. Each chapter focuses on a particular purpose for which writers composed dialogue texts.

The first chapter, "Dialogue as Christological Debate," examines the various literary forms employed for dialogues. This classification of form and content reveals how authors communicated their ideas using dialogue. In terms of purpose, why write dialogues? In terms of agency, who wrote dialogues? In terms of utility, what was the value of the literary form for its author and readers? In terms of form and content, how did dialogues change over time? Then the chapter offers a brief overview of the literary genre and its features, moving from biblical uses of dialogue to its use for Christological debates until the seventh century. These developments offer several conclusions about pre-Islamic Christian approaches to other religions using the literary form.

The second chapter, "Dialogue as Divine Exegesis," traces the history and significance of dialogues in the Qur'an in the early seventh century. For the Qur'an, dialogue functioned as a divine exegesis of biblical and theological topics, working on multiple levels between divine authority, prophet, righteous believers, and skeptical questioners. The chapter highlights the significance of the Qur'an's relationship to the Jews and Christians in the context of these exchanges. Finally, the chapter considers the relationship between qur'anic dialogues and Christian Christological argumentation and the way the Qur'an internalizes Christian thought and practice in its own image to establish conventional forms of discourse with religious others.

The third chapter, "Dialogue as Conquest and Conversion," examines the literary form as a response to the Islamic conquest and an explanation of Christian conversion to Islam. The chapter provides an analysis of the religious challenges of the Islamic conquest to the end of the Umayyad period (634-750). The section examines the conditions for Christian discussion with nascent Islamic communities and the situations available for early Muslim

---

Islamochristiana notes new editions and manuscripts of texts as they are published.

conversation with Christians. These historical developments offer several conclusions about Christian and Muslim approaches to other religions and how to interpret dialogue as a historical phenomenon. The following section analyzes a dialogue that commemorates a meeting between the Christian Patriarch John and a Muslim emir soon after the Islamic conquest.[15] Then the chapter examines three Shi'ite dialogues which commemorate early conversations between 'Ali and Christian leaders in the context of conversion to Islam.[16]

The fourth chapter, "Dialogue as Competing Historiographies," examines how Muslims and Christians used the literary form of dialogue to reconstruct images of the Prophet and his relationship to Christians and their doctrines. After the Qur'an, the oldest Islamic dialogues between Muslim characters and Christians belong to the eighth-century biographical accounts of the life of Muhammad. Composed by Muhammad Ibn Ishaq (d. ca. 767) and transmitted via Ibn Hisham (d. ca. 833), one story depicts Christian Arab leaders from Najran in conversation with Muhammad.[17] The

---

[15] The latest edition is in Michael Penn, "John and the Emir: A New Introduction, Edition and Translation," *Le Muséon* 121 (2008): 65-91. See also an edition and English translation by Abdul-Massih Saadi, "The Letter of John of Sedreh: A New Perspective on Nascent Islam," *Karmo* 1/1 (1998): 18-31 (Arabic and Syriac); and 1/2 (1999): 46-64 (English). An earlier study and text was produced by François Nau, "Un colloque du patriarche Jean avec l'émir des Agaréens et faits divers des années 712 à 716 d'après le ms. du British Museum Add. 17193," *Journal Asiatique* 11/5 (1915): 225-279. For an English translation of Nau's text, see N. A. Newman, ed., *The Early Christian-Muslim Dialogue: A Collection of Documents from the First Three Islamic Centuries, 632-900 A.D.; Translations with Commentary* (Hatfield, PA: Interdisciplinary Biblical Research Institute, 1993), 7-46.

[16] See the chapter on 'Ali's discussions with Christians in Muhammad Baqir ibn Muhammad Taqi al-Majlisi, *Bihar al-Anwar al-Jami'a li-Durar Akhbar al-A'imma al-athar*, 4 vols. (Beirut: Dar al-Fiqh lil-Tiba'ah wa-al-Nashr, 1421/2001), 4:247-258.

[17] See the English translation in Alfred Guillaume, *The Life of Muhammad: A Translation of Ishaq's Sirat Rasul Allah* (London: Oxford University Press, 1955, reprint 2006), 270-272. For the Arabic text, see

chapter also examines a popular story found in both Christian and Muslim narratives, which imagines an encounter between Muhammad and a Christian monk named Sergius-Bahira.[18]

The fifth chapter, "Dialogue as Theological Education and Dialectic," reveals how Christians and Muslims used the literary form as part of their education systems. Dialogues helped to explain doctrine, provide answers to critics' questions, and employ philosophical dialectic. The chapter begins with an analysis of the early eighth-century Syriac dialogue between the Monk of Bet Hale and an Arab notable.[19] Then the work examines the use of rational argumentation in the discussion between Patriarch Timothy of the Church of the East and the caliph al-Mahdi in 781.[20] Some dia-

---

Ibn Hisham, *Al-Sirat al-Nabawiyya*, ed. Mustafa al-Saqqa et al., 4 vols. (Beirut: al-Maktabat al-'Ilmiya, 1990), 2:162-163.

[18] There are several versions of the story in Syriac and Arabic, among other languages. For the latest editions and English translations, see Barbara Roggema, *The Legend of Sergius Bahira: Eastern Christian Apologetics and Apocalyptic in Response to Islam* (Leiden: Brill, 2009). Roggema completed a meticulous study of four different recensions of the Sergius-Bahira material.

[19] There is no complete edition and translation available of this text, although there are several studies. See Gerrit Reinink, "Bible and Qur'an in early Syriac Christian-Islamic Disputation," in *Christians and Muslims in Dialogue in the Islamic Orient of the Middle Ages*, ed. Martin Tamcke (Beirut: Ergon Verlag, 2007), 57-72; Gerrit Reinink, "Political Power and Right Religion in the East Syrian Disputation between a Monk of Bet Hale and an Arab Notable," in *The Encounter of Eastern Christianity with Early Islam*, eds. Emmanouela Grypeou, Mark Swanson and David Thomas (Leiden: Brill, 2006), 153-169; Sidney Griffith, "Disputing with Islam in Syriac: The Case of the Monk of Bet Hale and a Muslim Emir," *Hugoye: Journal of Syriac Studies* 3/1 (2000): 1-19. It is also available online at the website: http://syrcom.cua.edu/Hugoye/Vol3No1/HV3N1Griffith.html.

[20] A Syriac manuscript and English translation were published by Alphonse Mingana, ed., "The Apology of Timothy the Patriarch before the Caliph Mahdi," *Bulletin of the John Rylands Library* 12/1 (1928): 137-298. Arabic versions of the encounter, which were likely translated from the Syriac, have also been published by Louis Cheikho, "Al-Muhawara al-diniya allati jarat bayna al-khalifa al-Mahdi wa Timotheus al-jathaliq," *al-Machriq* 19 (1921): 359-374, 408-418; Hans Putman, *L'église et l'islam sous*

logues between the eighth Imam ʿAli ibn Musa al-Rida (d. 818) and Arab Christians reveal Islamic interest in dialectic.[21]

The sixth chapter, "Dialogue as Hagiography," looks at the literary genre as a form of rhetorical enjoyment and memory making for the heroes of Muslim and Christian communities. One account magnifies Wasil of Damascus in a discussion with Byzantine leaders.[22] The Shiʿite tradition also includes some Muslim-Christian dialogues acclaiming Hisham ibn al-Hakam and a Christian patriarch named Bariha who converts to Islam.[23] The Imam Musa al-Kazim was commemorated in his wise responses to a monk and a nun from Najran. Finally, several short Arabic dialogues belonging to Theodore Abu Qurra recognize his charismatic personality while engaging in debate at the court of Caliph al-Maʾmun.[24]

The seventh chapter, "Dialogue as Scriptural Reinterpretation," examines the new and creative ways Muslims and Christians placed their communities within another scriptural worldview. The ninth-century imam al-Rida presented some innovative biblical criticism to his Christian discussion partner in one dialogue. Abraham of Tiberias reinterpreted the Qurʾan in light of Christian theology

---

Timothée I (780-823): étude sur l'église nestorienne au temps des premiers ʿAbbasides; avec nouvelle édition et traduction du Dialogue entre Timothée et al-Mahdi (Beirut: Dar el-Machreq [distribution, Librairie orientale], 1975).

[21] These dialogues are in Muhammad Baqir al-Majlisi, *Bihar al-Anwar*, 4:404-434. An English translation for one of them is available in David Thomas, "Two Muslim-Christian Debates from the Early Shiʿite Tradition," *Journal of Semitic Studies* 33 (1988): 53-80.

[22] Sidney Griffith, "Bashir/Beser: Boon Companion of the Byzantine Emperor Leo III; the Islamic Recension of His Story in Leiden Oriental Ms 951 (2)," *Le Muséon*, 103 (1990): 293-327. Griffith's study, edition and translation were reprinted as the eleventh chapter in Sidney Griffith, *The Beginnings of Christian Theology in Arabic: Muslim-Christian Encounters in the Early Islamic Period* (Aldershot: Variorum, 2002).

[23] This article includes a translation as well as the dialogue mentioned above from al-Rida. See David Thomas, "Two Muslim-Christian Debates from the Early Shiʿite Tradition," 53-80.

[24] John Lamoreaux is presently working on a study, edition and translation of this ninth-century work entitled *Against the Outsiders*.

during a dialogue in Jerusalem around 820.²⁵ Finally, the debate of Theodore Abu Qurra with Muslim dialectical theologians at the court of caliph al-Ma'mun, held in the year 829, is a prominent example of how Christians had come to use qur'anic sources to commend their particular religious worldview.²⁶ The interpretive framework illustrates how dialogues redefined the community's orthodoxy and promoted the reinterpretation of qur'anic and biblical material in order to praise religious truth. These features highlight the ways in which religious encounters shaped social identity through the dynamism of dialogue.

The conclusion, "The End of Dialogue," examines the texts of the eleventh to thirteenth centuries leading up to the Crusades, when the use of the dialogue form began to decrease. Elias of Nisibis (d. 1046), a Metropolitan for the Church of the East, wrote down seven discussions between himself and the Muslim vizier Abu al-Qasim al-Husayn ibn 'Ali al-Maghribi (d. 1027).²⁷ During

---

²⁵ The critical edition and French translation are available in Giacinto Bulus Marcuzzo, *Le Dialogue d'Abraham de Tibériade avec 'Abd al-Rahman al-Hashimi à Jérusalem vers 820* (Rome: Pontificia Universitas Lateranensis, 1986). An English translation, made from a German translation prior to the critical edition, was published by N. A. Newman, ed., *The Early Christian-Muslim Dialogue*, 269-353. The German edition was made by Kurt Vollers, "Das Religionsgespräch von Jerusalem (Um 800 D) aus dem Arabischen Übersetzt," *Zeitschrift für Kirchengeschichte* 29 (1908): 29-71, 197-221.

²⁶ An English translation of the critical edition is available in Wafik Nasry, *The Caliph and the Bishop: A 9th Century Muslim-Christian Debate: Al-Ma'mun and Abu Qurrah* (Beirut: CEDRAC, 2008).

²⁷ New critical editions of most of the dialogues have been published by Samir Khalil Samir, "Deux cultures qui s'affrontent: une controverse sur l'i'rab au XI. siècle entre Elie de Nisibe et le vizir Abu l-Qasim," *Mélanges de l'Université Saint-Joseph* 49 (1975/1976): 619-649; Samir Khalil Samir, "La réfutation de l'astrologie par Élie de Nisibe," *Orientalia Christiana Periodica* 43 (1977): 408-440; Samir Khalil Samir, "Le Premier Entretien d'Élie de Nisibe avec le vizir al-Maġribi sur l'Unité et la Trinité," *Islamochristiana* 5 (1979): 31-117; Samir Khalil Samir, "Langue arabe, logique et théologie chez Élie de Nisibe," *Mélanges de l'Université Saint-Joseph* 52 (1991/1992): 229-367; Samir Khalil Samir, *Foi et Culture en Irak au XIe*

the Crusader period, George the monk entered a dialogue with Muslim scholars in Aleppo, Syria. The chapter highlights some of the most significant themes in the literary form. Dialogues were accounts of hope for future generations, teaching tools for their audience, apologetics for students, vehicles of empowerment for minority historiographies, entertaining stories that inculcated socio-cultural values, and stories that prevented or encouraged conversion to other religious communities. The literary form sheds considerable light on the history of Christian-Muslim encounters, particularly in illustrating the relationship between the communities and identity formation in the early medieval Middle East. On close inspection, Christian and Muslim dialogues from the early Islamic Middle East can serve as both a guide and a warning about the religious uses of dialogue.

---

siècle: Elie de Nisibe et l'Islam (Aldershot, England: Variorum, 1996); Samir Khalil Samir, "Iliyya al-Nasibini (975-1046 A.D.) wa-l-wazir Abu-l-Qasim al-Maghribi (981-1027 A.D.)," *al-Machriq* 77 (2003): 83-105, 297. The first Arabic edition is in Louis Cheikho, "Majalis Iliya mutran Nisibin," *al-Machriq* 20 (1922): 33-44, 112-122, 267-272, 366-377, 425-434.

1 Dialogue as Christological Debate

ORIGINS

The dialogue form made its first appearance in the earliest stages of written literature.[28] By the beginning of the second millennium BC, authors were already composing dialogues in cuneiform Sumerian. Examples of dialogue literature appeared later in Akkadian, Egyptian, Greek, Persian (Pahlavi), Hebrew, Aramaic, Syriac, and eventually in Arabic. Dialogues were already part of the curriculum at academies and schools in the Ancient Middle East.[29] The earliest examples of this style of writing in the Mediterranean are found in

---

[28] Dialogue can be analyzed through form and/or content. Analyzing the form of a dialogue answers the questions: Why was the dialogue composed? In what style of writing was the text composed? For whom was the text written? How was the dialogue to be presented? Examples of literature in which dialogues are used include hymnography, poetry, dramatic and homiletic literature, and prose literature, which encompasses historical writing, chronicles, apocalypses, biographies, hagiographies, dogmatic theology, and texts made up exclusively of dialogue between characters. The final literary form is the focus of this study.

Classifying dialogues according to content involves an assessment of the characters and the setting within the narrative. The content may include colloquial dialogues, legal and judicial dialogues, wisdom and precedence disputations, theodicy and lebensmüde, philosophical and speculative dialogues, and apologetic and polemical dialogues. The last category of dialogue is the focus of this study.

[29] See Karel van der Toorn, "The Ancient Near Eastern Literary Dialogue as a Vehicle of Critical Reflection," in *Dispute Poems and Dialogues in the Ancient and Mediaeval Near East*, 59-75, especially 64.

Greek philosophical dialogues. In contrast to the use of dialogues to advance a story plot, literary dialogues presented the plot as a way to advance characters' ideas. For Greek writers such as Plato, the form was an intellectual display of rational argumentation between the questioner and respondent. Based on the assumptions of objectivity, rationality, and teaching authority, the dialogue form was meant to persuade and convince others of specific truths, offer apologetics, and present intelligible accounts of their worldview. Using dialectic and rhetoric, dialogues were meant to mimic human conversation while leading their audience toward a specific intellectual goal.[30]

Ancient authors adopted the dialogue genre because of the beneficial characteristics of its form. Dialogues solve a problem through the process of questions and answers in a discussion. The dialogue form created a relationship between characters, such as a master and disciple link. Ancient dialogue literature portrayed realistic participants, as conversation partners needed identities. Only then could the author negotiate the path of his own identity with that of the discussants. In many dialogues, a contest would ensue between the characters. They engaged in debate using polite or adversarial rhetoric to argue against one another or to consider innovative answers to a problem.[31] As the champion of the author's dialogue, the master was in control of the discussion with the disciple. At the end of the dialogue, the merits of the competing claims were weighed against one another, and the dialogue came to a conclusion. Many texts used a political leader or impartial observer as the judge between the speakers.

Different types of dialogue texts proliferated in the Ancient Middle East and Mediterranean. Colloquial dialogues were popular

---

[30] For more on the early Greek use of Socratic dialogues, see Charles Kahn, *Plato and the Socratic Dialogue: The Philosophical Use of a Literary Form* (Cambridge: Cambridge University Press, 1996), 1-35.

[31] See the introduction in G. J. Reinink and H. L. J. Vanstiphout, eds., *Dispute Poems and Dialogues in the Ancient and Mediaeval Near East: Forms and Types of Literary Debates in Semitic and Related Literatures* (Louvain: Department Oriëntalistiek, 1991), 1-6.

texts that recorded as brief exchanges between characters. Some colloquial dialogues were set in the workplace and they sometimes they had a humorous intent. Legal and judicial dialogues were set in a court where the characters were typically the prosecutor and the defendant. The stories were concerned with issues of law, morals, and the final judgment. Wisdom and precedence dialogues were between inanimate objects, such as flowers or the months of the year. The two types differed because debates about wisdom discussed the values of a particular merit, while precedence dialogues argued for the superiority of one object over another. Theodicy dialogues involved a human or the human soul speaking with a divine power. They concentrated on the relationship between humanity and difficulties that are beyond their power. The genre includes discussions about why bad things happen to good people – the most prominent of these dialogues being the biblical Book of Job. Philosophical and speculative dialogues focused on two human characters in discussion about a particular matter in the search for specific knowledge concerning the subject. The Socratic dialogues, among other Greek works, belong to this subtype of the genre. The goal of these dialogues was not for precedence or triumph, but rather for a colloquy that would result in new insights or truths.

Originally these dialogues were used exclusively by the educated elite such as philosophers, poets, playwrights, and political leaders. But the dialogue form proliferated among the common class because of its accessibility, its use of everyday language, and its adaptability to many different contexts. The genre underwent numerous developments, adaptations, and reinterpretations dependent upon its literary environment. Scholars have noted that the dialogue structure in the Ancient Middle East remained relatively stable in form, yet adaptable to the ethnic, political, and religious concerns of the authors who employed the genre for various purposes. The history of the dialogue structure is traceable from Ancient Middle Eastern literature down to the early Islamic period; however the differing features of the literary content within the genre are dependent upon the author's environment in relation to time and geography.³² In this way the earlier dialogues were the geographical and spiritual antecedents to Christian and Muslim dialogues. They followed a formal link with earlier compositions on the basis of the genre's structure, although the authors modified the particular content of the dialogue according to their own theological concerns.

The widespread evidence of dialogues within Mediterranean and Middle Eastern cultures suggests that Muslim and Christian authors consciously embraced existing forms of the genre. Their dialogues were not a unique development in literary history but they were a part of the cultures of the region. Several scholars have shown that dialogue genre was prevalent prior to the Islamic period because it was accessible to the common and literate classes through its style of depicting real conversations.³³ Dialogue litera-

---

³² See the introduction in Reinink and Vanstiphout, eds., *Dispute Poems and Dialogues in the Ancient and Mediaeval Near East*, 1-3.

³³ See Reinink and Vanstiphout, eds., *Dispute Poems and Dialogues in the Ancient and Mediaeval Near East*, 5. They state:

> Very often the genre, which was apparently used by a literate class, seems to be addressed to the common people, or to the market place and street; and in some instances it seems even to be felt to "belong" there. An attractive line of evolution, presented here with much caution and only as a line for further research, might consist of pointing out that the tradition in Mesopotamia was strong enough to carry the form from the second millennium down to the first, and even beyond the demise of cuneiform culture as such, and thus well down into the Common Era. The line of transmission, by the way, was a double one: the Aramaic as well as the Persian linguistic area show the enduring popularity of much Mesopotamian material till a very late date. On the other hand, as a popular genre the structure underwent new thematic developments, and might then reascend into higher, e.g. liturgical, spheres (see the Syriac examples), accompanied sometimes by an evolution from "quodlibetal" or value-free opposition to well-defined and prejudged oppositions. Such a view of the evolution would account for the adaptations the structure has undergone in different times, places and cultures. It does not greatly affect the linear descent of the genre in the formal sense, albeit that some formal features may also be adapted to new functions and contexts. This approach seems

ture was not a unique creation of each society or a direct descendent of earlier cultures, but rather an adaptable genre that spoke to the needs and contexts of peoples from different periods and locations. Dialogue was a successful literary form because of its cross-pollination at the religious, social, and economic levels.

DIALOGUE AND CHRISTOLOGY IN THE BIBLE

Historically speaking, Christians and Muslims have exhibited great interest in religious conversation. They integrated religious others into their writings about culture, history, and practical concerns. Religious identities were fundamentally bound to the types of conversations they had with those who espoused a different worldview. For instance, Syriac and Arabic-speaking Christians were among the first writers to describe and analyze the emerging Islamic religion and its rulers. During subsequent centuries, Muslims adopted existing literary structures and fashioned new literary styles, such as oral traditions, in order to describe the rise of Arab tribes into a vast Islamic empire. The ongoing dialogue was an inherent part of the process of developing an identity, and the dialogue text represented one manifestation of this. Nowhere was this development of dialogue via identity more profound for Christians than in the Bible.

For early Christian believers, there were two important levels of dialogue. First there were the written narratives of the Bible that included dialogues between biblical figures. The Book of Job is the only biblical text to use the dialogue form exclusively. The Book of Job was a dialogue on theodicy (the problem of evil in a world with a just God).[34] The story introduces Job as a blameless and righteous man who feared God. When the Lord commends Job because of his faith, Satan replies that it is only because of God's blessings. Satan is then permitted to take these things away from Job, in order

---

certainly more satisfactory than the polygenesis theory by which the genre would have sprung up at different places and at different times and in different cultures – more or less as a literary universal."

[34] The structure of Job shows that literary dialogues already had established thematic and structural prototypes in the Ancient Middle East.

to test his reaction. The rest of the story is a dialogue between Job and others regarding his situation. When the first calamities befall Job, he tears his clothing, shaves his beard, and prays: "Naked I came from my mother's womb, and naked shall I return; the Lord gave, and the Lord has taken away; blessed be the name of the Lord."[35] But in the following sections, Job converses with his wife and three friends on the subject of theodicy – how can a just God permit such actions to befall his servant? Each section is a lengthy dialogue between Job and his friends, who offer consolation in the form of wisdom about what has happened to him. Job responds that they would not think philosophically if they were in his place. When the three men end their conversation with Job, he feels he is justified, but does not acquiesce to their counsel. Another speaker, Elihu, comes forward to dialogue with Job, reminding him of God's greatness and that Job is wrong to question the justice of the Lord. Finally, the Lord enters into dialogue, asking Job: "Where were you when I laid the foundation of the earth? Tell me, if you have understanding."[36] In response, Job acknowledges that the Lord is omnipotent and omniscient. He acknowledges that humans cannot understand the ways of the Lord and he chooses to repent. The dialogue closes with the Lord judging in favor of Job and restoring his blessings twice over.

In Job's dialogue with others, we learn how the literary form was used to introduce multiple perspectives as a series of free and unmerged voices.[37] The conversations depict the protagonist as a hero who answers the questions of his conversation partners. Each speaker critiques Job's response to his predicament, while the Lord offers a closing word on the situation. From a structural perspective, the Lord is the impartial moderator and judge of the discussion. In this case, the Lord does not regulate the discussion but presents a conclusion, allowing Job to be the victor after his re-

---

[35] Job 1:21
[36] Ibid., 38:4
[37] For more on Job and the use of dialogue, see Carol Newsom, "The Book of Job as a Polyphonic Text," *Journal for the Study of the Old Testament* 97 (2002): 87-108.

pentance. These archetypal structures in Scripture would justify their use in later religious literature.

The second level of dialogue engaged in by early Christians was the dialogue between the text, its readers, and the ways of interpreting them in time. For instance, the very act of canonizing the Christian Bible as a set of books inspired by God was an act of dialogue; it proclaimed that the Holy Spirit had spoken with created beings relationally through these specific texts (and not through others).[38] By way of those books, a dialogue between humanity and divinity occurred on a new level between the texts and their readers. For example, early Christians read the conversations between God and creation, particularly in Genesis, as dialogical exchanges that were perpetually relevant for the Church and its sacramental relationship to God.[39] These books were to be read dialogically with each other – that is, Paul's letter's had entered into dialogue with Genesis, or John Chrysostom's homilies had entered into dialogue with the Gospel according to Matthew. Early Christian interpretations of how these scriptures fit together theologically were part of the Christian attempt to understand Jesus Christ and elaborate on his identity.

Returning to the first level of dialogue, there is no complete literary dialogue in the New Testament. However, the Gospel writers recorded several dialogues between Jesus and his adversaries. These exchanges highlight three important qualities in dialogues that became more important in subsequent centuries: they estab-

---

[38] In terms of dialogic theology, the Hebrew Bible is a continuous dialogue between God and his chosen people. Many of God's conversations with Adam, Noah, Abraham, Isaac, Jacob, and others follow a literary pattern for human participation in a dialogue with the divine. Dialogue is therefore seen as sharing in the truth of God, especially when God shares the truth with his chosen people. See Walter L. Reed, *Dialogues of the Word: The Bible as Literature According to Bakhtin* (New York: Oxford University Press, 1993).

[39] For a summary of the dialogical aspect of biblical texts, see Gerhard Sauter, "Dialogik II," in *Theologische Realenzyklopädie*, ed. Gerhard Krause and Gerhard Müller (New York: Walter de Gruyter, 1981), 8:703-709.

lished patterns of Christian response to criticism; they crafted a theological vocabulary for early Christological language about Jesus Christ; and they expressed Christian identity through dialogue that interiorized Jewish and Hellenistic worldviews as inseparable components of Christian discourse.

Many of Jesus' dialogues recorded in the Gospels were based on a brief question to which he responded with an extended parable or wisdom saying. For instance, the synoptic Gospels of Matthew, Mark, and Luke recorded several encounters between the Pharisees, the scribes, and Jesus.[40] But very few examples included a discussion partner who spoke more than once. One exception was Jesus' encounter with Satan in the synoptic parallels Luke 4:1-13 and Matt. 4:1-11. While wandering in the desert prior to his public ministry, the devil tries to tempt Jesus. The devil attempts to coax Jesus to produce bread, worship him, and prove he was the Son of God. Jesus responds to the temptations with wisdom sayings in the form of a religious disputation. When the devil asks him to turn a stone into bread, Jesus responds with a biblical verse: "It is written, 'Man shall not live by bread alone.'" The passage suggests that Jesus found recourse to his message and identity in the words of Scripture. This biblical approach to dialogue would become an essential aspect of interreligious dialogue in later periods.[41]

---

[40] In the synoptic parallels Matt. 9:1-8/Mark 2:1-12/Luke 5:17-26, Jesus argues with scribes about forgiving the sins of a paralytic man. Jesus responds that the Son of Man has power to do such things on earth. This brief exchange is a question and response which typify Gospel argumentation. Another example of a disputation occurs in the parallels Matt. 12:1-8/Mark 2:23-28/Luke 6:1-5, where Jesus' disciples are accused of violating the Sabbath by plucking heads of grain. Jesus responds with a scriptural analogy from 1 Sam. 21:3-6, in which David is given holy bread to eat despite the fact that the bread was reserved for the priests alone.

[41] Prophetic prediction, in which one verse was interpreted in light of another verse, was another common method of scriptural argumentation found in early Christian writings. Early Christian authors amassed Old Testament biblical verses and used them for distinctive Christian doctrines, such as the divinity of Jesus. This style of interpretation via proof text developed into an entire genre, known as testimony collections.

Authors also used analogies in their dialogues as a way of pointing to a particular truth. In the synoptic parallel Matt. 15:21-28/Mark 7:24-30, Jesus encounters a Syro-Phoenician Canaanite woman who implores him to help her possessed daughter, to which he responds, "It is not fair to take the children's bread and throw it to the dogs." Jesus' mission was for the chosen people of Israel. Undeterred, however, she points out: "Yes, Lord, yet even the dogs eat the crumbs that fall from their master's table." Pleased with the woman's apt analogy and determination, Jesus heals her daughter on account of her faith (and her sound analogical reasoning).

In Luke 10:25-37, Jesus converses with a lawyer. The lawyer's first question concerns the criteria for inheriting eternal life. Jesus reminds him of the law in Deut. 6:5 and Lev. 19:18 about human conduct in the world ("You shall love the Lord your God with all your heart, and with all your soul, and with all your might" and "You shall love your neighbor as yourself"). But the lawyer asks him for the definition of one's neighbor. Jesus offers the parable of the Good Samaritan as a response to the question about who is one's neighbor – whoever is within reach and shows mercy.

Christological debate was a significant theme included in many Gospel dialogues. For example, the chief priests and the elders are part of a dispute with Jesus concerning his authority in the synoptic parallels Matt. 21:23-27/Mark 11:27-33/Luke 20:1-8. In another dialogue from Matt. 22:15-22/Mark 12:13-17/Luke 20:20-26, Jesus is challenged to answer a question concerning tribute to Caesar as a test of his authority. In Matt. 26:59-68/Mark 14:55-

---

See Mark Swanson, "Apologetics, Catechesis, and the Question of Audience in 'On the Triune Nature of God' (Sinai Arabic 154) and three Treatises of Theodore Abu Qurrah," 113-134; David Bertaina, "The Development of Testimony Collections in Early Christian Apologetics with Islam," in *The Bible in Arab Christianity*, ed. David Thomas (Leiden: Brill, 2007), 151-173; Mark Swanson, "Beyond Prooftexting: Approaches to the Qur'an in Some Early Arabic Christian Apologies," *Muslim World* 86 (1998): 297-319. For the patristic period, see Martin C. Albl, *'And Scripture Cannot Be Broken': The Form and Function of the Early Christian Testimonia Collections* (Leiden: Brill, 1999).

65/Luke 22:66-71, the Sanhedrin council debates with Jesus about whether he is the Messiah. In each case, the Gospel author uses the dialogue form to disclose Christian Christology within the Jewish context. The evidence suggests that the synoptic Gospel authors recognized the reality of a polemical milieu in which Jesus and the community sought to commend their faith. Thus, the Gospel writers used the dialogue form as one way of establishing apologetic and polemical responses to religious others and in support of the Christological claims made by the early Christian community.[42]

The Gospel according to John was unique in its presentation of Jesus. In the opening chapters, Jesus has discussions with Nicodemus (John 3:1-15) and with a Samaritan woman at Jacob's well (John 4:5-29). Both dialogues reveal the Christological status of Jesus to religious others, a Pharisee and a Samaritan, as the Living Water and the Source of Life.

In subsequent chapters, Jesus debates with Jews concerning his identity and mission. In John 6:41-59, Jesus calls himself the Bread of Life and alludes to the Eucharist as a way to explain his flesh and blood. His audience murmurs, grumbles, and complains about his witness. Unlike the manna, which the chosen people ate in the wilderness, and yet later died a human death, Jesus proclaims that one who would eat his bread would never die.

The longest dialogue in the Gospel involves Jesus and Pontius Pilate discussing Jesus' kingship (John 18:33-38). In comparison with Roman and Jewish rule, Jesus emphasizes the truth of his message is not a worldly political system:

> Pilate entered the praetorium again and called Jesus, and said to him, "Are you the King of the Jews?" Jesus answered, "Do you say this of your own accord, or did others say it to you about me?" Pilate answered, "Am I a Jew? Your own nation

---

[42] For a study of the Jewish-Christian encounter in the earliest periods, see Claudia Setzer, *Jewish Responses to Early Christians: History and Polemics, 30-150 C.E* (Minneapolis: Fortress Press, 1994). See also the chapters in M. J. Edwards, Martin Goodman, and S. R. F. Rowland Christopher Price, eds., *Apologetics in the Roman Empire: Pagans, Jews, and Christians* (Oxford: Oxford University Press, 1999).

and the chief priests have handed you over to me; what have you done?" Jesus answered, "My kingship is not of this world; if my kingship were of this world, my servants would fight, that I might not be handed over to the Jews; but my kingship is not from the world." Pilate said to him, "So you are a king?" Jesus answered, "You say that I am a king. For this I was born, and for this I have come into the world, to bear witness to the truth. Every one who is of the truth hears my voice." Pilate said to him, "What is truth?"

The Book of Acts contains some religious dialogues as well. The deacon Stephen disputes with the Freedmen synagogue members in Acts 6:8-9 concerning the Christological status of Jesus, which culminates in his death by stoning. In Thessalonica, Paul debates with members of the Jewish community concerning the meaning of the scriptures and how they should be read in light of Christological claims about Jesus (Acts 17:1-4). When he travels to Athens, Paul follows the same method and debates with the Athenian community as well as in the market streets. Paul even engages in debate with Epicurean and Stoic philosophers on these matters.

Acts 26 records a dialogue between Paul, King Agrippa, and the governor Porcius Festus. The dialogue follows the form of a court exchange, where the person on trial attempts to prove the truth of a religion before skeptical leaders. The encounter emphasizes the Christian need to make Christological claims about Jesus in the context of first-century Judaism and its prophetic tradition:

> Agrippa said to Paul, "You have permission to speak for yourself." Then Paul stretched out his hand and made his defense.... "To this day, I have had the help that comes from God, and so I stand here testifying both to small and great, saying nothing but what the prophets and Moses said would come to pass." And as he thus made his defense, Festus said with a loud voice, "Paul, you are mad; your great learning is turning you mad." But Paul said, "I am not mad, most excellent Festus, but I am speaking the sober truth. For the king knows about these things, and to him I speak freely; for I am persuaded that none of these things has escaped his notice, for this was not done in a corner. King Agrippa, do you believe the prophets? I know that you believe." And Agrippa said to Paul, "In a short time you think to make me a Christian!" And

Paul said, "Whether short or long, I would to God that not only you but also all who hear me this day might become such as I am – except for these chains" (Acts 26:1-7, 24-29).

The twenty-sixth chapter of Acts provides the most complete New Testament example of a dialogue. In terms of content, the topic concerned the Christological assertions of Christianity and it was written for apologetic as well as religious purposes. With regard to its form, the literary dialogue was intended as a written text to be read for an audience or to be read personally. Its purpose was to strengthen the nascent Christian community, but also to encourage dialogue with the world through evangelization.[43]

Early Christian writers used dialogue to explore the identity and authority of Jesus in debate with Jews within the historical contexts of first-century Judaism and the Roman Empire. Often their focus was to commend Jesus' message and his status as the Messiah. While the dialogue form was not the most significant genre used by early Christians, the concept of dialogue was quite important. Later Christian readers used these patterns for understanding their identity in relation to religious others. Biblical texts established that Christian identity was dependent upon a dialogical encounter. In the process of dialogue with these other voices, early Christian readers were called into a relationship with the religious commitments of first-century Judaism. This furthered their theological worldviews that proclaimed Jesus as the Messiah. In subsequent centuries, Christians would continue to use the dialogue in Christological debate not only with Jews and pagans, but with other Christian communities.

THE MELKITES, JACOBITES, AND CHURCH OF THE EAST

Following the New Testament, Christian authors would fully exploit the dialogue as a way of communicating their identity through

---

[43] For reading this particular dialogue between Paul and the Roman leaders in Acts as a new cultural worldview of evangelization, see C. Kavin Rowe, *World Upside Down: Reading Acts in the Graeco-Roman Age* (Oxford: Oxford University Press, 2009), 53-87.

religious encounter.[44] Among early Greek authors, Justin Martyr (d. 165) composed his *Dialogue with Trypho the Jew*,[45] and three other Jewish-Christian dialogues are extant: Athanasius and Zacchaeus, Simon and Theophilus, and Timothy and Aquila.[46] Latin dialogues include the second-century *Octavius* by the Roman convert Marcus Minucius Felix,[47] and several philosophical dialogues by Augustine (d. 430),[48] Sulpitius Severus (d. 420),[49] and Pope Gregory the Great

---

[44] For a closer study of the dialogue genre among early Christian writers, see Manfred Hoffmann, *Der Dialog bei den Christlichen Schriftstellern der Ersten Vier Jahrhunderte* (Berlin: Akademie-Verlag, 1966). He lists the dialogues as either apologetic, martyr literature, dogmatic-polemic, or philosophical. See also Bernd Reiner Voss, *Der Dialog in der frühchristlichen Literatur* (Munich: Wilhelm Fink Verlag, 1970); P.L. Schmidt, "Zur Typologie Und Literarisierung Des Frühchristlichen Lateinischen Dialogs," in *Christianisme Et Formes Littéraires De L'antiquité Tardive En Occident: Huit Exposés Suivis De Discussions*, ed. Alan Cameron and Manfred Fuhrmann (Geneva: Vandoeuvres, 1976), 101-190; Alain Le Boulluec, ed., *La Controverse Religieuse et ses Formes* (Paris: Cerf, 1995).

[45] For Justin Martyr, see Philippe Bobichon, ed., *Justin Martyr, Dialogue Avec Le Tryphon: Edition Critique* (Fribourg: Academic Press Fribourg, 2003); Michael Slusser, ed., *Dialogue with Trypho* (Washington, D.C.: Catholic University of America Press, 2003).

[46] See William Varner, ed., *Ancient Jewish-Christian Dialogues: Athanasius and Zacchaeus, Simon and Theophilus, Timothy and Aquila: Introductions, Texts, and Translations* (Lewiston, NY: E. Mellen Press, 2004). Ariston of Pella wrote *The Dialogue between Jason and Papiscus* in the mid-second century but it is no longer extant.

[47] See Bernhard Kytzler, *M. Minuci Felicis: Octavius* (Stuttgart and Leipzig: B.G. Teubner, 1992). An English translation is available in Graeme W. Clarke, *The Octavius of Marcus Minucius Felix* (New York: Newman Press, 1974).

[48] Augustine composed a series of philosophical dialogues in 386-387 while preparing for Baptism. See Ludwig Schopp et al., eds., *The Happy Life, Answer to Skeptics, Divine Providence and the Problem of Evil, Soliloquies* (New York: Cima Publishing Company, 1948). Augustine also wrote a dialogue *On Free Will*.

[49] Sulpitius Severus wrote three books of dialogues, most notably concerning the life of his colleague Saint Martin of Tours. A translation is

(d. 604).[50] Other authors composed intra-Christian dialogues, including the *Dialogue with Heraclides* by Origen (d. ca. 254),[51] the *Symposium, or on Virginity* by Methodius of Olympus (d. ca. 311),[52] and three dialogues called *Eranistes* by Theodoret of Cyrrhus (d. ca. 457).[53] Other early Christian writers used the genre as a polemical instrument against Gnostics and Manichaeans, such as the *Dialogue on True Faith in God* by Origen.[54] There are many more dialogues attributed to Arius, Gregory Thaumaturgos, Pseudo-Athanasius, Hegemonius, and Gregory of Nyssa.[55] Fusing Greek philosophical themes, Aristotelian dialectic, and Christian theology, authors in the first four centuries used dialogues to debate with Jews, defend Christianity from pagan attacks, demonstrate Christian reasonable-

---

available in Alexander Roberts, ed., *Sulpitius Severus, Vincent of Lerins* (Grand Rapids, MI: Eerdmans, 1982).

[50] Pope Gregory the Great composed four books of dialogues between himself and his deacon Peter on the lives of the Italian saints. For a translation into English see Odo John Zimmerman, ed., *Saint Gregory the Great: Dialogues* (Washington, DC: Catholic University of America Press, 1959, reprint 2007).

[51] The critical edition is in Jean Scherer, ed., *Entretien d'Origèn avec Héraclide* (Paris: Cerf, 1960, reprint 2002); the English translation is in Robert Daly, ed., *Treatise on the Passover and Dialogue of Origen with Heraclides and His Fellow Bishops on the Father, the Son, and the Soul* (New York: Paulist Press, 1992).

[52] See the English translation in Herbert Musurillo, ed., *Methodius: The Symposium, a Treatise on Chastity* (Westminster, MD: Newman Press, 1958; reprint 1988).

[53] See the English translation in Gérard Ettlinger, ed., *Theodoret, Bishop of Cyrrhus: Eranistes* (Washington, DC: Catholic University of America Press, 1975; reprint 2003).

[54] See Robert A. Pretty and G. W. Trompf, eds., *Dialogue on the True Faith in God: De Recta in Deum Fide* (Louvain: Peeters, 1997). On Christian-Manichaean encounters, see Guy Stroumsa and Sarah Stroumsa, "Aspects of Anti-Manichaean Polemics in Late Antiquity and under Early Islam," *Harvard Theological Review* 81 (1988): 37-58. A lost third-century dialogue with the Montanist Proclus is another example of the use of the genre by early Christians against heretical groups.

[55] For more on these dialogues, see Manfred Hoffmann, *Der Dialog bei den Christlichen Schriftstellern der Ersten Vier Jahrhunderte*.

ness in the Roman Empire, reflect on philosophical issues, explore different theological views on matters of Christian thought and practice, and critique Gnostic and Manichaean claims.

By the fifth century, dialogues held a prominent place in Christian literature, whether in Latin, Greek, or Syriac.[56] One way that dialogues were used was as records of debates between Christological foes.[57] Between the Orthodox Church councils of Ephesus in 431, Chalcedon in 451, and Constantinople II in 553 and the Church of the East synods of Dadisho in 424, Acacius in 486, and Mar Aba in 544, there arose a growing estrangement between Christian communities of the eastern Mediterranean and Middle East. In fact, the developing schisms between Christian communities only became fully formed after the rise of Islam, during the seventh, eighth and ninth centuries, when the Councils of Constantinople III in 681, Nicea II in 787 and the Synodicon of Orthodoxy in 843 fully established Byzantine Orthodoxy and signified the end of attempts at reunion between Christian Churches in the region.[58]

There were three Christian groups involved in these theological discussions, with each community given a polemical name by the others: Chalcedonians, Monophysites, and Nestorians. They

---

[56] On the relationship between Greek and Syriac and their shared literary tradition of dialogues, see chapters VI-XI in Sebastian Brock, *From Ephrem to Romanos: Interactions between Syriac and Greek in Late Antiquity* (Aldershot, England: Ashgate Variorum, 1999).

[57] See Richard Lim, *Public Disputation, Power, and Social Order in Late Antiquity* (Berkeley: University of California Press, 1995). Lim argues that the rise of rhetoric and dialectic in public disputations transformed dialogue from an intellectual display into a social event determined by hierarchy (the holy man) and consensus (the Church).

[58] For a survey of the Christological debates and the differences of terminology as described for the Chalcedonians, Monophysites, and Nestorians, see Alois Grillmeier, *Christ in Christian Tradition*, vol. 2 in 4 Parts (Atlanta: John Knox Press, 1975-1995). Part one covers the reception history of the Council of Chalcedon from each community's perspective. Part two focuses on the Orthodox tradition in sixth-century Constantinople, while part four focuses on the tradition of the Coptic and Ethiopic Churches after Chalcedon.

were separated not only by Christology but by theology, liturgy, language, geography, and ethnicity. Each of these factors played a role in the polemical nature of their debates and the resulting dialogue texts. As the three largest Christian communities of Late Antiquity, their histories were deeply tied to the Christological debates of early Christianity and the Councils that rendered decisions that were either orthodox or heretical, depending upon one's point of view.[59]

The Chalcedonians, also known as the Orthodox, were primarily adherents living within the Byzantine Empire. They were also known as Byzantine or Greek Orthodox, and later by Muslims as Rum (Roman) Orthodox. Most Orthodox Christians lived in the Eastern Mediterranean, including Greece, Asia Minor, Syria, and Palestine. The heart of the Church in the Middle East was located at the patriarchates of Jerusalem and Antioch, with a minority in Alexandria. The polemical term Chalcedonian came from the Council of 451, which proclaimed that Jesus Christ was perfectly the same in divinity and in his humanity, true God and true man, composed of rational soul and body. For them, Jesus Christ had both a human and divine nature, as well as a human and divine will, yet he was one essence as the incarnate hypostasis of the eternal Son, which possessed the fullness of both natures.[60] Following the rise of Islam and the council of Constantinople II in 681, the Orthodox Christians living under Islamic rule came to be called 'Melkites' (imperialists) by their Christological opponents.[61] The Melkites were Arab Orthodox, who used Arabic as a literary language, adhered to the Church councils, used the Byzantine liturgical

---

[59] For more on these groups in the Middle East and early Islamic times, see Sidney Griffith, *The Church in the Shadow of the Mosque*, 129-140.

[60] For more on Byzantine Patristic theology, see John Meyendorff, *Byzantine Theology: Historical Trends and Doctrinal Themes* (New York: Fordham University Press, 1974), especially 19-41.

[61] For more on the legacy of these controversies, see Sidney Griffith, "'Melkites,' 'Jacobites,' and the Christological Controversies in Arabic in Third/Ninth-Century Syria," in *Syrian Christians under Islam: The First Thousand Years*, ed. David Thomas (Leiden: Brill, 2001), 9-55.

rite, and were in communion with the Byzantine Orthodox who lived outside of the Islamic realm. In addition to the Melkites, Georgian Christians were also part of the Orthodox communion living under Islam.

The polemical term Monophysite referred to the Coptic, Ethiopic, and Jacobite (West Syrian) Churches that professed the Christological teaching of Cyril of Alexandria (d. 444) as interpreted by subsequent theologians such as Severus of Antioch (d. 538) and Philoxenus of Mabbug (d. 523).[62] Also called Miaphysites, the communities taught that Jesus Christ, while human and divine, had a single incarnate nature as God the Word. In the aftermath of the Islamic conquest, the Coptic Church, and the Syriac-speaking West Syrian Church (which, after the sixth-century, were called 'Jacobites' after their bishop Jacob Baradeus) became two prominent Christian communities participating within the life of the caliphate. In the ninth century, the Armenian Church would also join this communion of churches.

The Nestorians, who did not identify themselves by this polemical term but called themselves simply the Church of the East, lived under the Sasanian Persians before the rise of Islam.[63] They are also referred to as East Syrians by scholars, in contrast to the West Syrian Jacobites. I will use this non-polemical term in the book, rather than the polemical term Nestorian. In terms of geography, the East Syrians were the largest Church in the world by the seventh century. They had communities in the Middle East, including Iraq, Arabia, and Central Asia as well as India and China. Following the school of Antioch led by Greek theologian Theodore of Mopsuestia (d. 428) and the later Syriac theologians Narsai (d. 503) and Babai the Great (d. 628), the Church of the East taught that

---

[62] Particularly influential theologians for the Church were Patriarch Severus of Antioch (d. 538), Philoxenus of Mabbug (d. 523), and Jacob Baradeus (d. 578).

[63] For surveys of the Church of the East, see Christoph Baumer, *The Church of the East: An Illustrated History of Assyrian Christianity* (London: I.B. Tauris, 2006); and Samuel Hugh Moffett, *A History of Christianity in Asia: Volume I* (San Francisco: Harper, 1992).

Jesus Christ had a union of two natures and their two essences (hypostases) in one person.[64] Contrary to most historical books, the rise of Islam did not signal an end to Christian evangelization by Eastern Christians. In fact, the Church of the East sent missionaries among certain Turkic and Mongol tribes and entered China by the end of the seventh century.

In addition to these three significant groups, the Maronites were a community of Syriac-speaking Christians who lived primarily in what is now Lebanon. The Maronites, who came into communion with the Catholic Church during the Crusader period, were originally neo-Chalcedonians who believed that while Jesus Christ was made of human and divine natures, he had a single divine will – the term for this theological claim is monothelitism. Even after the rise of Islam, Maronites were still considered theologically different from the other communities, although their location in the mountainous regions of Lebanon meant they participated less in the intellectual ferment of the early Islamic Middle East.[65]

DIALOGUE AND CHRISTOLOGY IN LATE ANTIQUITY

Among these Christian communities, the dialogue form was used with practical questions in mind. The dialogue rose to prominence because of its important background in the Greek and Syriac traditions, its capacity for presenting the new comprehensive systems of theological learning, its usefulness for apologetics and polemics, its role in the education system, its relation to the Bible and early Christian literature, its significance for recounting discussions at Church councils, and its facility for depicting Christological de-

---

[64] For more on the Christology of the Church of the East, see Sebastian Brock, "The Christology of the Church of the East in the Synods of the Fifth to Early Seventh Centuries: Preliminary Considerations and Materials," in *Studies in Syriac Christianity: History, Literature, and Theology* (Aldershot, England: Ashgate Variorum, 1992), Chapter XII.

[65] On Maronite history and literature, see Matti Moosa, *The Maronites in History* (Piscataway, NJ: Gorgias Press, 2005).

bate.⁶⁶ Dialogues were meant to be practical compositions that promoted a community's orthodoxy and condemned heretical interpretations of faith and practice (e.g., the Melkites, Jacobites, and the Church of the East).⁶⁷

Literary dialogues from this period were typically drawn from real conversations with theological opponents. Averil Cameron argues that the Christological debates in the pre-Islamic period gave rise to the literary dialogue as an amenable way of transmitting the essence of these discussions. Sixth-century records include Orthodox dialogues with Copts and Jacobites in Constantinople during 531/2, the monk Sabas' arguments against Origenism in 531 in Constantinople, Chalcedonian debates with Copts and Jacobites in 532, a debate between Paul the Persian and Photeinos the Manichaean in Constantinople, and conference reports from Chalcedonian discussions with Persians and with Jacobites in 561.⁶⁸ There were also several debates held under the patronage of the Sasanian court, such as a dialogue between East Syrians and West-Syrian Jacobites in Ctesiphon in 612. The debate between Maximus the Confessor and Pyrrhus, as well as the debate following the Council of Constantinople II in 681, confirms that oral and written dialogues continued well into the Islamic era in the eastern Mediterranean.⁶⁹

---

⁶⁶ Averil Cameron, "Disputations, Polemical Literature and the Formation of Opinion in the Early Byzantine Period," 91-108, esp. 100.

⁶⁷ See Richard Lim, *Public Disputation, Power, and Social Order in Late Antiquity*. He argues that the fifth-century debates had shifted the dialogue genre from pure Aristotelian dialectic to formal debate with an emphasis on orthodox piety as a criterion for argumentation.

⁶⁸ See for instance Sebastian Brock, "The Conversations with the Syrian Orthodox under Justinian (532)," *Orientalia Christiana Periodica* 47 (1981): 87-121; the debate between Paul and Photeinos in J.-P. Migne, ed., *Patrologiæ cursus completus: Series Græca* (Paris: J.-P. Migne, 1864-1865), 88:529-552; and Antoine Guillaumont, "Justinien et l'Église de Perse," *Dumbarton Oaks Papers* 23/24 (1969-1970): 39-66.

⁶⁹ See Joseph Farrell, *The Disputation with Pyrrhus of Our Father among the Saints, Maximus the Confessor* (South Canaan, PA: St. Tikhon's Seminary

Averil Cameron has pointed out a link between the sixth-century culture of debate and its subsequent importance in the first centuries Christian-Muslim encounters.[70] The impetus for Christian-Muslim dialogues, according to Cameron, came out of the religiously plural context of the Mediterranean and Middle East:

> Thus there is no single explanation for the prevalence of the literary disputation in the early Byzantine period, but rather a range of interlocking ones. Travel of Eastern Orthodox and sometimes Nestorians to Constantinople, resort to asylum in the imperial palace and the frequency of translation all made it certain that there would be much interrelation between such writings in Greek and in Syriac, without having to look for direct debts; similarly, the political circumstances which made debate necessary at the same time tend to obscure the line between literary and non-literary or documentary. The very prevalence of such debate almost in everyday experience made it all the more understandable, I suggest, that some writers used it for fictitious or more purely literary purposes, and that many subjects which might have lent themselves to other literary forms (hagiographical narrative, for instance) were now treated in the form of a disputation.[71]

By the early seventh century, dialogues had become perhaps the most popular literary genre in theological writing. Set within a new religious context, the literary genre provided a means to express the supremacy of one's community and contend against religious interlocutors. Thus Greek and Syriac dialogues reflected the historical background of intense theological debate during Late Antiquity.[72]

Press, 1990). For the Greek see J.-P. Migne, ed., *Patrologia Graeca* 91:287-354.

[70] Avril Cameron, "Disputations, Polemical Literature and the Formation of Opinion in the Early Byzantine Period," 102-103.

[71] Avril Cameron, "Disputations, Polemical Literature and the Formation of Opinion in the Early Byzantine Period," 104.

[72] On these controversies in a general historical context, see John Meyendorff, *Imperial Unity and Christian Divisions: The Church, 450-680 A.D.* (Crestwood, NY: St. Vladimir's Seminary Press, 1989).

In the Syriac tradition of the Middle East, the dialogue had been well established since the time of the Christian philosopher Bar Daysan (d. 222).[73] Late Antique Syriac authors also employed the literary form for poetic liturgical dialogues and theological disputations.[74] Approximately fifty Syriac dialogue works are extant today.[75] Many of the works incorporate biblical characters. For instance, an anonymous Syriac dialogue between the two thieves who were crucified between Jesus Christ served as a discourse between Reason (represented by the bad thief) and Faith (represented by the good thief).[76] Other Syriac works constructed their disputes as precedence poems between personifications such as the months of the year, the cup and the wine, or grace and justice. Fifth-century writers John of Apamea (John the Solitary), Thaumasios, and the East Syrian teacher Narsai (d. c. 502) also composed liturgical dialogues. Some Syriac dialogue poems recast biblical characters in dramatic conversations between Cain and Abel, Mary and the An-

---

[73] H. J. W. Drijvers, ed., *The Book of the Laws of Countries: Dialogue on Fate of Bardaisan of Edessa* (Piscataway, NJ: Gorgias Press, 2006).

[74] Sebastian Brock has contributed greatly to our knowledge of Syriac dispute dialogues in liturgical poetry. On the history of the genre, see Sebastian Brock, "The Dispute Poem: From Sumer to Syriac," *Bayn al-Nahrayn* 7 (28) (1979): 417-426; and Sebastian Brock, "The Dispute between Soul and Body: An Example of a long-lived Mesopotamian Literary Genre," *ARAM* 1 (1989): 53-64. For a survey of the genre, see Sebastian Brock, "Syriac Dispute Poems: The Various Types," in *Dispute Poems and Dialogues in the Ancient and Mediaeval Near East*, 109-119. See also Sebastian Brock, "Dialogue Hymns of the Syriac Churches," *Sobornost* 5:2 (1983): 35-45; Sebastian Brock, "Dramatic Dialogue Poems," in *IV Symposium Syriacum 1984: Literary Genres in Syriac Literature*, ed. H. J. W. Drijvers et al. (Rome: Pont. Institutum Studiorum Orientalium, 1987), 135-147; Sebastian Brock, "The Sinful Woman and Satan: Two Syriac Dialogue Poems," *Oriens Christianus* 72 (1988): 21-62; and Sebastian Brock, "1. Syriac Poetry on Biblical Themes: 2. A Dialogue Poem on the Sacrifice of Isaac (Gen 22)," *The Harp* 7 (1994): 55-72.

[75] For a list and classification, see Sebastian Brock, "Syriac Dispute Poems: The Various Types," 116-119.

[76] Sebastian Brock, "The Dialogue between the Two Thieves," *The Harp* 20 (2006): 151-170.

gel, Mary and the Magi, and John the Baptist and Christ.[77] Jacob of Sarug (d. 521), considered the most notable Syriac poet after Ephrem (d. 373), composed many narrative poems in the dialogue form, including one between the Synagogue and the Church. These poetic dialogues were also popular in Greek literature, as seen in the form of the kontakion liturgical poem promoted by the famous Byzantine hymnographer Romanos the Melodist (d. ca. 556).

Syriac and Greek dialogue poems were different in their form from later disputation texts. They were composed as poetry rather than prose. Their intended audience was in the church, rather than in an academic or monastic school setting. The poetic dialogue was primarily a part of the liturgical year; it was an expression of the life of the Church and the way of life for those who sang or listened to the liturgy. As Sebastian Brock has pointed out, poetic and homiletic dialogues reflect the wider phenomenon of the form's popularity in Syriac as well as Greek.[78] But as will be discussed in the following chapter, poetic dialogue was also used in qur'anic Arabic.

Syriac Christians were also using the dialogue genre for the purpose of Aristotelian dialectic and theological debate.[79] The Church of the East taught with dialogue literature (*drasha* in Syriac) as part of the curriculum at the schools of Nisibis, Seleucia-Ctesiphon, and Gundeshapur (Bet Lapat).[80] Syriac-speaking Jacobite authors preserved Christological debates between Chalcedoni-

---

[77] See Sebastian Brock, *A Brief Outline of Syriac Literature* (Kottayam, India: St. Ephrem Ecumenical Research Institute, 1997). See examples of Marian dialogues in Sebastian Brock, *Bride of Light* (Kottayam, India: St. Ephrem Ecumenical Research Institute, 1994).

[78] Brock, "Syriac Dispute Poems: The Various Types," 116.

[79] On the dialogue form in Syriac and Persian during the Sasanian period, see Joel Thomas Walker, *The Legend of Mar Qardagh: Narrative and Christian Heroism in Late Antique Iraq* (Berkeley: University of California Press, 2006), 164-205.

[80] On the school of Nisibis and Syriac learning, see Adam Becker, *Fear of God and the Beginning of Wisdom: The School of Nisibis and Christian Scholastic Culture in Late Antique Mesopotamia* (Philadelphia: University of Pennsylvania Press, 2006); Adam Becker, *Sources for the History of the School of Nisibis* (Liverpool: Liverpool University Press, 2008).

ans and their community.[81] Syriac authors also employed the literary form for martyrs' literature and saints' lives.[82] According to Joel Walker, Syriac Christian literature played a significant role in the philosophical and theological exchange between the Byzantine and Sasanian Empires, particularly during the reigns of Justinian (527-565) and Khusro I (531-579). Studying the legend of Mar Qardagh in particular, Walker argues for close relations between Syriac and Greek Christian authors in their use of the dialogue form.[83] Texts with titles such as *Against the Magi in Nisibis*, *Disputation against a Heretical Bishop*, and *Disputations against the Severians, Manichaeans, Cantaye, and Mandraye* all suggest the presence of the genre in the Middle East, and a concern for religious disputation and Christological debate in particular.[84] Syriac authors such as John of Ephesus and Babai have preserved accounts suggesting that the Sasanian rulers Khusro I and his grandson Khusro II (590-628) both encouraged dialogues between the West-Syrian Jacobites and the East-Syrian Church of the East.

CONCLUSION

Late Antique Christian authors in the Mediterranean and Middle East increasingly came to use the dialogue genre for interreligious and intra-religious Christological debates in the two centuries preceding the rise of Islam. The writers typically employed the literary genre as a defense of their theological position and a commenda-

---

[81] See Averil Cameron, "New Themes and Styles in Greek Literature: Seventh-Eighth Centuries," in *The Byzantine and Early Islamic Near East: Problems in the Literary Source Material*, ed. Averil Cameron and Lawrence Conrad (Princeton: Darwin Press, 1992), 1:81-105, esp. 98-99.

[82] See the dialogues in the Persian martyrs and the martyrs of Najran in Sebastian Brock and Susan Ashbrook Harvey, eds., *Holy Women of the Syrian Orient* (Berkeley: University of California Press, 1987), 63-121.

[83] Joel Thomas Walker, *The Legend of Mar Qardagh*, 169.

[84] These texts, written by Mari the Persian (fifth century), Isho'yahb of Arzon (d. 595), and Nathaniel of Shirzor (d. 618), respectively, are mentioned in the *Catalogue of Ecclesiastical Writers* composed by the medieval Syriac author Abdisho of Nisibis. For sources see Joel Thomas Walker, *The Legend of Mar Qardagh*, 170.

tion of their view of orthodoxy or their view of Christianity (against Judaism) as the true religion. Many Syriac Christian writers used the dialogue form to support their Christological views against the Chalcedonian Orthodox. Overall, they used the dialogue form as a method of inquiry and spiritual expression. The evidence indicates that the dialogue genre was already a significant form for interreligious debates prior to the Islamic conquest.

In the pre-Islamic period, Christological debates had an invigorating effect on the dialogue form and they encouraged its use in a divided climate of heated discussions. They were popular for their use in political intrigues, conferences and councils, formal and informal debates, intra-Christian debates and debates with Jews and the Zorastrian Persians. The evidence indicates that even prior to the Islamic conquest, rising religious and social tensions between Jews, Christian communities, and other religious groups served as a catalyst for the amplified use of literary dialogues. For instance, Christian dialogue with Jews in the pre-Islamic era became a model for early approaches to Muslims, using the same dialogue form and often the same content.[85]

The rise of Islam came about when dialogue, as both a literary form and a concept, was part of the cultural ferment. In the midst of new systematizations of theology and theological debates, and the ways of regulating authority through Scripture, the Councils, and the interpretations of the Fathers of the Church, dialogues were one way of addressing the social and religious anxieties of Christians. They contributed to the fashioning of new religious identities among the Orthodox Chalcedonian Melkites, West-Syrian

---

[85] Some examples of Jewish-Christian dialogues from this period include the *Trophies of Damascus*, a Chalcedonian-Jewish dialogue held in 681 in the presence of other Christians, pagans, Muslims, and Samaritans. See Gustave Bardy, ed., *Les Trophées de Damas: Controverse Judéo-Chrétienne du Viie Siècle* (Paris: Firmin-Didot, 1927), 171-292. Another notable Jewish-Christian dialogue from the eighth century reveals how Jewish-Christian interaction changed following the Islamic conquest. See Allison Peter Hayman, *The Disputation of Sergius the Stylite against a Jew*, 2 vols (Louvain: Secretariat du CorpusSCO, 1973).

Jacobites, and the East-Syrian Church of the East. In the effort to maintain and develop their cultural and intellectual identities, Christian authors composed dialogues in order to exert control over their opponents and to link their ideal of a pristine past with a hope for future security and authority. It should not be surprising to discover that the Qur'an and its monotheistic followers were also drawn into this dialogue.[86] The hostilities between religious communities would not only affect the evolution of the literary form among Christians; the crosspollination of the dialogue form was soon to be reflected in the Qur'an's Christological formulations.

---

[86] Peter Brown argues for contextualizing Muhammad within the Late Antique concept of a holy man who was God's intermediary and a bearer of a divine message, rather than de-historicizing seventh-century Arabia. See Peter Brown, *Society and the Holy in Late Antiquity* (Berkeley: University of California Press, 1982), 103-104, 148-152.

2   Dialogue as Divine Exegesis: The Case of the Qur'an

Reading the Qur'an as Dialogue

Dialogue is one of the prominent forms that the Qur'an uses to communicate its message.[87] Many of its verses have a dialogical structure in which the Qur'an debates with polytheists, Jews, and Christians.[88] The Qur'an uses dialogue to respond to these opponents and commend itself to its listeners. Qur'anic dialogues clarify, prove, and/or reveal signs of its divine authority while stressing the hostile nature of its dialogue partners.[89] The fact that the Qur'an

---

[87] For more on literary approaches to the Qur'an, see the essays in Parts I and II in Issa Boullata, ed., *Literary Structures of Religious Meaning in the Qur'an* (Richmond: Curzon Press, 2000); and the essays in Colin Turner, ed. *The Koran: Critical Concepts in Islamic Studies, vol. 2: Themes and Doctrines: Form, Content, and Literary Structure* (London: RoutledgeCurzon, 2004).

[88] The dialogues in the Qur'an can be classified according to their form and content. On the basis of form, which focuses on performance and audience, the Qur'an used poetic and homiletic content to communicate orally to a live audience. On the basis of content, which focuses on the characters, the Qur'an used legal/judicial dialogues and apologetic/polemical dialogues with its opponents. Qur'anic material was directed at Christian interlocutors as homiletic content censuring their faith and practice. This material is not restricted to a single time period or portion of the Qur'an and it covers a variety of theological topics. On the Qur'an's dialogues as poetic content in response to a Christian audience, see Irfan Shahid, "Islam and *Oriens Christianus*: Makka 610-622 AD," 9-31.

[89] See Jane D. McAuliffe, "'Debate with Them in the Better Way': The Construction of a Qur'anic Commonplace" in *Myths, Historical*

preserved these dialogues suggests that they were meant to communicate divine knowledge in response to challenges posed by skeptics. Since the Qur'an attaches significance to dialogue as a form of communication, it may indicate that religious interactions between discussion partners acted as a catalyst for its emergence.[90]

Qur'anic dialogue works on a number of different levels throughout the past, present, and future.[91] For example, Q 5:116-118 is framed in a past dialogue between Jesus and God:

> And God said: "Jesus, son of Mary, did you say to your people: 'Take me and my mother as gods, apart from God?'" He replied: "Glory be to you. It is not given me to say what is untrue. If I said it, you would have known it. You know what is in my soul, but I do not know what is in yours. You are indeed the Knower of the Unseen. I told them only what you com-

---

Archetypes and Symbolic Figures in Arabic Literature, ed. B. Embaló, et al. (Beirut: 1999), 163-188, esp. 163-169.

[90] Dialogue is particularly important because it preserves the dynamism of prophetic discourse as an oral recitation, rather than as a written text. Some scholars examine the phenomenon of dialogue as reception history, meaning that they study the canonized text of the Qur'an through later historical events and interpreters. This methodology is amenable for scholars to analyze the written Qur'an in the context of responses by later Muslims. Other scholars approach the Qur'an on textual, literary, and historical-critical levels (prior to its canonization and codification, in its oral or early textual state). From these perspectives, the Qur'an contains a multiplicity of heterogenous dialogues originating from particular times and places. For more on how this method has impacted the field of Islamic studies, see Chase Robinson, "Reconstructing Early Islam: Truth and Consequences," esp. 115-118. For Robinson, the Qur'an was practical and pragmatic, while later commentary and legal literature was reflexive — regardless of what may have been important to early Believers, the later community determined what was important and systematized the past according to their needs.

[91] Mustansir Mir has written on dialogue in the Qur'an, but he studied only dialogues of past characters and their affinities with analogous biblical dialogues. See Mustansir Mir, "Dialogue in the Qur'an," *Religion and Literature* 24 (1992): 1-22; and Mustansir Mir, "Dialogues," 1:531-535.

manded me: 'Worship God, your Lord and mine', and I was watcher over them while I was among them, but when you took me to yourself, you became the Watcher over them; for you are the Witness of everything. Should you punish them, they are surely your servants. But should you forgive them, you are truly the Mighty, the Wise."[92]

There are several levels of dialogue working in this section. First, this is a dialogue between Jesus and God, which occurred at some point after Jesus' time on earth. It could represent a past, present, or future dialogue between Jesus and God. Second, it implies a present dialogue in which Christians advocate taking Jesus and his mother as gods. Third, God reports this dialogue he had with Jesus to the Prophet in a dialogue. Fourth, the Prophet reports the reported dialogue in dialogue with his audience. Because of the complexity of these levels of dialogue, it is important to differentiate reports of conversations set in the distant past from dialogues with the Qur'an's listeners. This chapter will focus on the level of dialogue between the Qur'an and its seventh-century Christian discussion partners.[93]

---

[92] For the translations of the Qur'an in this book, I used my own own reading of the Arabic along with Majid Fakhry, *An Interpretation of the Qur'an, English Translation of the Meanings: A Bilingual Edition* (New York: University Press, 2002).

[93] For one perspective on the polytheist, Jewish, and Christian audiences, see Jacques Waardenburg, "Towards a Periodization of Earliest Islam According to its Relations with Other Religions," in *The Qur'an: Style and Contents*, ed. Andrew Rippin (Aldershot: Ashgate Variorum, 2001), 93-115. According to Waardenburg:

> A third striking fact is that, contrary to the Qur'anic texts directed against the polytheists and the Jews, which seem to reflect real debates in which Muhammad used any argument he could find in the arsenal of the beliefs of the other party, the Qur'anic texts against the Christians are rather wishy-washy and give the impression of a man shouting at an enemy who is far away.

This chapter argues that the Qur'an demonstrates a closer interest and knowledge of Christian material than allowed for by Waardenburg.

There are three significant features that emerge when considering how the Qur'an uses dialogue in its discussions with Christians. First, the formulaic statements "They say A, say: B" in the Qur'an act as divine exegesis of biblical material, themes, and history while challenging Jewish and Christian interpretive methods.[94] Divine exegesis is the visible sign of the transcendent God (the self-referential qur'anic word beginning with "say").[95] The Qur'an's divine exegesis confirms its revealed authority while negotiating with the interpretive rights of earlier recipients of revelations. As Nicolai Sinai has noted:

> The Qur'an, not unlike other scriptures, grew out of a process of a community's successive appropriation of earlier traditions and thus forms a heterogeneous composition. A vast though undetermined body of narratives, theological concepts and beliefs was received and lengthily debated by an emerging community. With the emergence of the Qur'an, one set of such recounting came to acquire an authority analogous to that of the Bible itself. Unlike the latter, however, the Qur'an materialized in an environment familiar with pre-existent notions of sacred books, and consequently had to stake its own claim to authority in terms of these precedents. The Qur'anic consciousness of its own scripturality in turn shaped the kind of text that was evolving, and determined its literary and theological configuration. The Qur'anic revelations were from very early on subject

---

[94] The argument that dialogues in the Qur'an function as divine exegesis has some parallels with the arguments found in Nicolai Sinai, "Qur'anic Self-Referentiality as a Strategy of Self-Authorization," in *Self-Referentiality in the Qur'an*, ed. Stefan Wild (Wiesbaden: Otto Harrassowitz, 2006), 103-134. Sinai points out on page 124 that "the text stages itself as a kind of divine targum" that translates the heavenly book of revelation with its own interpretation. In this sense, God is originator, translator, and interpreter of the Qur'an.

[95] The verses of the Qur'an carry this connotation in the Arabic phrase "sign of God" or *ayat Allah*.

to a kind of gravitational pull exerted by the notion of scripture.⁹⁶

Second, the Qur'an engages in a sustained dialogue with Christians concerning eschatology, the true religion, biblical and post-biblical literature, and Jesus' relation to God.⁹⁷ For instance, the Qur'an teaches its listeners the following about Jesus: he was born of a virgin, he is a word and a spirit from God, he confirmed the Jewish scriptures, he fulfilled some of the old Jewish law, and he taught monotheism. In his life and ministry, Jesus was opposed by Jews who tried to kill him, he was supported by his disciples, and God raised him up to himself. But the Qur'an argues with Christians in four significant ways: first, it argues that Jesus is not God or Lord. Second, it denies that Jesus is the Son of God. Third, the Qur'an claims Jesus is not part of a Trinity to be worshipped along with Mary. Fourth, it asserts Jesus was not crucified. When the Qur'an makes these exegetical claims, it uses the dialogue form to instruct its listeners about Jesus' prophethood and to challenge claims to his divinity.⁹⁸ This dialogue reveals the Qur'an as an engaged participant in the broader Christological debates of the Late Antique Middle East and reveals its close relationship to the broader cultural ferment of the historical period.⁹⁹

---

⁹⁶ Quoted in Angelika Neuwirth, "Orientalism in Oriental Studies? Qur'anic Studies as a Case in Point," *Journal of Qur'anic Studies* 9 (2007): 115-127, esp. 119.

⁹⁷ I use the term 'Qur'an' when referring to the pre-canonical sections because the Qur'an understood itself as a recitation (*qur'an*) and as a scripture even in its oral state during the lifetime of the Prophet. This does not mean that when I use the term 'Qur'an' I am referring to it as a literary whole. Rather, one can speak of the Qur'an even in its incomplete form during the process of its formation in the seventh century.

⁹⁸ For a comprehensive survey, see Geoffrey Parrinder, *Jesus in the Qur'an* (New York: Barnes & Noble, 1965; reprint Oxford: Oneworld, 1995); and Neal Robinson, "Jesus," 3:7-21.

⁹⁹ Angelika Neuwirth has argued that scholars need to move beyond interpretations of the Qur'an based solely on later commentaries. Instead, she argues that this method was the product of de-historicization initiated by John Wansbrough. In order to be fair to the Qur'an, scholars must

Third, the Qur'an's polemical attitude toward religious others was preserved due to its exalted status as Scripture. The patterns of debate and dialogue in the Qur'an became the normative Islamic approach to interactions with Christians and their holy books.[100] Early Islamic identity was therefore bound up in the process of dialogue and debate with Christians as later codified within the text.[101] Subsequent literary dialogues were shaped by these qur'anic dialogue encounters in terms of form and content.[102]

The earliest sources for Muslim-Christian encounters are these dialogues embedded in the Qur'an.[103] Many of these encounters

---

historicize the pre-canonical text in the same ways that biblical scholars have done with the Hebrew Bible and the New Testament. By historicizing the Qur'an within the Late Antique context and the wider culture, Islam will no longer be excluded from the western narratives that privilege Judaism and Christianity as historical antecedents to the West and denigrate Islam as a de-historicized 'other'. See Angelika Neuwirth, "Orientalism in Oriental Studies? Qur'anic Studies as a Case in Point." For more on historical studies of the Qur'an, see the collection of essays in "Part Two: Contextualizing the Qur'an" in Angelika Neuwirth, Nicolai Sinai, and Michael Marx, eds., *The Qur'an in Context: Historical and Literary Investigations into the Qur'anic Milieu* (Leiden: Brill, 2010); and the essays in Gabriel Said Reynolds, ed., *The Qur'an in its Historical Context*.

[100] In respect to the Qur'an's perception of Christian scriptures, see Andrew Rippin, "Interpreting the Bible through the Qur'an," in *Approaches to the Qur'an*, ed. G. R. Hawting and Abdulkader A. Shareef (London: Routledge, 1993), 249-259.

[101] For an introduction to these later forms of argument, see Louis Gardet and Marshall Hodgson, "Hudjdja," in *Encyclopaedia of Islam, Second Edition* (Leiden: Brill, 1971), 3:543-545; E. Wagner, "Munazara," 7:565-568.

[102] On scholarly models applied to Muslim interactions with others, such as influence, migration, diffusion, appropriation and crosspollination, see James M. Montgomery, "Islamic Crosspollinations."

[103] On the Qur'an's view of Christians and Christianity, see Sidney Griffith, "Christians and Christianity," in *Encyclopaedia of the Qur'an*, ed. Jane Dammen McAuliffe (Leiden: Brill, 2001), 1:307-316; Samir Khalil Samir, "The Theological Christian Influence on the Qur'an: A Reflection," in *The Qur'an in its Historical Context*, ed. Gabriel Reynolds (London: Routledge, 2008), 141-162; David Marshall, "Christianity in the

belong to the Medinan period (622-632) based on the traditional dating of the verses, although there remain many difficulties in dating verses with absolute certainty.[104] The general nature of these qur'anic dialogues and the lack of historical context should be kept in mind when trying to apply their meaning to other dialogue literature. It is difficult to be certain about the confessional identity of the Qur'an's Christian discussion partners. Indeed, the Qur'an is more concerned with its own divine message.[105]

THE QUR'AN'S USE OF DIALOGUE

During the course of a dialogue, the Qur'an presents the arguments of a particular opponent and then offers responses through a series of exegetical rejoinders. In protecting the essential aspects of its divine message, the Qur'an interprets earlier religious narratives

---

Qur'an," in *Islamic Interpretations of Christianity*, ed. Lloyd Ridgeon (New York: St. Martin's Press, 2000), 3-29; and Jane Dammen McAuliffe, "Christians in the Qur'an and Tafsir," in *Muslim Perceptions of Other Religions: A Historical Survey* (New York: Oxford University Press, 1999), 105-121. For a historiographical survey, see Jaakko Hämenn-Anttila, "Christians and Christianity in the Qur'an," 21-30.

[104] Most dialogues in the Qur'an are said to belong to the third Meccan and Medinan periods, using Theodor Nöldeke's model for dating the occasions of the revelations. See Theodor Nöldeke, *Geschichte des Qorans*, 3 vols. (Leipzig: T. Weicher, 1909-1938; repr. Hildesheim: Olms, 1961). This may suggest that Christianity did not have a significant influence in Mecca, or it may suggest that the later commentators dated the material to the Medinan period based on their readings of eighth-century biographical material about Muhammad. Since Meccan-dated verses already mention Christian doctrine, the dating issue is problematic and a matter of controversy.

[105] Sidney Griffith has noted that the Qur'an explains, praises, and blames its conversation partners from its narrative center. According to Griffith, the audience must have been acquainted with scriptural and religious literature via oral accounts in Arabic. The Qur'an does not borrow or quote these texts, but alludes to their content for its own purposes. See Sidney Griffith, "Christian Lore and the Arabic Qur'an: The 'Companions of the Cave' in *Surat al-Kahf* and in Syriac Tradition," 109-137, esp. 116.

through an allusive discourse and exegesis. The Qur'an is aware of the human capacity for argumentative debate: "We have set forth for the people in this Qur'an every manner of example, but man is the most contentious being" (Q 18:54).[106] The dialogue form within the Qur'an serves at least two purposes: first, it instructs its listeners about practical matters in debate with religious others, and second, it constructs an exegetical framework for descriptive and evaluative polemic against theological rivals.[107] Q 58 has been given the title "The Disputation."[108] The Qur'an uses dialogue as a vehicle to debate and to convince its listeners of its divine message.[109]

As a dramatic communication, qur'anic dialogue presupposes knowledge of stories that are external to its recitation, such as biblical material or apocryphal literature.[110] After assuming the contextual knowledge of its listeners, the Qur'an uses the dialogue as a method of appeal to its audience. The dialogues are meant to encourage, persuade, or critique listeners through a dramatic story.

---

[106] See Angelika Neuwirth, "Structural, Linguistic and Literary Features," in *The Cambridge Companion to the Qur'an*, ed. Jane Dammen McAuliffe (Cambridge: Cambridge University Press, 2006), 97-113, esp. 108.

[107] For a description of debates in the Qur'an, see Jane D. McAuliffe, "Debate and Disputation," 1:511-514. McAuliffe points out that the root *jadala* and its cognates appear 29 times within the Qur'an.

[108] For descriptions of argumentation in the Qur'an, see Rosalind Ward Gwynne, *Logic, Rhetoric, and Legal Reasoning in the Qur'an: God's Arguments* (London: RoutledgeCurzon, 2004); Kate Zebiri, "Argumentation," in *The Blackwell Companion to the Qur'an*, ed. Andrew Rippin (Malden, MA: Blackwell, 2006), 266-281; Rosalind Ward Gwynne, "Sign, Analogy, and the *Via Negativa*: Approaching the Transcendent God of the Qur'an," in *Sacred Tropes: Tanakh, New Testament, and Qur'an as Literature and Culture*, ed. Roberta Sterman Sabbath (Leiden: Brill, 2009), 53-63.

[109] Louis Gardet, "Al-Burhan," 1:1326-1327.

[110] Sometimes referred to as the phenomenon of intertextuality by scholars, the Qur'an expects its listeners to be familiar with biblical stories. For more on this topic, see the essays in John Reeves, ed., *Bible and Qur'an: Essays in Scriptural Intertextuality* (Atlanta: Society of Biblical Literature, 2003).

For instance, one of the silent narratives in the Qur'an is the legend of Alexander the Great. Kevin van Bladel argues convincingly that the Syriac apocalyptic text, known as the *Alexander Legend*, was composed around 629-630. The *Alexander Legend* must have made its way into the community at Mecca or Medina, where Muhammad was asked whether it should be considered a prophetic work.[111] Q 18:83-102 has not preserved the original Syriac text, but it presumes that its audience is aware of the text and retells part of the story. The verses are a striking example of crosspollination with the wider Syriac Middle Eastern culture of the seventh century.

The Qur'an also makes use of dialogue as an effective method for communicating stories of religious obstinacy against its truth claims. Several dialogues involve God's messengers debating with opponents who reject God's signs and bring judgment upon themselves. In Q 23:23-30, Noah gives his people the message to fear and worship God to the exclusion of other gods. They respond with skepticism since he was human. As in the biblical story, God commands Noah to build the ark and fill it with two of each kind of animal, whereupon the wrongdoers are drowned. Thus the Qur'an rebukes its opponents, often using the dialogue form, because they ignore the prophetic message.[112]

THE QUR'AN'S CHRISTIAN AUDIENCE

The Qur'an is particularly aware of its ongoing dialogue with Jews and Christians, who are named the "People of the Book" (*Ahl al-Kitab*) thirty-one times within its suras.[113] When it specifically mentions Christians, they are called "Nazarenes" (*nasara*) which comes from the Greek term transmitted through the Syriac *Nasraya*.[114] On

---

[111] The account is not in the form of a dialogue, so it is not treated in detail here, although its existence in the Qur'an indicates that a dialogue must have taken place. See Kevin van Bladel, "The *Alexander Legend* in the Qur'an 18:83-102," 175-203.

[112] Jane D. McAuliffe, "Debate and Disputation," 512.

[113] See Georges Vajda, "Ahl Al-Kitab," 1:264-266.

[114] See Sidney Griffith, "Christians and Christianity." This is also discussed in Arthur Jeffery, *The Foreign Vocabulary of the Qur'an* (Baroda:

one occasion, Christians are called the "People of the Gospel" (Q 5:47).[115] Approximately ninety-three verses in the Qur'an directly address Christian themes.[116] The attention given to Christianity indicates the widespread presence of Christian groups within the pre-Islamic Arabian milieu.[117]

Most likely, these Christians belonged to three groups. The Melkite Chalcedonians belonged to the Orthodox tradition and were under Byzantine patronage. Most of their communities were located in the regions of Palestine and Syria, and they spoke mostly Syriac (or Palestinian Aramaic), Greek, or Arabic.

The Church of the East (East Syrian) was a minority Church under the Sasanian Empire, although some lived under Byzantine influence in the frontier regions near Arabia. These Syriac-speaking communities were located primarily in the Middle East, including north and eastern Arabia, where the Lakhmids were the dominant Christian community at al-Hira, and along the Persian Gulf at Oman, Bahrain, and Qatar.[118]

Oriental Institute, 1938; reprint, Leiden: Brill, 2006). On the historical background and meaning of this term in Syriac, see Sebastian Brock, "Christians in the Sassanian Empire: A Case of Divided Loyalties," *Studies in Church History* 18 (1982): 1-19 (reprinted as chapter 6 in his book *Syriac Perspectives on Late Antiquity* (London: Variorum Reprints, 1984).)

[115] The Arabic word for Gospel, *injil*, is a transliteration, most likely from the Ge'ez *wangel* that was adopted into Arabic as a loanword. The Ethiopic term originally transliterated the Greek *euangelion*. See Wolf Leslau, *Comparative Dictionary of Ge'ez (Classical Ethiopic)* (Wiesbaden: Otto Harrassowitz, 1991), 615.

[116] For a chronological order and classification of these verses, see Michel Hayek, *Le Christ de L'islam: Textes Présentés, Traduits Et Annotés* (Paris: Éditions du Seuil, 1959), 31-45.

[117] For maps and a study of archaeological data in Late Antique Arabia and the presence of Christians throughout the region, see Barbara Finster, "Arabia in Late Antiquity: An Outline of the Cultural Situation in the Peninsula at the Time of Muhammad," 61-114.

[118] See Isabel Toral-Niehoff, "The 'Ibad of Al-Hira: An Arab Christian Community of Late Antique Iraq," 323-347; Joseph Elders, "The Lost Churches of the Arabian Gulf: Recent Discoveries on the

The West Syrian communities were predominant in the region surrounding Arabia: Syriac-speaking Jacobites were found in Palestine, Syria, and throughout the Arabian Peninsula (such as the Ghassanids), while the Ge'ez-speaking Ethiopian Christians were found in Ethiopia and South Arabia (particularly Yemen, which had both Arab Christian Jacobites and Ethiopians). In fact, there were a number of Arab Christian members of tribes such as the Ghassan, Lakhm, Kalb, Tayy, Tamim, Ibad, Kinda, Taghlib, Shayban, Judham, and others throughout the peninsula.[119] Christians of diverse geographies, theologies, and languages were likely participants in the seventh-century qur'anic dialogues.[120] Recent textual and material evidence indicates that Arabia was not an arid land of

---

Islands of Sir Bani Yas and Marawah, Abu Dhabi Emirate, United Arab Emirates," *Proceedings of the Seminar for Arabian Studies* 31 (2001): 47-58.

[119] Barbara Finster has argued that the Arab Christian presence and impact on pre-Islamic Arabia is clear in terms of architecture, art, manuscript production, and applied arts. See Barbara Finster, "Arabia in Late Antiquity," 75. See also Irfan Shahid, *Byzantium and the Arabs in the Sixth Century*, 2 vols. (Washington, DC: Dumbarton Oaks Research Library and Collection, 1995).

[120] The dialogues with Christians in the Qur'an have led to many works being written on the existence of Christianity in pre-Islamic Arabia. For instance, it is supposed that Ethiopian Christianity and its presence in Yemen and South Arabia would have produced contact between Christians and pagans along the caravan routes, including Mecca. Others claim that Byzantine trade influenced the area, as seen in Irfan Shahid, "Byzantium in South Arabia," *Dumbarton Oaks Papers* 33 (1979): 23-94. For a discussion of pre-Islamic Christianity on the Arabian peninsula, see Richard Bell, *The Origin of Islam in Its Christian Environment* (London: Macmillan, 1926); Louis Cheikho, *Al-Nasraniyya wa-Adabuha bayna 'Arab al-Jahiliyya* (Beirut: Dar al-Mashriq, 1989); and J. Spencer Trimingham, *Christianity among the Arabs in Pre-Islamic Times* (London: Longman, 1979). Some theorists claim that Jewish-Christian groups or other heretical Unitarian Christians lived in the area, although this adds an unnecessary complication, since all of the evidence of Christianity in the Qur'an can be explained in terms of the predominant communities of the region.

ignorance, but a location tied to the cultures of the Late Antique Mediterranean and Middle East.[121]

Most qur'anic dialogues that dealt with Christians are dated to the third Meccan and Medinan periods of Muhammad's lifetime, although many scholars are wary of asserting precise dates for the occasions of the verses.[122] The audience likely included one or more particular Christian groups from either the Syriac tradition (Jacobite or Chalcedonian) or the Ethiopic tradition. Some scholars hypothesize three stages of development in the relationship between the Believers and Christians in the Qur'an.[123] At first, the encounters convey a sense of companionship against common enemies, even acknowledging the virtues of priests and monks (5:82-83).[124] In the second stage, the qur'anic dialogues initiate a challenge to Christians through theological argumentation about Jesus' origin, mission, and life (e.g., Q 3:48-56). During the final stage, Christian doctrinal claims and their refusal to acknowledge the Qur'an's divine authority make Christianity incompatible with qur'anic exegesis (e.g., Q 5:51).[125] The principal dialogues with

---

[121] For instance, Robert Hoyland has argued that epigraphic evidence demonstrates a long tradition of Arabic language use prior to Islam. See Robert Hoyland, "Epigraphy and the Linguistic Background to the Qur'an," 51-69.

[122] Scholars involved in the *Corpus Coranicum* project to produce a critical edition of the Qur'an are very interested in historical reconstructtion. One example for reconstructing early Meccan verses is Nicolai Sinai, "The Qur'an as Process," 407-439. See also the essays in "Studies on the Text" in Stefan Wild, ed., *The Qur'an as Text* (Leiden: Brill, 1996). For a critical view of traditional dating as a projection of later biographical material back into a reconstructed imagined past, see Gabriel Said Reynolds, *The Qur'an and Its Biblical Subtext*, 3-36.

[123] See the paradigm in Jean-Marie Gaudeul, *Encounters & Clashes*, 15-19.

[124] See in Q 5:82: "You shall find those who say: 'We are Christians' the closest in affection to the Believers. For among them are priests and monks, and they are not arrogant."

[125] Some scholars point to the defeat at Mu'ta (629) and the invasion of Tabuk (630), both against Christian opponents, as changing points in the Qur'an's attiude toward Christian faith and practice. See Jacques

Christians in the Qur'an occur in the second and third stages of this development.

The Qur'an participates in dialogue through protest against other competing religious statements and in favor of its own exegesis.¹²⁶ Religious dialogue with Jews and Christians is condoned by the Qur'an which advises its listeners to: "Call to the way of your Lord with wisdom and fine exhortation and debate with them in the best manner" (Q 16:125).¹²⁷ Civility should govern discussions with Jews and Christians: "Do not debate with the People of the Book except in the best manner, except for the wrongdoers among them" (Q 29:46).

The Qur'an utilizes dialogues as a means to contest Christian faith and practice while simultaneously reinforcing its particular brand of monotheism. For instance, the Qur'an criticizes Christian conceptions of Jesus' divinity in the dialogue between Jesus and God mentioned above (Q 5:116-119). The Qur'an claims to preserve the correct exegesis of Jesus' statement concerning his status as a prophet, rather than the Son of God. The Qur'an also responds to criticism regarding its message and divine authority. The Qur'an worries that a number of the People of the Book might turn the Believers back toward the Jewish or Christian faith (Q 2:135).¹²⁸ For the Qur'an, the People of the Book only do this out

---

Waardenburg, "Towards a Periodization of Earliest Islam According to its Relations with Other Religions," 103-104.

¹²⁶ On qur'anic awareness of Christian claims, see David Marshall, "Christianity in the Qur'an," and Jane Dammen McAuliffe, *Qur'anic Christians: An Analysis of Classical and Modern Exegesis* (Cambridge: Cambridge University Press, 1991); and Francis Peters, "*Alius* or *Alter*: The Qur'anic Definition of Christians and Christianity," *Islam and Christian-Muslim Relations* 8 (1997): 165-176.

¹²⁷ For a discussion of qur'anic matters of debate, see Jane D. McAuliffe, "'Debate with Them in the Better Way'."

¹²⁸ Q 2:135: "They say: 'If you become Jews or Christians, you hsall be well guided.' Say: 'Rather, we follow the religion of Abraham, who was upright and no polytheist.'"

of selfish envy (Q 2:109).¹²⁹ It alleges that they do not have good intentions for the Believers, for even though they were the People of the Book, they are sometimes associated with unbelievers (Q 2:105).¹³⁰ Through these polemical statements, the Qur'an forges a dialogue with Christians based on theological interpretation. The Qur'an's fear of Christians and their potential evangelization among the Believers challenges traditional notions of the Qur'an's religious context and reinforces its competition with other religious claims as part of a pluralistic Late Antique society.

The Qur'an incorporates many different styles of debate into its dialogue with Christians. In Kate Zebiri's classification of polemical characteristics in the Qur'an, she includes exhortation, rebuke or criticism, arguments, challenges, refutations of accusations against Muhammad or the Qur'an, discrediting opponents by means of a critical aside or by declaring them to be liars, threatening or warning of temporal or otherworldly punishment, declarations of woe, curses, satire, rhetorical or hypothetical questions, exclamations, and emphatic denials or denunciations.¹³¹ While some of these dialogues are directed at polytheists, hypocritical Believers, or Jews, the Christians also faced many of these charges in the Qur'an.¹³² The Qur'an exhorts the People of the Book to "come to a common word between us and you, that we worship none but God, do not associate anything with him, and do not set

---

[129] Q 2:109: "Many of the People of the Book wish, out of envy, to turn you back into unbelievers after the truth had become manifest to them. But pardon and overlook, until God makes known his will. Surely God has power over all things."

[130] Q 2:105: "Neither the unbelievers among the People of the Book nor the polytheists wish to see any good sent down to you from your Lord."

[131] Kate Zebiri, "Polemic and Polemical Language," 4:114-125, esp. 116-117. See also Kate Zebiri, "Towards a rhetorical criticism of the Qur'an," *Journal of Qur'anic Studies* 5 (2003): 95-120.

[132] For a discussion of Jewish dialogues and an analysis of their characteristics in the Qur'an and subsequent literature, see John Wansbrough, *The Sectarian Milieu: Content and Composition of Islamic Salvation History* (Oxford: Oxford University Press, 1978), 18-19.

up each other as lords besides God" (Q 3:64). One of the most prominent criticisms of Christian Christology comes from Q 4:171:

> O People of the Book, do not exceed the bounds of your religion, nor speak of God except the truth. Christ Jesus the son of Mary is only God's messenger and His Word, which he imparted to Mary and a Spirit from Him. So believe in God and His messengers and do not say "three." It is better for you to refrain, for how could God who is One God (glory to Him!) have a son?[133]

The Qur'an argues that Christ's Gospel did not include monasticism, which Christians invented (Q 57:27).[134] Jews and Christians are challenged to produce evidence for their claim that no person shall ever enter paradise unless that person was a Jew or a Christian (Q 2:111, mentioned below). In response to accusations about the derivation of the Qur'an, it claims a divine origin in line with the Torah and the Gospel as its proof (Q 3:3-4).[135] The

---

[133] It seems that the statement criticizes those who say "three" means tritheists, which would not apply to any of the mainstream Christian groups in their expression of Trinitarian doctrine. On the other hand, it may be more likely that the Arabic is a calque of the Syriac appellation for Christ, *tlithaya*, which means "the treble one." Since the Qur'an also employs this phrase in Q 5:73 as "third of three," it indicates that the Qur'an argues with Christians about Christological claims with an awareness of their Syriac language. See Sidney Griffith, "Syriacisms in the "Arabic Qur'an": Who were "those who said 'Allah is third of three'" according to al-Ma'ida 73?" in *A Word Fitly Spoken: Studies in Mediaeval Exegesis of the Hebrew Bible and the Qur'an*, eds. Meir M. Bar-Asher, Simon Hopkins, Sarah Stroumsa, and Bruno Chiesa (Jerusalem: Ben-Zvi Institute, 2007), 83-110.

[134] Q 57:27: "As for the monasticism which they invented, for we did not prescribe it for them, seeking thereby to please God, they did not observe it properly, so we rewarded those of them who believed, but many of them are sinful."

[135] Q 3:3, 4: "He has revealed the book to you in truth, confirming what came before it… and he has also revealed the proof." The Arabic word *furqan*, which was later given the meaning "proof" or "evidence" is a calque on the Syriac word *purqana*, which means "ransom" or "salvation,"

Qur'an declares that the People of the Book deliberately conceal the truth in spite of their knowledge about it (Q 3:71-73, mentioned below).[136] Those who reject the Qur'an among the People of the Book are threatened with eternal Hell-Fire (Q 98:6). It declares that if only they believed and were righteous, God would have "blotted out their iniquities and admitted them to gardens of bliss" (Q 5:65). A proclamation of woe is given for the Christian sects who differ from the Believers concerning God (Q 19:36-37).[137] If any Christian argues about the origin of the qur'anic message, the Qur'an says to pray to God for his curse to come upon the liars (Q 3:59-61, mentioned below). The Qur'an rhetorically asks its Christian interlocutors why they reject the signs of God, despite the fact they have witnessed them and know they are true (Q 3:70, 98). The Qur'an utilizes exclamations to show that while Christians attempt to deceive the Believers, they deceive themselves (Q 3:69).[138] Finally, qur'anic verses contain emphatic denunciations, such as in Q 9:30: "The Christians say: 'Christ is the Son of God.' That is their statement with their mouths; they emulate the statement of those who disbelieved earlier. May God destroy

---

see J. Payne Smith, *A Compendious Syriac Dictionary* (Oxford: Oxford University Press, 1903; reprint, Winona Lake, IN: Eisenbrauns, 1998), 439. Q 25 also has this word as its title. For a controversial discussion of Syriac loanwords in Arabic, see Christoph Luxenberg, *Die Syro-Aramäische Lesart Des Koran: Ein Beitrag Zur Entschlüsselung Der Koransprache* (Berlin: Das Arabische Buch, 2000). The English translation is Christoph Luxenberg, *The Syro-Aramaic Reading of the Koran: A Contribution to the Decoding of the Language of the Koran* (Berlin: Han Schiler, 2007). For a case study critique of one of Luxenberg's theses, see Stefan Wild, "Lost in Philology? The Virgins of Paradise and the Luxenberg Hypothesis," 625-647. See also Arthur Jeffery, *The Foreign Vocabulary of the Qur'an*.

[136] Q 3:171: "People of the Book, why do you confound truth with error and knowingly conceal the truth?"

[137] Q 19:36-37: "God is truly your Lord and my Lord, so worship him. That is the straight path. Yet, the sects among them differed. Woe to those who have disbelieved from the spectacle of a Great Day!"

[138] Q 3:69: "A party of the People of the Book wished that they would lead you astray. They only lead themselves astray without perceiving it!"

them! How they are perverted!" The following section will analyze specific qur'anic verses that use the dialogue form to communicate its message to Christians.[139]

DIALOGUES WITH CHRISTIANS IN THE QUR'AN

The Qur'an's dialogues likely preserve real oral discourses that occurred between Christians and the emerging community of Believers. Often these exchanges are preserved with only a single phrase, and sometimes only a single word spoken by Christians. In many cases, the qur'anic verses follow the pattern of "They say A, so say B" in response to the particular Christian view.[140] Dialogue required some acknowledgement of the Christian voices. For our purposes, this section will focus on dialogues where the Christian speaker's words are present in the Qur'an.

When the Qur'an enters into a dialogue with Christians, it is typically concerned with matters of Christian doctrine. The dialogues can be classified into four categories: eschatology, the true religion, post-biblical literature, and Christology related to the Incarnation and the Trinity. In each section, the Christians commend a particular truth to which the Qur'an responds with a rejoinder. It appears likely that these verses were occasional answers during a one-time historical encounter, with the Christian claims and qur'anic responses patterned after real discussions. The dialogues reveal the Qur'an as a referential recitation that presumes its listeners have knowledge of biblical traditions.[141]

---

[139] For a survey of qur'anic views of religious others, see Jacques Waardenburg, *Muslim Perceptions of Other Religions: A Historical Survey* (New York: Oxford University Press, 1999), 1-17.

[140] The form has some affinities with the genre of question-and-answer literature, which relies on an oral character to lend credence to the discourse. For its literary antecedents in the Eastern Christian tradition, see Bas ter Haar Romeny, "Question-and-Answer Collections in Syriac Literature," in *Erotapokriseis: Early Christian Question-and-Answer Literature in Context.*, ed. Annelie Volgers and Claudio Zamagni (Louvain: Peeters, 2004), 145-163.

[141] On some of the problems with self-referentiality as a concept, and some of the potential for understanding the Qur'an's references in

In the category of eschatology, which is concerned with the end of time and salvation, Q 2:111 preserves a discussion with some Christians. Will there be a resurrection? What is Paradise for a Believer? How does it differ from its parallels in Judaism and Christianity? How will God elect the Believers for eternal life? When will the end come?[142] The Qur'an recounts: "They say, 'None shall enter Paradise except one who is a Jew or a Christian.' These are their claims. Say: "Produce your evidence, if you are speaking the truth!" In response to the universal and exclusivist claims made by Jews and Christians, the Qur'an sought to assert its own principles for salvation. This dialogue also indicates that Christians in the Prophet's audience were explaining their competing eschatological views of Paradise and their criteria for salvation (e.g., Q 2:80; 3:24).[143]

In the category of the true religion, qur'anic dialogues preserve Jewish and Christian arguments while calling for a restoration of the monotheist faith given to Abraham.[144] Q 2:135-142 includes a series of responses to qur'anic adversaries:

> They say: "If you become Jews or Christians, you shall be well-guided." Say: "Rather, we follow the religion of Abraham, who was upright and not a polytheist." ... Or do you say: "Abraham, Ishmael, Isaac, Jacob and the Tribes were Jews and Christians?" Say: "Who knows better, you or God?" ... The

---

relation to Syriac Christian terms, see Daniel Madigan, "The Limits of Self-Referentiality in the Qur'an," 59-69. Nicolai Sinai has argued that the process through which the Qur'an came to be self-referential was its dialogues with its audience. See Nicolai Sinai, "Qur'anic Self-Referentiality as a Strategy of Self-Authorization."

[142] For this question in a qur'anic dialogue, see Q 7:187, and 34:29-31.

[143] Q 2:80 is also related to eschatology, though it does not refer to a dialogue with Christians: "And they say: 'The Fire will only touch us for a few days.' Say: 'Have you received a pledge from God, and God does not revoke His pledge, or are you imputing to God what you do not know?'"

[144] See the study of Michael Lodahl, *Claiming Abraham: Reading the Bible and the Qur'an Side by Side* (Grand Rapids, MI: Brazos Press, 2010); and Louis Gardet, "Iman," 3:1170-1174.

ignorant among the people will say: "What caused them to turn away from their former direction of prayer?" Say: "To God belongs the East and the West. He guides whom He wills towards the Right Path."

The Qur'an admonishes its listeners to speak of Abraham, Jesus, and the other biblical figures as prophets who transmitted an identical message, while Jews and Christians fail to recognize its continuity and fulfillment in the Qur'an, arguing they already believed in God's revelation.[145] We also learn from the dialogue that Christians were evangelizing and encouraging conversion during this time. It may be that they were using biblical interpretation and theological reflection to explain their continuity with God's chosen people in the Bible. They were also aware of some of the Believers' practices that were similar to those of Jews, such as prayer toward Jerusalem.

According to the Qur'an, the true religion had never changed. For example, Q 2:140 preserves a debate between Jews and Christians that the Qur'an is supposed to resolve in order to prove it is of divine origin:

> "Do you claim that Abraham and Ishmael and Isaac and Jacob and their descendants were Jews or Christians?" Say: "Do you know more than God? Who is more unjust than he who conceals a testimony given to him by God? For God is not ignorant of what you do."

The Qur'an is posed with the question of adjudicating between the claims of Judaism and Christianity, while still contending that it represents the true religion. By asserting its continuity with Abrahamic monotheism and insisting that Jews and Christians conceal testimonies concerning this fact, the Qur'an rejects their claims to possess full religious truth.[146] At the same time it ignores the

---

[145] For dialogues with Jews on the true religion, see for example Q 2:88, 2:91, 2:170.

[146] For another example, see Q 2:113: "The Jews say: 'The Christians promote nothing' and the Christians say: 'The Jews promote nothing' while they both recite the Scripture. Those who do not know speak

question of superiority between Jews and Christians. The audience for this dialogue may have been a Jew or a Christian who brought this question forward as a test. Regardless, it demonstrates the Qur'an's knowledge of the salvific claims of the local Christians.

Another exchange with the People of the Book occurs in Q 3:71-73. In this section, the Qur'an deals with issues implying an ambiguous relationship between Christians and the Qur'an's Believers:

> People of the Book, why do you confound truth with error and knowingly conceal the truth? Some of the People of the Book say: "Believe what is revealed to the Believers at the beginning of the day, but disbelieve it at its end. Perhaps [the Believers] will turn back; but do not believe anyone except for whoever follows your religion." Say: "Right guidance is God's guidance, consisting in one's being granted something like what you [Believers] have been granted." Or would they dispute with you about your Lord? Say: "The rest is in God's hand. He grants it to whomever He wills, for God is infinite, all-knowing."

The dialogue seems to indicate that some Christians (as well as Jews) were part of the early movement, while others were part of the local Christian community and the Believers' movement simultaneously. The dialogue preserved here shows that individuals had real connections with one another on the levels of oral and written communication.

The Qur'an also explains the characteristics of the true religion with a dialogue about God's children. In the biblical tradition regarding Abraham, Jews and Christians affirm that he had belonged to their respective communities. However, the Qur'an claims that Abraham was in fact a monotheist like the early Believers (Q 2:135). The dialogue reminds its listeners that Jews and Christians have no special status in God's view:

---

likewise. God will judge between them on the Day of Resurrection about that which they differ."

The Jews and the Christians have said, "We are God's children and His beloved ones." Say: "Why then does He punish you for your sins?[147] Rather, you are human beings whom He has created. He forgives whom He wills and punishes whom He wills. God has dominion over the heavens and the earth and what is between them, and to Him is the return" (Q 5:18).[148]

In the category of post-biblical literature, qur'anic dialogues include discussions about its prophetic inspiration. The Qur'an needs to authenticate its divine origin when asked: How do we properly know God's characteristics? Will there be a bodily resurrection?[149] How can you verify your divine knowledge?[150] One dialogue preserved in the Qur'an recalls the Christian legend of the

---

[147] Jewish and Christian biblical narratives contain extended discussions and explanations of suffering and the history of God disciplining his people in order that they repent. For the Qur'an however, their justifications were irreconcilable with the qur'anic understanding of God's covenantal role and rule in history.

[148] As John Wansbrough has remarked, Islamic salvation history might be termed 'election history', due to the absence of eschatological features or any apprehension concerning the potential course of the future or concern for the conclusion of linear historical time. The example above demonstrates how qur'anic expressions reveal a self-assured confidence vis-à-vis interreligious polemics and the ultimate success of the community. See John Wansbrough, *The Sectarian Milieu*, 148.

[149] See Q 10:38, 11:13, 11:35, 16:24, 16:101-103, 21:5, 25:4-5, 32:3, 34:43 and several more instances for dialogues about whether the Qur'an was a revelation or a forgery. On specific Christian or Jewish informants contributing to the Qur'an, see Claude Gilliot, "Reconsidering the Authorship of the Qur'an: Is the Qur'an Partly the Fruit of a Progressive Work?" in *The Qur'an in its Historical Context*, 88-108.

[150] One example of a dialogue which challenged the Qur'an's authority is preserved in Q 6:91 (see also Q 28:48):
> They do not show regard for God's power when they say: "God has not revealed anything to a human being." Say: "Who revealed the Scripture which Moses brought as a light and guidance to mankind? You put it in scrolls which you reveal, while you conceal much, but you are taught what neither you nor your fathers knew." Say: "God." Then leave them to revel in their nonsense.

Companions of the Cave (Q 18:9-26), also known as the Sleepers of Ephesus.[151] According to the Christian legend, found in pre-Islamic Greek and Syriac versions, a number of young men took refuge in a cave during the persecutions of Christians during the third century (the number of men varies according to the different versions of the story). God made them sleep in the cave for about three hundred years, and when they woke up, they thought it had only been a short time. When the young men went back to their city of Ephesus, which was now Christian, the people were astonished and interpreted the event as a miracle from God that proved the truth of the resurrection. But someone asks for the exact number of sleepers within the cave in order to challenge the divine knowledge of the Qur'an:

> They say: "[There were] three, their dog was the fourth," [or] they say: "five, their dog was the sixth." And they say: "Seven, their dog was the eighth." Respond: "My Lord knows best their number. No one knows them, except for a few. So do not dispute about them, except regarding what is clear, and do not question regarding any of them." (Q 18:22)

The exchange reveals how discussions of Christian texts challenge the Qur'an. The speaker, who was likely a Syriac Christian with access or knowledge of the variant texts, presents the Qur'an with different versions of the Sleepers of Ephesus. Since there was no consensus on their number, it was a way to assess the Qur'an's access to divine knowledge and exegetical authority.[152] This ongoing dialogue served a purpose in creating the Qur'an's self image and was a catalyst in its process of self discovery. Some of the most

---

[151] See Sidney Griffith, "Christian Lore and the Arabic Qur'an: The 'Companions of the Cave' in *Surat al-Kahf* and in Syriac Tradition."

[152] Another example that shows the awareness of the Qur'an about legendary material is Q 3:78: "And there is a group of them who twist their tongues while reciting the Scripture, so that you might suppose it is part of the Scripture, but it is not from Scripture. They say it is from God, but it is not from God. They speak a falsehood against God knowingly."

prominent dialogues in this respect are the discussions concerning God's oneness and Christology.[153]

In the category of Christology, the Qur'an is particularly concerned with emphasizing the transcendence of God. It seeks to distance Jesus from claims that he was divine through reinterpretations of biblical and post-biblical Christian literature. The most prominent problem for qur'anic theology is the idea that Jesus was the Son of God. For the Qur'an, God could have no physical offspring since humanity and divinity were mutually exclusive. Therefore, if it could be proven that Jesus was human, this would settle the argument. For instance, Q 43:81 told its listeners: "Say: 'If the Merciful One had a Son, then I would be the first of the worshippers'." In addition, there is a brief dialogue on this matter in Q 2:116: "They say: 'God has begotten a son.' Glory be to Him, rather to Him belongs what is in the heavens and the earth, all are obedient to Him." Thus the qur'anic dialogue appeals to a created Jesus within the theological understanding of God's transcendence.[154] The Qur'an commends Jesus' identity as son of Mary to the exclusion of divine sonship as part of its divine exegesis.[155] The references to God's son are likely from Christians (or possibly polytheists), and show that Christians in the period were explaining the doctrine of the Incarnation.

---

[153] There may be reason to believe that the Qur'an's first arguments for monotheism were aimed at pagans who claimed the jinn as God's partners, and later this criticism was applied to Christians through the Qur'an's Christological critique (e.g., Q 6:100-101).

[154] For more on the Qur'an's argumentation with Christians, see Kate Zebiri, "Argumentation."

[155] This section only treats the qur'anic dialogues regarding Jesus. Much more information is available in Geoffrey Parrinder, *Jesus in the Qur'an*. On Mary's role in the theological argument, see Michael Marx, "Glimpses of a Mariology in the Qur'an: From Hagiography to Theology via Religious-Political Debate," 533-564; Neal Robinson, "Jesus and Mary in the Qur'an: Some Neglected Affinities," *Religion* 20 (1990): 161-175; reprinted in Andrew Rippin, ed., *The Qur'an: Style and Contents* (Aldershot, England: Ashgate Variorum, 2001), 21-35.

Other dialogues record the tensions between Christian Christological claims and the Qur'an's rejection of these ideas. For fear of associating a created being with God, Q 5:17 rebuffs Christian claims:

> Those who say, "Christ the son of Mary is God" disbelieve. Say: 'Who could prevent God in any way if he wanted to destroy Christ, the son of Mary, and his mother, together with everyone who is on earth?'"

Q 3:59-61 implies that Christians were entering into debate to support their claims to Jesus' divinity:

> Whoever debates with you about [Jesus] after the knowledge that has come to you, say: "Come, let us call our sons and your sons, our wives and your wives, ourselves and yourselves. Then let us pray and call down God's curse upon the liars."[156]

In this dialogue with Christians, the Qur'an records not only the disagreement, but enters into a second dialogue with itself through re-presentation of an earlier Christological reading (Q 19). It is also presumably in response to a dialogue with Christians. Thus, the Qur'an's Christological critiques are developed through dialogical encounters with a Christian audience.

A similar statement appears in Q 5:72 when the Christians declare that Christ, the son of Mary, is God. But in this verse the respondent was the qur'anic Jesus, who commends worship of God alone and emphasizes divine transcendence. In each verbal exchange concerning Jesus, the Qur'an rejects his divinity and sonship because they are in conflict with its prophetology.[157] Even

---

[156] For more on this sura and Christology, see Angelika Neuwirth, "The House of Abraham and the House of Amram: Genealogy, Patriarchal Authority, and Exegetical Professionalism," 499-531. Neuwirth argues that Q 3 was a re-reading of Q 19 in order to respond to Christological controversies, assuage Christian Believers, and counterbalance the Jewish family of Abraham with the Christian family of Jesus and Mary.

[157] On the construction of prophetic types see Uri Rubin, "Prophets and Prophethood," 4:289-307.

when entering into dialogue with the Jews, the Qur'an reaffirms this claim about Jesus.[158]

During the emergence of the Believers' community, the Qur'an gave its first listeners a fruitful opportunity for interactions in the arena of Christological debate. This audience of listeners certainly included knowledgeable Christians who explained their theological doctrines on the Incarnation. The Qur'an is anxious to instruct its faithful listeners and critique its opponents much as was found at the same time in the Byzantine Empire's Christological debates.[159] The Qur'an's preoccupation with monotheistic doctrine and its relationship to Christian claims about Jesus is a significant part of the Qur'an's development, especially if we take its dialogue sections as authentic fragments of real seventh-century debates.[160]

CONCLUSION

During the seventh century, the Qur'an was born out of an environment that was deeply tied to the biblical worldview.[161] As described in the previous chapter, Christian dialogues were taking

---

[158] Q 4:157, the well-known verse on the crucifixion, is possibly part of a dialogue with a group of Jews, or a reflection on Jewish teaching. See Todd Lawson, *The Crucifixion and the Qur'an: A Study in the History of Muslim Thought* (Oxford: Oneworld, 2009).

> They say: "We have killed Christ Jesus, the son of Mary and the messenger of God." They did not kill him or crucify him, but it appeared so to them. Those who differ about him are in doubt about it. Their knowledge does not go beyond conjecture, and they did not kill him for certain.

[159] See Averil Cameron, "New Themes and Styles in Greek Literature: Seventh-Eighth Centuries," 100. Cameron is basing her assessment on the work of Adel Théodore Khoury, *Les théologiens byzantins et l'Islam. Textes et auteurs. VIIIe-XIIIe s.* (Louvain: Nauwelaerts, 1969), 15-30.

[160] Angelika Neuwirth has posited a liturgical setting for the Qur'an, which would be one reason why it contains dialogue responses to both believing and skeptical listeners. See Angelika Neuwirth, "Structure and the Emergence of Community," 140-158.

[161] For a detailed study of this topic, see Gabriel Said Reynolds, *The Qur'an and Its Biblical Subtext* (London: Routledge, 2010).

place during Late Antiquity throughout the Middle East and Mediterranean, in literary as well as oral forms.[162] These oral patterns of dialogue in the Qur'an were a product of the wider cultural cross-pollination of the seventh-century Middle East.

The Qur'an utilized dialogue as a significant literary form for communicating its message. Some characteristics of these dialogues include their brevity, their attention to simple points of doctrine, their assumption of knowledge about biblical and post-biblical material, and the emphasis on the didactic potential of such dialogues in light of real exchanges with Christians. On a practical level, qur'anic dialogues were designed to reveal the imperfections of Judaism and Christianity and show the Qur'an's superior access to divine knowledge and authority above the Torah and the Gospel.[163] The dialogues sought to instruct the listener about the unity of God, the prophetic continuity which links the Qur'an's divine message with earlier scriptures, and the gift of eternal salvation through submission and good works. Qur'anic dialogues were not systematic presentations of either Christian or Believer ideals. This limits

---

[162] Syriac Christians were composing and reciting dialogues in liturgical settings, which have led some scholars to suggest an analogous relationship to the Qur'an's original liturgical setting. See Fred Leemhuis, "A Koranic Contest Poem in Surat As-Saffat?" in *Dispute Poems and Dialogues in the Ancient and Mediaeval Near East*, 165-177. He argues on pages 176-177:

> It is sufficiently well known that the literary debate played an important role in Syriac Christianity. Especially within a homiletic and liturgical framework it is indeed frequently met with. It would be improbable if nothing of it had seeped through to the surroundings of the Apostle of Islam. If the Koran really was meant as an Arabic lectionary – and we have the word of the Koran for it that it was – then it is probable that the sura as a liturgical unit is based on and has assimilated the forms of liturgical address that were present in its environment. Thus it is not really very astonishing that we also find vestiges of debate literature and even something which looks somewhat like a contest poem.

[163] On the Qur'an as a sign of divine authority rather than a book, see Daniel Madigan, *The Qur'an's Self-Image: Writing and Authority in Islam's Scripture* (Princeton: Princeton University Press, 2001).

the conclusions scholars can draw about the Christian voices preserved in the Qur'an's dialogues.

The Qur'an built its authority precisely on its ability to refer to scriptural accounts as earlier modes of revelation while insisting that its exegesis was the only proper one, at least in terms of its Christological reading of Jesus.[164] God was the divine exegete who provided the Prophet with access to the heavenly book of revelation in order to respond, reinterpret, and re-read Jewish and Christian scriptures. The Qur'an's exegetical authority over earlier revelation grew in complexity as the emerging community developed the idea that earlier scriptures had been changed. The doctrine of corruption (*tahrif*) sought to discredit Jewish and Christian argumentation from their scriptures on the basis that such scriptures had been changed by later communities, thereby losing their guaranteed access to truth.[165]

Based on this analysis, dialogue in the Qur'an was significant because it opened possibilities to divine exegesis via prophetic revelation in response to opponents. The Qur'an was shaped by this process of self-reflexive prophetic discourse that was ultimately concerned with its own status as Scripture. The Qur'an not only spoke of revelation, but talked about itself as revelation to its dia-

---

[164] As Nasr Hamid Abu Zayd and Angelika Neuwirth have also argued, the qur'anic re-reading of Marian material in Q 19 through Q 3 demonstrates the Christological concerns and activities of a Qur'an that commented not only on biblical and post-biblical apocryphal material, but upon its own discourse on Christology. Angelika Neuwirth, "The House of Abraham and the House of Amram: Genealogy, Patriarchal Authority, and Exegetical Professionalism," 518-519 and 525-526.

[165] On the doctrine of corruption, see Jean-Marie Gaudeul and Robert Caspar, "Textes de la Tradition Musulmane concernant le Tahrif (Falsification) des Écritures," *Islamochristiana* 6 (1980): 61-104; Hava Lazarus-Yafeh, *Intertwined Worlds: Medieval Islam and Bible Criticism* (Princeton, NJ: Princeton University Press, 1992). See Christian responses in Clare Wilde, "Is There Room for Corruption in the 'Books' of God?" 225-240.

logue partners.[166] The dialogue portions of the Qur'an reveal it as a divine exegete precisely where it commented upon itself, its characteristics, its dialogue partner's ideas, their scriptures, and their traditions. This polyphony of voices – God, Prophet, Opponent, Believer, biblical character – preserved in its reported speech, unveils some of the historical and cultural crosspollinations that took place in the seventh century.

The dialogue form merits further study from scholars as an impetus for the emergence of the Qur'an itself. Paradoxically, these dialogues were both a source of divine authority and a source of anxiety. On the one hand, the responses to specific Christian questions confirmed the Qur'an's authority to interpret earlier revelations and proclaim its own message. The Qur'an's self-acknowledged relationship with Jewish and Christian scriptures meant dialogues could authenticate its doctrines and criticize the perceived insufficiencies of Christian faith. Engaging the religious ferment of the early seventh century became one of the significant reasons for the recitations. On the other hand, the Qur'an's Christian audience argued that this dialogue was deficient – precisely because it was an oral recitation rather than a written Scripture like the Hebrew Bible or the New Testament. As a revelation that was living and incomplete, and open to reinterpretation, the Qur'an was treated with skepticism by the Christians remembered in its dialogues.

---

[166] See Stefan Wild, "Why Self-Referentiality?" in *Self-Referentiality in the Qur'an*, 1-23.

3 Dialogue as Conquest and Conversion

The seventh-century Islamic conquest and the subsequent religious conversions deeply affected Christians and Muslims in terms of their literary imaginations. In the wake of the conquest, conversions were few in number and did not have an effect on daily life for most Christian communities. But at the beginning of the eighth century, the Umayyad caliphs began policies of Arabization and Islamicization which initiated real change.[167] Conversions only became more prevalent during the ninth century in urban locations, and even later in rural areas. However, the fear of conversion to Islam was very real for Christians, and the attention shown to the matter in literary works from the period reinforce this perception.[168] Christian-Muslim relations shifted according to communal ties of family and kinship, and the changing religious identities of the period permanently marked the character of religious affiliation in the Middle East. What was a Christian majority in the Middle East slowly became a minority group, with many urban Christians converting to Islam during the ninth and tenth centuries. Many

---

[167] See for instance Daniel Dennett, *Conversion and the Poll Tax in Early Islam* (Cambridge, MA: Harvard University Press, 1950).

[168] See Gerrit Reinink, "Following the Doctrine of the Demons: Early Christian Fear of Conversion to Islam," in *Cultures of Conversions*, ed. Jan Bremmer, Wout van Bekkum and Arie Molendijk (Leuven: Peeters, 2006), 127-138. He argues that the appearance and purpose of the literary dialogue form in Christian-Muslim debate was to prevent Christian conversion to Islam.

rural areas remained Christian beyond the Crusader period.[169] For both Christians and Muslims, the memories of conquests and conversions would affect their interest in literary dialogues. Following a discussion of the conditions for dialogue in the early Islamic Middle East, the chapter will examine several dialogues set within the context of conquest and conversion, and will shed light on how authors used the literary form to draw attention to these themes in their writings.

CONDITIONS FOR CHRISTIAN DIALOGUE IN THE AFTERMATH OF THE ISLAMIC CONQUEST

Initial Christian observations of the Islamic conquest, beginning in 634, did not demonstrate knowledge of the emergence of a new religion.[170] On the contrary, Christian reactions to the territorial gains were analyzed through writings that focused on the internal concerns of the Melkite Arab Orthodox (Chalcedonian), the West Syrian Jacobites, and East Syrian Church of the East (Nestorian).[171]

---

[169] According to Richard Bulliet, up to one third of local populations converted during the ninth century. However, since the quantitative data comes mostly from urban areas, it is reasonable to assume that conversions occurred at a slower pace in the rural areas, some of which have remained Christian until this day. See Richard Bulliet, *Conversion to Islam in the Medieval Period: An Essay in Quantitative History* (Cambridge, MA: Harvard University Press, 1979); Nehemia Levtzion, "Conversion to Islam in Syria and Palestine and the Survival of Christian Communities," in *Conversion and Continuity: Indigenous Christian Communities in Islamic Lands, Eighth to Eighteenth Centuries*, ed. Michael Gervers and Ramzi Jibran Bikhazi (Toronto: Pontifical Institute of Mediaeval Studies, 1990), 289-311; Gerrit J. Reinink, "The Beginnings of Syriac Apologetic Literature in Response to Islam," *Oriens Christianus* 77 (1993): 165-187.

[170] See Abdul-Massih Saadi, "Nascent Islam in the Seventh Century Syriac Sources," 217-222. Some scholars assert that the interest in taking Christian lands north of Yathrib (Medina) began during Muhammad's lifetime with the battles at Mu'ta (629) and Tabuk (630).

[171] There is an abundance of material that describes the Syriac sources for the seventh century. For secondary literature on Syriac historical literature in the seventh century, see Sebastian Brock, "Syriac Sources for Seventh-Century History," *Byzantine and Modern Greek Studies* 2 (1976): 17-

Each confession had a different response to the Islamic conquest.¹⁷² The various Christian communities used a variety of literary genres, including apocalyptic literature, chronicles, and letters to respond to the conquests.¹⁷³ In general, Christian attention was primarily directed toward the preservation of legal, financial, and religious structures for their respective communities.

From the Melkite Chalcedonian perspective, the writings of the Jerusalem patriarch Sophronius were representative of their protest against the "Saracens" who had prevented Christians from making their pilgrimage from Jerusalem to Bethlehem in order to commemorate the birth of Jesus Christ on 25 December 634. Sophronius was likely unaware of the motives of the "Saracens" whom he called "godless" and "God-haters."¹⁷⁴ Similar responses are found in the *Dialogue of Jacob the Newly Baptized*, which looks toward the end of the trials against the faithful Orthodox, as "there

---

36; Sebastian Brock, "Syriac Historical Writing: A Survey of the Main Sources," *Journal of the Iraqi Academy* 5 (1979/1980): 297-326; Sebastian Brock, "Syriac Culture in the Seventh Century," *ARAM* 1/2 (1989): 268-280. Another perspective is found in Hugh Kennedy, "Change and continuity in Syria and Palestine at the time of the Moslem conquest," *ARAM* 1/2 (1989): 258-267. On early religious views of Islam, see Robert Hoyland, *Seeing Islam as Others Saw It: A Survey and Evaluation of Christian, Jewish, and Zoroastrian Writings on Early Islam* (Princeton, NJ: Darwin Press, 1997).

¹⁷² See Sebastian Brock, "Syriac Views of Emergent Islam," in *Studies on the First Century of Islamic Society*, ed. G. H. A. Juynboll (Carbondale: Southern Illinois University Press, 1982), 9-21. Also, see the bibliography of earliest Syriac sources in Michael Penn, "Syriac sources for the study of early Christian-Muslim relations," *Islamochristiana* 28 (2003): 59-78.

¹⁷³ For instance, see Cynthia Villagomez, "Christian Salvation through Muslim Domination: Divine Punishment and Syriac Apocalyptic Expectation in the Seventh and Eighth Centuries," *Medieval Encounters* 4 (1998): 203-218.

¹⁷⁴ See the section on Sophronius and the bibliography in Alan Guenther, "The Christian Experience and Interpretation of the Early Muslim Conquest and Rule," *Islam and Christian-Muslim Relations* 10 (1999): 363-377, esp. 366-367. See also Daniel Sahas, "Sophronius, Patriarch of Jerusalem," 120-127.

was no truth to be found in the so-called prophet, only the shedding of men's blood."[175]

From the West Syrian Jacobite perspective, the conquest was sometimes viewed as a response to the oppressive measures of Byzantine ecclesiastical policy established by the emperor Heraclius (d. 641) against non-Chalcedonians.[176] However the writings demonstrate little knowledge of an Islamic religious movement.[177] Instead, Syriac chronicles used polemics against the other churches as a way to explain the rise of Arab power.[178]

The Church of the East had a unique relationship with the conquerors since their community lived completely under Islamic rule.[179] One of the earliest East Syrian responses commended the Arabs for permitting religious freedom for Christians, as seen in the letters of Isho'yahb III (d. 659).[180] On the other hand, some of

---

[175] See Vincent Déroche and Gilbert Dagron, "Doctrina Jacobi nuper baptizati," *Travaux et mémoires (du Centre de Recherche d'Histoire et de Civilisation byzantines)* 11 (1991): 17-273; and Johannes Pahlitzsch, "Doctrina Iacobi nuper baptizati," 117-119.

[176] See Michael Morony, "History and Identity in the Syrian Churches," in *Redefining Christian Identity: Cultural Interaction in the Middle East since the Rise of Islam*, ed. J.J. van Ginkel, H.L. Murre-van den Berg, and T.M. van Lint (Leuven: Peeters, 2005), 1-33.

[177] For instance, a record of the Arab conquest from 637 was composed by an observer on the first folio of a gospel codex. Another account from a Jacobite perspective describes the confrontation between the Byzantine armies and the Arabs around 640. For translations see Palmer, Brock, and Hoyland, eds., *The Seventh Century in the West-Syrian Chronicles*, 1-4, 13-23.

[178] Ibid.

[179] For a history, see Jean Maurice Fiey, *Chrétiens syriaques sous les Abbassides surtout à Bagdad, 749-1258* (Louvain: Secrétariat du CorpusSCO, 1980). For a compilation of articles on Syriac Christianity in this period, see Gerrit J. Reinink, *Syriac Christianity under late Sasanian and early Islamic rule* (Aldershot, England: Ashgate Variorum, 2005).

[180] For a discussion on Isho'yahb III, see William Young, *Patriarch, Shah, and Caliph: A Study of the Relationships of the Church of the East with the Sassanid Empire and the Early Caliphates up to 820 A.D., with special reference to available translated Syriac sources*, 85-99. He mentions relations with Muslims

his fellow bishops did not share his perspective. East Syrian leadership was preoccupied with internal matters. They had little awareness of the Believers as a distinct faith. Other East Syrian chroniclers revealed similar concerns for their own confessional community.[181]

In sum, Christian literature from the period provides evidence to the contrary of the notion that the conquering Arab armies were welcomed by Eastern Christians as liberators from an oppressive Byzantine church policy.[182] Although Jacobites deemed the Chalcedonian Orthodox heretical, most of their anger was directed at particular Byzantine rulers rather than the at population at large. The Melkite, Jacobite, and Church of the East communities initially responded to the Islamic conquest by using established biblical terms and patterns to create a theological justification for the attacks. The sources only come to the gradual realization that the Arab conquerors already had a religion and intended to remain in the land during the latter portion of the seventh century.[183]

Middle Eastern Christian awareness of the Believers' community as a distinct religion entered its first stages through encounters with Muslim rulers who enforced their laws according to qur'anic norms. Later seventh-century Christians seemed to have been aware that the Arab conquerors were tied to Jewish principles and

---

in two letters, in Rubens Duval, ed., *Iso'yahb Patriarchae III Liber epistularum*, 2 vols. (Louvain: Secrétariat du CorpusSCO, 1962), 1:92-97, 247-255.

[181] A chronicler from the Church of the East writing ca. 40/660 describes his community's initial encounter with the Arabs. The text is reproduced in Ignazio Guidi, E. W. Brooks, and Jean-Baptiste Chabot, eds., *Chronica minora*, 6 vols. (Paris: E Typographeo Reipublicae, 1903. Reprint, Louvain: Secrétariat du CorpusSCO, 1955-1961), 1:15-39.

[182] See also the treatment of the conquest by Sidney Griffith, *The Church in the Shadow of the Mosque*, 23-28. Griffith argues that the seventh-century Christian sources viewed the conquest as a disaster for which their own sins or the heretical actions of other churches were primarily responsible.

[183] For a brief survey of seventh-century Jewish and Christian sources, see Harald Suermann, "Early Islam in the Light of Christian and Jewish Sources," 135-148.

biblical ideas, such as the prophets and the Torah. However, they remained ambivalent toward this new leadership and its place in history. Christians used biblical language from the Book of Daniel to describe the Arabs in apocalyptic terms, pointing to the end of time and the final return of the Messiah. They used existing political terms as well, such as king (*malka*), head (*risha*), and commander (*amira*).[184]

As for the name of the conquerors, Eastern Christians initially used the old term "Tayyaye," which described the pre-Islamic Arab nomads. As a term derived from the Arab tribe of the Tayy, it originally carried a derogatory connotation for uneducated and rural Arabs, although it became a common term for Muslims in early Christian discourse. The other frequent term used by Christian authors was the word *hanpe*, which contained a double meaning within the Syriac and Arabic context. In Syriac, the word meant "pagan." However the Syriac *hanpe* was cognate with the Arabic word *hanif*, which was used in the Qur'an to indicate a monotheist believer. Thus the Syriac descriptor *hanpe* could be applied accurately to Muslims while including another meaning altogether.[185]

Sidney Griffith has pointed out another term with a double meaning in Syriac and Arabic that revealed Christians' growing understanding of the Arabs as the community of Believers. According to the Book of Genesis, Arabs were the descendents of Hagar, Abraham's concubine with whom he conceived a child (Gen. 16:1-16). After fleeing from Abraham's jealous wife Sarah, Hagar was given a promise in 16:10-11:

> The angel of the Lord also said to her, "I will so greatly multiply your descendants that they cannot be numbered for multitude." And the angel of the Lord said to her, "Behold, you are

---

[184] Sebastian Brock, "Syriac Views of Emergent Islam," 20.

[185] The singular or plural of the adjective *hanif* occurs twelve times in the Qur'an, with seven of those associated with Abraham as the model of true faith. Abraham is mentioned as the model *hanif* in Q 2:135, 3:67, 3:95, 4:125, 6:161, 16:120, 123. For more on Syriac terminology, see Sidney Griffith, *Syriac Writers on Muslims and the Religious Challenge of Islam* (Kottayam: St. Ephrem Ecumenical Research Institute, 1995), 8-14.

with child, and shall bear a son; you shall call his name Ishmael; because the Lord has given heed to your affliction."

Readers of Scripture immediately recognized the claims of the Arab conquerors to have fulfilled the promise given to them by God in Gen. 21:13: "And I will make a nation of the son of the slave woman also, because [Ishmael] is your offspring." Ishmael had twelve sons who were the ancestors of the Arab tribes, according to Gen. 25:12-18 (cf. Gen. 17:20; 1 Chron. 1:29-31).[186] Linking the biblical story of Hagar with the Arabs, Syriac writers called them "Hagarenes" in Syriac (*mhaggraye*).[187] Originally, the term sought to distinguish the Arab people, who considered themselves descendents of Hagar, from the chosen Jewish people, who were considered descendents of Sarah and her son Isaac. What gave the word its double meaning was the fact that the Arabic root was used as a self-description by seventh-century Arabs who settled in the new conquered territories as "Emigrants" (*muhajirun*).[188] In other words, Syriac writers could use the term to refer to the Arabs with an older polemical expression ("Hagarenes") while simultaneously using the Arabic word used by Believers to identify their community.[189] The use of this term by Christians was likely a conscious at-

---

[186] Hagar's name also appears in Baruch 3:23 as a reference to the "sons of Hagar." In the New Testament, Paul utilizes Hagar's name typologically in Galatians 4:24-25 to describe Hagar as the old covenant of the present Jerusalem of the world, who is in slavery. For Paul, Christians belong to the new covenant which belongs to the heavenly Jerusalem, thus making the faithful free from slavery.

[187] On the meaning of the term, see Patricia Crone, "The First-Century Concept of 'Hiǧra'," *Arabica* 41 (1994): 352-387.

[188] In Islamic tradition, the term first applies to those who fled Mecca for Yathrib (Medina) marking the *Hijra*. Regardless of the origin of the term, the fact remains that Syriac-speaking writers heard Muslims who settled in their lands refer to themselves as *muhajirun* and took the term to apply to those who had immigrated into the Fertile Crescent.

[189] The use of the designation Hagarenes and *muhajirun* has led some scholars to postulate a conscious identification with the biblical story and a later date in the formation of an Islamic identity that was originally more Samaritan and/or Jewish in character. See Patricia Crone and Michael

tempt on their part to describe and evaluate the new Arab emigrants who were settling in the Middle East.[190]

During the second half of the seventh century, Christians began to speak of "Muslims" and "Islam" rather than simply Believers of a generic puritanical monotheistic faith. Christian awareness of Islamic doctrines was restricted because of several limitations. Greek- and Syriac-speaking Christians encountered communication difficulties with Muslims which inhibited further dialogue between the two groups. Although they are both Semitic languages, Syriac and Arabic are mutually unintelligible; indeed, there were many cultural and educational divisions that compounded the language rift. For instance, most Christian Arab tribes were bilingual communities which typically celebrated their liturgy in the dominant intellectual language of Syriac or in Greek according to their liturgical Church rite. Arabic was not a liturgical or literary language for Middle Eastern Christians until nearly two centuries after the advent of Islam.[191] This information leads one to believe that the dialogues held between Muslims and Christians developed gradually as more Christians learned Arabic, as there is no record of Muslims learning Syriac for the purpose of engaging Christian faith and practice.

Christian discussions with Muslims were restricted in the theological arena due to the lack of an Arabic Bible and proper technical terminology for intellectual learning in Arabic.[192] Chris-

---

Cook, *Hagarism: The Making of the Islamic World* (Cambridge: Cambridge University Press, 1977).

[190] Griffith, *Syriac Writers on Muslims and the Religious Challenge of Islam*, 9-14.

[191] In relation to the development of Arabic in Palestine, see Sidney Griffith, "From Aramaic to Arabic: the Languages of the Monasteries of Palestine in the Byzantine and Early Islamic Periods," *Dumbarton Oaks Papers* 51 (1997): 11-31; the article was repinted in Sidney Griffith, *The Beginnings of Christian Theology in Arabic*, Chapter 10. See also Kate Leeming, "The Adoption of Arabic as a Liturgical Language by the Palestinian Melkites," *ARAM* 15 (2003): 239-246.

[192] Anton Baumstark was the first person to argue that a pre-Islamic biblical lectionary based on the Christian Palestinian lectionary must have

tians had to develop theological expressions in Arabic before they could move beyond spoken encounters and engage in theological dialogue. Because of this, it appears likely that Christians during the seventh century were limited in their literary output in Arabic by the lack of a biblical and secular material composed in the language.[193]

Middle Eastern Christians initially thought of Muslims as their intellectual inferiors due to the limitations of the Arabic language and due to the language's lack of significance within the Hellenistic literary realm. Christians who encountered Muslims disdained their beliefs for their perceived heresy. This suspicion or religious indifference limited initial discussions, since Christians were primarily concerned with political and financial interests related to their communities while living under Arab hegemony.

---

been available for the Arabic-speaking communities among the Ghassanids or the Lakhmids at al-Hira in the east. This is based on the fact that some rubrics in Arabic translations retained the older Palestinian structure that was predominant in pre-Islamic times. See Anton Baumstark, "Das Problem eines vorislamischen christlich-kirchlichen Schrifttums in arabischer Sprache," *Islamica* 4 (1929-1931): 562-575. Irfan Shahid argues for the existence of the Arabic Bible in the region of Najran. See Irfan Shahid, *The Martyrs of Najrân: New documents* (Brussels: Soc. des Bollandistes, 1971).

[193] Debate continues between scholars on the matter of the origins of the first Christian scriptures to be translated and composed in Arabic. Sidney Griffith has argued that the first translations of scripture into Arabic were part of a later eighth- and ninth-century strategy by Christian apologists to counteract the Qur'an; they were not based on pre-existing biblical or liturgical material in Arabic but on new endeavors that sought to stem the tide of conversions that increased when the Abbasid Empire began to offer complete socio-political participation to Christians and others who would convert to Islam. Griffith argues that the endeavor to translate the New Testament into Arabic was initiated by the Palestinian monastic communities during the early Abbasid period, based upon manuscript evidence. See Sidney Griffith, "The Gospel in Arabic: An Inquiry into its Appearance in the First Abbasid Century," *Oriens Christianus* 69 (1985): 126-167.

Christian perceptions of the Believers' movement were characterized by their own experiences in earlier polemical discourses with Jews, pagans, and the other "heretical" Christian communities (depending upon whether a Christian belonged to the Melkites, Jacobites, or Church of the East). The basis of Christian discourse with other religions came from its Scripture, theology, and liturgy; however their encounter with Muslims was decidedly unique in that Muslims consciously co-opted the meaning and interpretation of the Bible while challenging the theological reflections of the three Christian communities, particularly in the areas of Christology and Trinitarian doctrine.[194]

As eighth-century Christians cultivated a greater awareness of Islam, they increasingly engaged the political power of Islamic leaders and their administration.[195] Because of their minority status in Islamic lands, Christian authors had to identify and reinforce the community against the dominant Islamic religious structure that shaped the culture and politics of the Middle East. Literary dialogues were exploited for use by Christians as a spoken outlet of protest against social and religious tensions in the caliphate. Since public roles of power in the political realm were in the hands of Muslims, Syriac and Christian Arabic authors used dialogue texts as a means of trying to control the intellectual field. Writers were able to emphasize educational aspects of Christian culture, while Muslims held political and social control. Christian authors engaged in a fight for literary dominance as a means of countering this influence over Christian identity. For the Christian composers, their texts

---

[194] On the legacy of this exchange in the area of Christology, see Mark Beaumont, *Christology in Dialogue with Muslims: A Critical Analysis of Christian Presentations of Christ for Muslims from the Ninth and Twentieth Centuries* (Carlisle: Paternoster, 2005). For examples of reinterpretations, see Michael Penn, "Monks, Manuscripts, and Muslims: Syriac Textual Changes in Reaction to the Rise of Islam," *Hugoye: Journal of Syriac Studies* 12 (2009): 235-257.

[195] For examples of such interactions in extant texts, see Lejla Demiri and Cornelia Römer, eds., *Texts from the Early Islamic Period of Egypt: Muslims and Christians at their First Encounter* (Vienna: Phoibos, 2009).

proclaimed the significance of Christian civilization within the caliphate.

There were three main classes that promoted Christian discourse with Islam: government officials, the hierarchies of patriarchs, metropolitans and bishops from the three Churches, and the monastic community. Those who wrote literary dialogues most often belonged to the latter two classes. It was also from these ranks of intellectuals that there was a development in Christian discourse with Islamic communities, especially among those who were known as dialectical theologians (*mutakallimun*).

As Middle Eastern Christians became more familiar with Muslims, a broad spectrum of attitudes toward Islam emerged during the Umayyad and early Abbasid periods. The diversity of responses indicates that Christians did not have a unified vision of Islamic communities. Some Christians in this period had no interest in Islamic faith and practice. These people ignored Muslim religious claims and concentrated upon their own social, political and financial concerns. Other individuals were openly hostile toward Islam but they refused to engage Muslims in literary debate or confront their claims. Still other Christians were willing to engage in discussions with different religious communities and commend the truth of their religion through literary means. Many Christian authors studied, described, analyzed, and evaluated Islam according to their own criteria of faith and reason. These Christian dialogue partners also had Muslim counterparts. The following section will examine how these Muslim intellectuals came to discuss religious topics with Christians.

Conditions for Early Muslim Dialogue with Christians

In its nascent stages, Muslim attitudes toward Christianity were governed by pre-existing qur'anic structures of polemical discourse. As discussed in the previous chapter, the Qur'an was particularly aware of its ongoing dialogue with Christians. This dialogue carried over into the Believers' community. The community's interest in other religions served as a foundation for discourse about common concepts of God, faith, and practice.[196] According to later qur'anic interpretation, Christians were permitted within Islamic lands as one of the communities who had received a revelation from God. As part of the protected People of the Book (*dhimmi*), the Christians were understood to have a prophet (Jesus) and a book (Gospel).[197] However, some factors limited early Muslim awareness of Christianity. Many of the early converts to Islam were speakers of Arabic or Persian. Christians who wrote in Greek, Syriac, Coptic, Armenian, or Georgian were at a disadvantage in terms of language. Also, the Arabic script was still developing a standard written form in the seventh century, and it continued to progress as a language, developing diacritical marks and vowel markings, over the course of the following two centuries.[198] Muslims obtained their information through practical necessity via oral encounters with Christians. Muslim contact with Christians developed only gradually as they began to incorporate their laws and practices into the wider environment of the Middle East.[199]

---

[196] There is an abundance of literature that deals with Muslims' perceptions of others in the early period as well as contemporary times. See especially Hugh Goddard, *Muslim Perceptions of Christianity* (London: Grey Seal, 1996); Kamal Salibi, ed., "Muslim Perceptions of Christianity--Christian Perceptions of Islam: The historical record," *Islam and Christian-Muslim Relations* 7 (1996): 7-93; Jacques Waardenburg, *Muslim Perceptions of Other Religions: A Historical Survey*; W. Montgomery Watt, *Muslim-Christian Encounters: Perceptions and Misperceptions* (London: Routledge, 1991).

[197] On the idea of Christians as subjugated *dhimmi* people, see Bat Ye'or, *The Dhimmi: Jews and Christians under Islam* (Rutherford: Fairleigh Dickinson University Press, 1985); Bat Ye'or, *The Decline of Eastern Christianity under Islam: From Jihad to Dhimmitude* (Teaneck, NJ: Fairleigh Dickinson University Press, 2002).

[198] See Beatrice Gruendler, "Arabic Script," 1:135-144; Claude Gilliot, "Creation of a Fixed Text," 41-57.

[199] For a comprehensive examination of Muslim perceptions of others in this period, see the article by Jacques Waardenburg, *Muslim Perceptions of Other Religions: A Historical Survey*, 18-68. See also Ahmad Shboul, "Byzantium and the Arabs: The Image of the Byzantines as Mirrored in Arabic Literature," in *Arab-Byzantine Relations in Early Islamic*

Nevertheless, early Muslim perceptions of Christianity were based upon descriptive and evaluative criteria established in the Qur'an. All subsequent judgments of Christianity were defined through the qur'anic lens and its interpretation of religious outsiders, even to the exclusion of reading the biblical text. Muslims utilized their scriptures as a means to refute Christian faith and practice while simultaneously establishing and reinforcing doctrinal aspects of Islam. Authors of literary dialogues used the Qur'an to construct an identity for their religious communities against competing Christian claims.[200] The evidence provided in the previous chapter indicated that Muslims already had an established paradigm in which to enter into conversation with Christians while employing the dialogue form. These earliest Islamic patterns of conversation reflected theological debates between the qur'anic message and Christian belief. Qur'anic models of debate influenced later Muslim perceptions of their discussion partners and their depiction in the dialogue form.

Early Muslim attitudes toward Christians were characterized by the idea of complete self-sufficiency. God's direct revelation rendered all other messages superfluous. Some argued that there was no benefit to critically engaging in religious discussions. Political expansion through military victories only perpetuated the sentiments of God's support for their endeavors. The qur'anic claim that Islam was the eternal and primordial monotheistic religion reinforced these ideas. For early Muslims, Islam was the perfect expression of God's religion while Christianity was an inferior and corrupted part of the eternal tradition.

Muslims believed that they understood Christian doctrine while Christians misinterpreted their own faith, particularly with regard to Jesus' identity. Early Muslims recognized from the Qur'an that Jesus was not divine; therefore, the qur'anic revelation supplied a more suitable interpretation than Christian Christolo-

---

Times, ed. Michael Bonner (Aldershot, England: Ashgate Variorum, 2004), 235-260.

[200] For a historical perspective of Muslim identity formation, see the first chapter in Hugh Goddard, *Muslim Perceptions of Christianity*.

gy.[201] Early Muslim claims separated Christian beliefs about Jesus Christ from their historical circumstances in order to emphasize Jesus as one of the Muslim prophets, thus, early Muslim perceptions were characterized by supersessionist views.[202] They expected Christians to accept qur'anic principles in order to share in the movement, to live within Islamic lands, and to submit to their political hegemony. For Muslims, Christians did not offer a convincing theological defense or a critique of Islamic doctrines. This feeling of self-assurance among Muslims of different communities revealed a faith that had its religious interpretations confirmed by its political authority.

According to Jacques Waardenburg, Muslims in the eighth and ninth centuries began to develop methods of perceiving, judging, and engaging Christians through descriptive and evaluative markers by way of socio-political, cultural, and religious structures.[203] He notes that these works were carried out primarily through four classes: the commentators (*mufassirun*), the traditionists (*muhaddithun*), the legalists (*fuqaha'*), and the dialectical theologians (*mutakallimun*). It was typically the theologians who engaged in composing literary dialogues, and so the claims in this book are restricted to these Muslim scholars. Proto-Sunni and Shi'ite authors encountered Melkite Chalcedonians, West Syrian Jacobites, and the East Syrian Church of the East who had established polemical traditions with each other. Here, early Muslim attitudes toward Christians were influenced by the critiques that Christians made of one another, which were adapted to Islamic rhetorical strategies for interreligious discourse.

As groups of Muslims came into contact with Christians, certain intellectuals participated in discussions concerning the Christian scriptures, faith, and practice. They commended their own

---

[201] On the qur'anic context of Q 4:157 and its interpretation by later commentators, see Todd Lawson, *The Crucifixion and the Qur'an*.

[202] These claims to superiority belonged to an idea developing within Islam concerning abrogation (*naskh*) and abrogated matters (*mansukh*).

[203] Jacques Waardenburg, *Muslim Perceptions of Other Religions: A Historical Survey*, 20.

doctrine, encouraged conversion, reinforced their community's link to divine authority, and refuted the claims of their religious adversaries. This group included Muslims who composed literary dialogues within the context of conquest and conversion. Therefore, it is important to remember that Christian and Muslim literary dialogues were written by this category of authors. The conclusions drawn from the analysis should be restricted to this limited group of like-minded writers.

JOHN OF SEDRA AND THE MUSLIM EMIR

The dialogue between Patriarch John and the Muslim emir is likely the oldest literary dialogue composed specifically to address Christian-Muslim relations.[204] The dialogue was reputedly composed by John's secretary in Syriac as a record of a discussion between John of Sedra, the Jacobite Patriarch of Antioch, and a Muslim emir on Sunday 9 May of the year 644.[205] Scholars continue to debate whether the dating of the text. Some argue for an eighth-century context.[206] Others believe that the document may reflect the real

---

[204] See Michael Penn, "John and the Emir: A New Introduction, Edition and Translation," and Abdul-Massih Saadi, "The Letter of John of Sedreh: A New Perspective on Nascent Islam." See also Penn, "Syriac sources for the study of early Christian-Muslim relations," 87-107; esp. 60-61; Louis Sako, "Bibliographie du dialogue islamo-chrétien: Auteurs chrétiens de langue syriaque," *Islamochristiana* 10 (1984): 273-292, esp. 277-278.

[205] Originally, François Nau dated the event to the year 639, but 644 fits best with further information of the Muslim emir's identity. See Harald Suermann, "The Old Testament and the Jews in the Dialogue between the Jacobite Patriarch John I and 'Umayr ibn Sa'd al-Ansari," in *Eastern Crossroads: Essays on Medieval Christian Legacy*, ed. Juan Pedro Monferrer-Sala (Piscataway, NJ: Gorgias, 2007), 131-141, esp. 133-134.

[206] Scholars for the eighth-century argument claim that the author is responding to Arab strategies to Arabize and Islamicize the society. These policies were instituted during the caliphates of the Umayyad rulers 'Abd al-Malik (d. 705) and al-Walid (d. 715). Michael Penn, "John and the Emir: A New Introduction, Edition and Translation"; Gerrit J. Reinink, "The Beginnings of Syriac Apologetic Literature in Response to Islam," 171; Sidney Griffith, "Disputes with Muslims in Syriac Christian Texts: From

encounter, but that later additions were inserted into the dialogue.²⁰⁷ Some scholars contend that the dialogue narrates a real event that took place between John of Sedra, the Jacobite Patriarch of Antioch (d. 648) and his discussion partner, the Muslim emir 'Umayr Ibn Sa'd al-Ansari, who was military governor of Homs (Emesa).²⁰⁸ Regardless of the historicity of the dialogue, it is an extremely valuable source for understanding the relationship between Christians and Muslims in light of the concept of conquest.²⁰⁹

Patriarch John (d. 648) to Bar Hebraeus (d. 1286)," in *Religionsgespräche im Mittlealter*, ed. Bernard Lewis and Friedrich Niewöhner (Wiesbaden: Otto Harrassowitz, 1992), 251-273; Patricia Crone and Michael Cook, *Hagarism*, 168.

²⁰⁷ See Barbara Roggema, "The Debate between Patriarch John and an Emir of the Mhaggraye: A Reconsideration of the Earliest Christian-Muslim Debate," 21-39.

²⁰⁸ See Harald Suermann, "The Old Testament and the Jews in the Dialogue between the Jacobite Patriarch John I and 'Umayr ibn Sa'd al-Ansari," and Abdul-Massih Saadi, "The Letter of John of Sedreh: A New Perspective on Nascent Islam." One source for this opinion is the account of the dialogue found in the twelfth-century Syriac history of Michael the Syrian and the anonymous Syriac chronicle of 1234, both of which use Dionysius of Tellmahre (d. 845) as a source. See Jean-Baptiste Chabot, ed., *Chronique de Michel le Syrien, Patriarche Jacobite d'Antioche (1166-1199)*, 5 vols. (Paris: Ernest Leroux, 1899-1924), 2:419-443. See also Jean-Baptiste Chabot, ed., *Anonymi auctoris Chronicon ad annum Christi 1234 pertinens* (Paris: E. Typographeo Reipublicae, 1916; reprint, Louvain: L. Durbecq, 1952), 1:263. The fact that the account is mentioned by Dionysius before 845 may only demonstrate that he knew of the text, not that he knew of an actual historical encounter. See Michael Penn, "John and the Emir: A New Introduction, Edition and Translation," 80.

²⁰⁹ On John of Sedra, see Ignatius Aphram Barsoum, *The Scattered Pearls: A History of Syriac Literature and Sciences*, trans. Matti Moosa, 2nd rev. ed. (Piscataway, NJ: Gorgias Press, 2003), 320-322. On the identity of the Muslim emir, see Samir Khalil Samir, "Qui est l'interlocuteur musulman du patriarche syrien Jean III (631-648)?," in *IV Symposium Syriacum 1984*, ed. H.J.W. Drijvers et al. (Rome: Pontifical Institute of Oriental Studies, 1987), 387-400. See also Harald Suermann, "Orientalische Christen und

The dialogue begins in the form of a letter written to a concerned person or community. The Jacobite patriarch and other Christian leaders had been summoned before the emir. The author reassures his audience that the emir's purpose is to ask John a series of questions regarding the Christian faith and practice. Over the course of the discussion, the emir asks John seven questions. First, the emir asks John if all Christians follow the same Gospel. John responds: "It is one and the same to the Greeks and the Romans and the Syrians and the Egyptians and the Ethiopians and the Indians and the Arameans and the Persians and the rest of all the peoples and languages."[210] On a theological level, John is concerned with a positive portrayal of Christian unity. The message of one Gospel served as a proclamation of its universality and an apologetic to the Islamic conquest and political pressures related to Christian divisions. On a legal level, John expresses the ability of Christians to govern themselves according to the criteria accepted by all Christians within the Gospel.

But the emir challenges John to account for the multiplicity of Christian groups despite the fact that there is a single Gospel. In response, he points out that just as "Emigrants/Hagarenes," Jews, and Christians accept the Torah but are divided, so too each group interprets Scripture differently. In the theological realm, John emphasizes the common scriptural foundations of Christians, while acknowledging that their interpretation is what separates them.[211] John subtly underscores the need for his Jacobite Christian group to be the proper judges in the interpretation of Christian scriptures.

---

der Islam: Christliche Texte aus der Zeit von 632-750," *Zeitschrift für Missionwissenschaft und Religionswissenschaft* 67 (1983): 120-136.

[210] Michael Penn, "John and the Emir: A New Introduction, Edition and Translation," 86.

[211] If the dialogue is a later text, then the author was aware of the fact that this same situation pertained to Muslim sects who argued about the proper interpretation of the Qur'an. Intra-Islamic polemicists used the category of heretics (*zanadiqa*) to claim that their community represented Islam faithfully based on their interpretive traditions (*sunna*).

Then the emir asks John if Christians consider Jesus Christ as equal to God. John explains how Jesus' human-divine relationship should be properly understood. He affirms that Christ was God and Word, eternal and without beginning, and became flesh for the salvation of mankind by the Holy Spirit and the Virgin Mary the Mother of God.[212] For John, emphasizing the divinity of Jesus Christ prevented any misunderstanding between Christian and Islamic conceptions of his identity.

In response, the emir challenges him about Jesus' divinity: "When Christ, who you say is God, was in Mary's womb, who bore and governed the heavens and the earth?"[213] John replies that if God descended to give the Law to Moses, then God is able to be present everywhere at all times. John concludes that the same explanation applies to Jesus Christ while he was in Mary's womb.

Then the emir asks whether Abraham and Moses belonged to Judaism, Christianity, or Islam.[214] For the emir, Christians did not properly follow the monotheistic message of the Believers and the prophets sent to them by God. But John, who is familiar with this tactic from Jewish-Christian debates, declares that all of the patriarchs, prophets, and righteous believers held to the same claims as the Christian faith that God is one. For John, the Incarnation of Jesus Christ revealed the true nature of God as Trinity. Previously, the people were not ready for his message since they had a tendency toward idol worship. The Jews proclaimed the truth in a reserved fashion through the Shema: "Hear, O Israel, the Lord our God is one Lord" (Deut. 6:4). For the patriarch, God reveals himself progressively in time as one God, the Father, Son, and Holy

---

[212] The statement resonated for Jacobites and Chalcedonians since his statement "Mother of God" was in contrast to the Nestorian claim that Mary should be called rather "Mother of Christ."

[213] Michael Penn, "John and the Emir: A New Introduction, Edition and Translation," 87.

[214] According to some scholars, early Muslims accepted the idea that the Torah was a revealed text since it belonged to the family of righteous believers. Fred Donner, "From Believers to Muslims: Confessional Self-Identity in the Early Islamic Community."

Spirit. John is explicit about the fact that there is no division in God. He was aware of the Jewish claim that Christians had ascribed a partner to God. As a strict monotheist, the emir would have agreed with this Jewish premise.

Next, the emir demands that John point out where the Torah mentions that Christ is God, born of the virgin, and that God had a son. The emir limits John to the Mosaic Law as a source (although the Christian Old Testament includes the Pentateuch, Prophets, and Writings).[215] The concept that the prophets in the Bible are inadmissible as scriptural proof would subsequently set the tone for Christian dialogue with Islam. Previously, Christian apologists developed testimony collections from their Bible to demonstrate the authenticity of Christian doctrines in dialogues with Jews. These testimony collections had to be re-evaluated and adapted to answer their Muslim interlocutors who did not agree with the authoritative nature of scriptures other than the Qur'an.[216]

---

[215] This evidence suggests several ideas about Muslim perceptions of dialogue during this period. First, it demonstrates that Muslims accepted the Torah as a partial source for revelation. Since the Torah was considered a divinely-revealed Scripture in Islam; it was worthwhile to examine its text. In the following centuries, Muslims would not avail themselves of the biblical text at all. It was only through the lens of the Qur'an that such stories would be read, based on their interpretations in the oral traditions (*hadith*). These interpretations would co-opt biblical narratives as the subtext for interpreting the Qur'an. The emir's willingness to look at evidence in the Torah for verification of Christian doctrines indicates that the composition came from an early stage in the Muslim-Christian conversation, when there was still reason to search its contents. The question also provides a hint at how Muslims would use the Old Testament and its Law in light of qur'anic interpretation. For the emir, only the first five books of the Christian Old Testament (the Pentateuch) were considered part of this divine witness given by God to Moses. Despite the fact that prophets came to Israel and that these prophets are mentioned in the Qur'an, he did not consider their narratives as part of God's proto-Islamic message.

[216] See David Bertaina, "The Development of Testimony Collections in Early Christian Apologetics with Islam"; and Mark Swanson, "Apologetics, Catechesis, and the Question of Audience in 'On the

For instance, John quotes Genesis as a proof of God's triune nature: "Then the Lord rained on Sodom and Gomorrah brimstone and fire from the Lord out of heaven" (19:24). Since "the Lord" appears twice in the verse, John argues that this is a reference to God's triune nature:

> The glorious emir asked that this be shown in the scripture. And without delay our father showed (this) in the full Greek and Syriac scriptures. For there were also present with us in (that) place some Hagarenes and they saw with their eyes those writings and the glorious name of "the Lord" and "the Lord." Indeed, the emir summoned a Jewish man who was [there] and was considered by them an expert of scripture. And he asked him if this was so in the wording of the Torah. But he answered, "I do not know exactly."[217]

In his seventh and final question, the emir asks John to explain Christian law.[218] John had to show the emir that the laws were written in the Gospel, or the Christian community would be required to follow Islamic law. He does not give a specific response to the question of how the Gospel governs Christian law. Instead, he affirms that the community's laws are based on the doctrines and commandments of Scripture, as interpreted by the early Church community and the canons of the Church. For John, these were virtuous, just, and worthy laws.

At this point, the Muslim emir concludes the discussion. The author mentions that the Chalcedonian Christians offered prayers

---

Triune Nature of God' (Sinai Arabic 154) and Three Treatises of Theodore Abu Qurrah."

[217] Michael Penn, "John and the Emir: A New Introduction, Edition and Translation," 88-89.

[218] Religious autonomy and tolerance was later allowed on the basis of interpreting the qur'anic verse from Q 5:47, "And let the People of the Gospel judge in accordance with what God has revealed in it." As a revealed law, the Islamic legal code determined the rules governing their Christian subjects following the Islamic conquest. John needed to offer a coherent and intelligible set of laws rooted in Scripture in order for Christians to maintain their own governance.

for the patriarch John and asked for prayers for the emir, John, and the other bishops of the synod who were present at the discussion.[219]

John is not a victorious hero for his community at the end of the discussion. Rather, a concern at the conclusion of the text is to emphasize the solidarity between the Chalcedonian and Jacobite communities in the face of the Islamic conquest. This tone of conciliation reflects the fact that shortly after the Islamic conquest Christians found themselves as a marginalized community which continued to make arguments against Muslims in a similar fashion to their approach with Jews.[220]

The story provides helpful information about the history of Christian-Muslim encounters through its presentation of early Islamic knowledge and interest in religious dialogue. The use of the literary form highlights several important points about its role in early dialogue. First, Muslims such as the emir were still seeking to interpret their own scriptures in light of other scriptures that were assumed to be revealed. The emir demonstrates a willingness to acknowledge the specific passages and the use of scriptures as grounds for an interreligious discussion. Second, the debate provides an initiation into the use of scriptural reasoning as a method, both as a starting point and as evidence for a rational argument. The dialogue includes only one concrete example of using scriptures in an apologetic manner. Third, the dialogue demonstrates a preoccupation with practical affairs in the day-to-day life of Christians in the decades following the Islamic conquest. The emir is concerned with Christian inheritance law, and if the Gospel contains the proper commandments and prohibitions. The emir claims that the law of the "Emigrants/Hagarenes" would be an alternative

---

[219] Scholars have been able to connect most of the bishops with historical figures from the mid-seventh century including Thomas, Severus, Sergius, Aitallaha, and John, who are mentioned in the dialogue. See Hoyland, *Seeing Islam as Others saw It*, 459-465, esp. 464.

[220] Harald Suermann, "The Old Testament and the Jews in the Dialogue between the Jacobite Patriarch John I and 'Umayr ibn Sa'd al-Ansari."

for the community if it did not have its own laws. Fourth, the literary dialogue between John and the emir is explicitly an internal document (a letter) that reveals little knowledge of religious others. The only exception is its use of traditional argumentation employed by Jews and Christians. It commends their patriarch's place as a speaker for all Christians and does not discuss Muslim doctrines. The text is not polemical in tone toward its Muslim interlocutors; rather the dialogue is an apologetic that is interested in presenting the Muslim leader in a favorable light. These qualities add verisimilitude to the literary dialogue and add to its charitable approach regarding the religious encounter.

In light of the Islamic conquest and the possibilities of conversion, the literary dialogue form was employed to explain the political, social, and religious realities of the new situation in the Middle East. The emir is in the position of authority throughout the discussion. He calls John to his audience to give an account of Christianity and to answer his questions. Despite the fact that he rarely speaks in the dialogue, the text renders his views just as accurately as what one might hear from a Muslim emir. He dismisses the group when he is finished. He has power over John's fate based on the author's concern for his well-being. The emir holds a position of power, but the dialogue frames the story in such a way that John is permitted to have the final word on each question. The emir is less of a discussion partner than a facilitator during the discussion. At the same time, this does not belittle his importance. The point of the dialogue is not a question of the true religion, but the question of proper governance in the wake of the Islamic conquest. In this respect, the dialogue between John and the emir used the literary form as a strategy for responding to the challenges resulting from the Islamic conquest.

'ALI AND THE BYZANTINE MONK

Many conversion stories were preserved in the genre called the "virtues of 'Ali." This literary genre was interested specifically in the miraculous, examples of divine knowledge, and superiority in debate with other religious groups. The authors were similarly interested in the incompetence of the proto-Sunni leadership as their Shi'ite theological claims. According to the claims of medieval authors, they had discovered dialogues recorded and transmitted via oral tradition, although their origins likely belong to later centuries.

In particular, medieval authors used 'Ali's miraculous knowledge of Judaism and Christianity as motifs for conversion.

Although written during later periods of mass conversion in the ninth to eleventh centuries, the dialogues between 'Ali ibn Abi Talib and different Christians were meant to look back into history at the power of conversion in the nascent Shi'ite community, and specifically to promote certain political and theological claims about 'Ali. As we shall see, often the literary dialogues between Christians and Muslims were tied to communal disputes between Muslims concerning matters of authority and theological orthodoxy.[221]

One important strategy employed in Muslim literary dialogues was Christian conversion to Islam. In the midst of internal disputes about authority and political power, several Shi'ite authors composed dialogues between 'Ali and Christians for several purposes. They used the form to demonstrate their power before Christians, show the proto-Sunni caliphal weakness in the face of Christian arguments, display 'Ali's ability to compel conversion through his special attributes of persuasion and knowledge, and most importantly, to reveal 'Ali's special status as the successor of the Prophet.

In the dialogue between 'Ali and the Byzantine monk, the story begins with a Byzantine delegation visiting Medina to meet Abu Bakr. A Christian monk is part of the entourage, and he goes to the mosque where Muhammad was buried, bringing with him gold and silver. After meeting Abu Bakr and the Medinans and Meccans in his party, the monk asks him: "Are you the successor of your prophet the messenger of God, and representative of your religion?"[222] Abu Bakr replies by asking for the monk's name, to which he answers that it is 'Atiq – which means "old man" in Arabic. When Abu Bakr asks him why he had such a name, he replies that he is so old that he knows no other name by which he is

---

[221] The text, preserved by a twelfth-century compiler of debates, was edited by Muhammad Baqir al-Khursan. See Ahmad ibn 'Ali al-Tabarsi, *Al-Ihtijaj*, 2 vols. (Najaf: Dar al-Nu'man, 1966), 1:307-308.

[222] Ahmad ibn 'Ali al-Tabarsi, *Al-Ihtijaj*, 1:307.

called. At this point, Abu Bakr asks him what he wants to debate, signifying the special place of the court for theological discussion. The monk replies with a test for his Islamic audience:

> I am from Byzantine territory. I came from it with a respectable amount of gold and silver. Therefore I would like to ask the representative of this community a question. If he answers me regarding it, then I will convert to Islam. Whatever he commands me, I will agree to, and I will split this money between you. But if he is unable to answer it, I will return home with what I have and I will not convert to Islam.[223]

Upon hearing this challenge, Abu Bakr asks him to initiate the debate. However, the monk refuses to begin the discussion, since he argues that they would not believe him on account of their pride and their numerical strength. Following the protocol of Christian-Muslim dialogue, both parties agree that no physical action will take place against the weaker member. When Abu Bakr gives the monk a guarantee that he is safe and no harm will come upon him, no matter what he says, the monk offers his riddle: "Tell me about something that God does not have, and is not from God, and God does not know of it."[224]

According to the dialogue, the caliph Abu Bakr trembles and does not offer an answer to the Christian monk. After a time of silence, Abu Bakr calls for 'Umar to enter the debate, who was an important figure and the second caliph after Abu Bakr's death. When he too is unable to respond, 'Uthman (the future third caliph) is brought in and the same thing happens again. In response to their incapacity to answer him, the monk asks: "Are the noble shaykhs speechless for Islam?" and when he gets up in order to leave, Abu Bakr exclaims, "Enemy of God, were it not for the promise, then the earth would be colored with your blood!"[225]

The first section of the dialogue reflects a Shi'ite commentary on the early leadership within the Believers' community. For the

---

[223] Ibid.
[224] Ibid.
[225] Ibid.

Shiʻite author, early proto-Sunni leadership was incompetent in matters of divine knowledge, charismatic authority, and temperament. The wise old Christian monk and his riddle had bested the most venerable leaders of the proto-Sunni movement.

The dialogue presumes that a number of other prominent Muslims were present for this important event, including Salman the Persian, an important transmitter of oral traditions for Shiʻites. In the story, he goes to ʻAli ibn Abi Talib who was sitting outside with his sons Hasan and Husayn. Then ʻAli enters the mosque where the discussion is taking place, and the monk asks for his name. Foreshadowing his special knowledge and charisma, ʻAli replies: "My name among the Jews is Elijah, and among the Christians Elias, and among my children ʻAli, and among my community Lion (Haydara)."[226] When the monk learns of his relationship to the Prophet, he tells him his companion is Jesus, and then asks the same riddle. Unlike the others, however, ʻAli demonstrates knowledge and authority in his response – immediately effecting the conversion of the Christian monk:

> ʻAli replied, "You made an error concerning the Knowing One. As for your statement 'what God does not have', God is one and he has no companion and no child. As for your statement 'it is not from God', there is nothing of God's oneness that is unjust. As for your statement 'God does not know it', he does not know any partners he has in the kingdom."

> Then the monk got up and cut off his belt and grabbed his head, and his eyes acknowledged what [ʻAli] had clarified. He said, "I testify that there is no god but God and I testify that Muhammad is the messenger of God, and I testify that you are the successor and the leader of this community, and the treasure trove and wisdom of religion, and the preeminent source of proof, for I recited your name in the Torah as Elijah, and in the Gospel as Elias, and in the Qurʾan as ʻAli, and in the books of the forefathers as Lion, and I found you as regent after the prophet, and the authoritative emir, and I proclaim the truth to

---

[226] Ibid., 1:308.

this gathering of others. Tell me, what do you and the people want?"[227]

Following the monk's conversion, he fulfills his promise to distribute his possessions among the poor and needy in Medina, never returning to Byzantine lands. The story ends with 'Ali's ability to convert the old Byzantine monk as the centerpiece of its narrative.

The Christian monk does not participate extensively in the narrative – in fact his only question was a riddle with no Christian connotations but clear Islamic references. The author is careful to demonstrate that the monk critiques the leadership of the proto-Sunni movement, but the monk never criticizes Islam. The dialogue does not show interest in theology, technical terminology, or historical details. Rather, it is particularly interested in the personality and virtues of 'Ali.

The subtext of the dialogue is not only about conversion but about Shi'ite theological claims. The literary form has an intra-religious use: the monk becomes the mouthpiece for an intra-Islamic debate concerning the true heirs of the Prophet in the religious and political realms. According to the monk, 'Ali exhibits the qualities of an authentic successor, a Commander of the Believers, a religious leader foretold in the scriptures and possessor of divine knowledge. His conversion in the dialogue demonstrates that even outsiders recognized 'Ali's claims, explicitly suggesting that the proto-Sunni community could not be trusted to distinguish between right and wrong in terms of religion or political leadership. In fact, Abu Bakr, 'Umar, and 'Uthman are incompetent in the areas that are most important for the community.

The dialogue presents itself as a contest of minds between an old Byzantine monk and the victorious 'Ali. The literary motif of conversion via debate became an important style applied by other Shi'ite authors. But why was the language of debate and conversion in reported speech about 'Ali's actions centuries earlier important for the later Shi'ite community? The dialogue form was valuable for

---

[227] Ibid.

the minority Shi'ite community because it presented their arguments on equal terms with Sunnis. Set in a debate settled only by intellectual argumentation and knowledge, Shi'ites believed that their claims merited a more convincing worldview than those claimed by their fellow Sunni traditionists and their schools. The dialogue was one way of expressing this confidence in literary terms. It was a way to share with a sympathetic audience as well as an idealized model for converting others. Another example of a Shi'ite-Christian dialogue will shed more light on these themes.

'ALI AND THE PATRIARCH

According to important Twelver Shi'ite traditionists of the eleventh century, 'Ali was also responsible for the conversion of an Arab Christian patriarch during a pivotal moment in the history of the early community.[228] But similar to the other narrative, it was part of the medieval genre that sought to magnify 'Ali through his knowledge, clarity, persuasiveness, and charismatic authority. Corollary to this goal was the attempt to denigrate the memory of the other early leaders, Abu Bakr and 'Umar, who were viewed as illegitimate usurpers of 'Ali's rightful place as Commander of the Believers.

The dialogue with the Patriarch begins immediately following the Prophet's death (632), when an entourage of Christians comes to Medina. According to the story, one of the Christians was a patriarch well-known among his Christian peers and well-schooled in dialectical reasoning. He had even memorized the entire Bible. In other words, he was one of the most intelligent and powerful Christians in the region. To convert someone like this would demonstrate the divine origins and authority of the Shi'ite tradition.

At the outset of the story, the patriarch is well disposed toward the Prophet's community. He notes that the Gospel contained verses mentioning that another messenger would come after Jesus. But the patriarch is concerned about something that also

---

[228] For this text, see Muhammad ibn al-Hasan al-Tusi, *Amali al-Shaykh al-Tusi*, 2 vols. (Najaf: Matba'at al-Nu'man, 1964), 1:222-225.

troubled the early Believers: who had the Prophet established as a regent to lead their community, and to instruct them on ambiguous matters? The patriarch asks to see this regent, in order to voice some of his objections. Then Abu Bakr and 'Umar engage in a dialogue with the patriarch:

> [The patriarch] said to him, "Tell us, successor, regarding your superiority over us in religion, for we came to ask about that." Abu Bakr said, "We are believers and you are unbelievers, and the believer is not like the unbeliever, and faith is not like unbelief." The Patriarch replied: "This claim justifies your argument, so tell me: are you a believer in God's view or in your own view?" Abu Bakr said, "I think I am a believer for I have no knowledge of God's view." The Patriarch replied, "Then how am I an unbeliever in your view based on the metaphor in which you are a believer – or am I an unbeliever in God's view?" He said, "I think you are an unbeliever, but I have no knowledge of the situation in God's view." The Patriarch replied, "Then I cannot show you my reliability without you doubting and I am not convinced by your religion. Tell me, do you have a place in the Garden, in which you are sure you are in it based upon your religion, in God's view?" He said, "By all means I expect that!" The Patriarch replied, "I can only show you that I am silent and fearful, in your view, so what is your superiority over me in terms of knowledge?"
>
> Then [the Patriarch] said to him, "Tell me, do you possess all of the knowledge of the prophet, delegated to you?" He replied, "No, but I know from him what part of his knowledge is necessary for me." He said, "But how do you determine the successor to the prophet, when you have not preserved the knowledge which his community uses for the argument to have his knowledge? How did your people set a precedent regarding this matter?" 'Umar said to him, "Stop with this annoyance, Christian, lest we spill your blood!" The Patriarch re-

plied, "This is not just for one who comes as a rightly-guided seeker."²²⁹

Similar to the story of 'Ali and the Byzantine monk, the Christian asks Abu Bakr questions which confuse him until he becomes enraged. But this dialogue contains more detailed dialectical questions, albeit exclusively ones that concerned later medieval Sunni and Shi'ite issues. Nevertheless, the discussion dealt with real dialectical arguments that took place between Muslims concerning the leader of the community and the principles of authority. The patriarch's questions were the type of questions Shi'ites likely asked in real formal debates.

Following the heated exchange, Salman the Persian gets up from the audience to bring 'Ali to debate with the Christian patriarch. The dialogue begins with 'Ali, whom the author calls the Commander of the Believers (*Amir al-Mu'minin*). The leader of the early Believers' movement was given this title. This is one example of the intra-Islamic polemics present in the dialogue.

The patriarch begins along the same line of questioning with 'Ali, although he deftly responds to these queries using arguments from revelation (the Prophet and the Qur'an). When 'Ali is asked whether he is a believer, he acknowledges that he believes in both his view and God's view as confirmed in his creed. The patriarch is skeptical of this argument; however, and declares that it is better to trust in God than the religious statement of a creed.

The second question is about salvation. Do Muslims know if they are saved? 'Ali replies that he will be with his prophet's community in the highest Paradise, as confirmed by the promise made in the revelation of the Qur'an given to the Prophet. Then the patriarch asks how 'Ali could guarantee the trustworthiness of this revelation, to which he replies that it was through signs and miracles. Once again, the skeptical patriarch declares that signs and miracles are a matter of dispute.

While 'Ali responds to the initial questions, his words are unpersuasive to the patriarch. Yet the discussion continues in a new

---

[229] Ibid., 2:222-223.

direction, in which 'Ali demonstrates his knowledge of divine matters in a more convincing fashion. This part of the dialogue moved from principles of authority to questions of theology. In the space of five short questions, the patriarch was converted to the teachings set forth by 'Ali. The patriarch first asks about God and his location and then how he communicates with humanity:

> ['Ali] said, "Christian, God is exalted above space, and he is beyond a place of being, so there is no descent or location. Now he is above that, he does not change from state to state."
>
> He replied, "Indeed, it is proper, wise one, and concise in reply. So tell me about God, is he perceived by means of the senses, in your view, encouraging right guidance in his instruction using senses, or how is it known that he does not command like that?" The Commander of the Believers said, "The Most High is the Almighty King that is described by means of space and time, or the senses perceive him, or it is measured by men, and the way to knowing him is his handicraft. The Splendid One has demonstrated intelligence, consisting in that which takes place before witnesses and is sensible from it."[230]

The third question moved the topic from dialogue about God to Jesus Christ. The patriarch asks 'Ali to explain his prophet's Christology. Was he in fact a created being, whose origin was in mankind? Did he reject Christ's divinity, and make him an inferior creature despite that which other religious communities claimed? 'Ali explains that he was a creature, with a physical form that changed states. For 'Ali, Jesus is a sinless prophet with the perfect approval of God, but he came from God in the same way as Adam: "He created him from dust, then he said 'Be' and it was" (Q 3:59).

The fourth and fifth questions related to 'Ali's special knowledge concerning the matter of the generation of Christ. When the patriarch asserts that he cannot refute 'Ali's arguments, he turns into a seeker asking for more insight to verify his claims. Upon hearing 'Ali's explanation, he is instantly converted:

---

[230] Ibid., 2:224.

[The patriarch] said, "You are correct! God is the one who sent forth Christ, and I did not look closely at what you told me about him, save God. I testify that there is no god but God and that Muhammad is the messenger of God and that you are the regent of the messenger of God and I will tell the people the truth about his position."

He converted those who were with him to his Islam, and they said, "We will return to our companions and we will report what we have discovered about this command and we will truly proclaim it."[231]

The theological questions in the latter portion of the dialogue do not employ dialectic, and resemble short creedal responses to the Christian patriarch in the form of confessional polemics. Despite the patriarch's prominence and knowledge of Christianity, he was converted by means of 'Ali's knowledge of Christian theology and charismatic authority. The story ends with a rationalization of why these conversions failed to make Shi'ism the dominant form of Islam. According to the dialogue, when 'Umar heard about the conversion, he praised them and told them to proclaim the entire Islamic message, except for the requirement to acknowledge the prophet's family. Rather, their first commitment was to the successor. After the patriarch and his entourage were dismissed, 'Umar ensured that that the situation was never mentioned again and he threatened punishment for anyone who talked about it. Despite 'Ali's virtues, 'Umar's machinations thwarted his claims to be acknowledged as Commander of the Believers.

The dialogue closes with a retrospective historical explanation of why conversion did not help the early Shi'ite community. First, 'Umar feared 'Ali and had considered killing him. He believed 'Ali wanted to sabotage the Believers' community and to encourage divisions among it. His actions were seen as part of the struggle for political and religious leadership within the early community. Second, 'Ali acknowledged that even when God made an argument clear for Christians and other Believers, their community would not

---

[231] Ibid., 2:225.

increase in number on account these actions. While dialogue with Christianity could bring about conversion, it would not bring about a change in the religio-political theology of the proto-Sunni community.

'ALI AND THE BISHOP OF NAJRAN

The dialogue between 'Ali and the Bishop of Najran was set during the rule of 'Umar ibn al-Khattab (634-644).[232] The historical presence of Christians in Najran is well-known, since the town in southwestern Arabia was a prominent Christian area with at least three churches known in pre-Islamic times.[233] The setting for the dialogue is in Medina, when the Bishop of Najran visits 'Umar in order to pay the poll tax.[234] 'Umar invites him to Islam, so the bishop answers with a theological question: If Paradise belongs to God and it is as wide as the heavens and the earth, where is hellfire located? But 'Umar remains silent and does not give an answer. The assembly present for the discussion even begs the Commander of the Believers to give an answer in order to prevent the bishop from discrediting Islam. But they all bow their heads in shame, for they cannot give a response.

At that moment, 'Ali enters the assembly and prepares to debate the bishop. Consistent with the themes of the "virtues of 'Ali" genre, he is acknowledged as "the perfect moon, the dispeller of darkness, and cousin of the messenger of mankind."[235] Indeed, this dialogue refers to him as the Imam, the instructor in divine matters. When the bishop asks 'Ali the same question about the location of hellfire he replies with an analogy. When night comes, where is the daylight? Then 'Ali uses his knowledge of biblical material to reveal

---

[232] For the Arabic text, see Shadhan ibn Jibra'il al-Qummi, *Kitab al-Fada'il* (Najaf: al-Maktabat al-Haydariya, 1950), 149-151.

[233] On the history prior to Islam, see Norbert Nebes, "The Martyrs of Najran and the End of the Himyar: On the Political History of South Arabia in the Early Sixth Century," 27-59.

[234] One of the manuscripts for this account has Bahrain, rather than Najran, as the origin of the Christian bishop.

[235] Shadhan ibn Jibra'il al-Qummi, *Kitab al-Fada'il*, 150.

God's control over night and day, and over the heavens and the earth. Referring to the story of Moses and the exodus out of Egypt, 'Ali argues that God split the sea and earth for Moses to cross, and the sun went down at that hour, and arose only after Pharaoh and his military were closed up in the sea and drowned.

The bishop agrees heartily with 'Ali, and so he asks him another riddle: What do people take from this world, yet it does not diminish but increases? 'Ali responds that the Qur'an and knowledge were the correct answer, to which the bishop agreed. Then he asks another riddle tied to biblical lore: Who was the first messenger that God sent who was not from the jinn and not from mankind? 'Ali replies that God had sent a raven when Cain killed his brother Abel. When it happened, God sent the raven to look in the ground in order to see how he kept his evil deed a secret.

Then the bishop questions 'Umar again, this time asking him where God is located. At this 'Umar becomes angry and refuses to give an answer. However, 'Ali steps in and gives an anecdotal account of a conversation he had with the Prophet:

> The Imam said: "One day, I was with the messenger of God when an angel came to him and wished peace upon him. He responded with the peace, and then he said, 'Where are you?' [The angel] replied, 'with my Lord, above in the seventh heaven'." Then another angel came to him and [Muhammad] said, 'Where are you?' He replied, 'with my Lord, lying down in the ground of the seventh lower level'. Then another angel came a third time and he asked him, 'Where are you?' He replied, 'with my Lord, in the rising of the sun'. Then another angel came and [Muhammad] said, 'Where are you?' He replied, 'I am with my Lord in the setting of the sun', because God is not devoid of any place, and he is not in anything, and nothing is higher, and nothing is from something. He is almighty upon his throne of the heavens and the earth, nothing is like him, while Christ is comprehensible. He is not far from the weight of a dust speck on the earth…"[236]

---

[236] Ibid., 151.

Although the oral tradition about the Prophet is a simple account of a miraculous event, this knowledge of the divine profoundly impacts the bishop instantly converting him. After hearing these words, he gives the testimony of faith, including a statement that 'Ali is the successor of the messenger of God and his regent. Upon this declaration, the dialogue ends with 'Ali smiling at him and offering him a greeting of peace.

CONCLUSION

The dialogues of conquest and conversion mentioned in this chapter remind us that medieval Christian-Muslim discourse was very concerned with the issue of conversion, real or imagined, for all Christian and Islamic communities. Openness to conversion was a real part of the fabric of the early Islamic Middle East in the wake of the Islamic conquest. The Shi'ite narratives preserved in these traditions employed the concept of conversion on multiple levels. First, the legends aggrandized the power that 'Ali had over the incompetent Abu Bakr, 'Umar and 'Uthman, who were portrayed as confused simpletons incapable of intellectual engagement. Second, the dialogues exalted Shi'ite intellectual prowess over their theological adversaries, particularly on principles of political and religious authority. 'Ali's virtues, wisdom, knowledge, and authority were self-evident proofs for the truth of the Shi'ite position against the claims of their Sunni rivals and their competing narrative of history. Third, the dialogues confirmed the power of the charismatic Shi'ite vision which compelled the conversion of outsiders, even Christian patriarchs, bishops, and monks. The depiction of 'Ali's intellectual abilities, political acumen, and familial ties were meant to confirm the medieval theological view of religious leadership by the imams and their ideal characteristics. For the Shi'ite communities of the Abbasid period, a coherent and popular expression of their theological claims was essential to maintaining and increasing religious and political power in the caliphate. Medieval authors of dialogues assumed that expressions of power relationships were an essential component to the legitimacy of religious authority. Despite lacking the religio-political power of the Sunni scholars and caliphate, medieval Shi'ite thinkers still composed dialogues in such a way as to tacitly assume that this power resided in the imamate. 'Ali's virtues and ability to convert others were not so much about Christianity and conversion as much as a historical memory that mirrored later medieval Shiʿite views of the conquest and early conversions.

The fact that these texts are primarily interested in intra-Islamic debates does not mitigate the interest in Christianity and conversion among the Shiʿite authors of dialogues. First, each dialogue includes a different member of the Christian hierarchy – a monk, a bishop, and a patriarch. Mentioning these positions indicates at least a superficial knowledge on the part of the authors. Second, there is at least some acquaintance with Christian argumentation in two of the dialogues, although they are mostly focused on Islamic questions. The patriarch's questions about whether Muslims knew they were believers, and whether they knew if they would be saved were both based on dialectical reasoning. Since the patriarch found ʿAli's responses based on revelation unconvincing, it may suggest some knowledge on the part of the author about Christian-Muslim exchanges on these issues. Third, the existence of the literary dialogues indicates the permeable boundaries between Christians and Muslims during this period. The literary form of dialogue had a special use for the Shiʿite community, but it also revealed their assumptions of religious pluralism and contacts with Christians (ideal or real). By defining Shiʿism in dialogue with Christian characters, authors made these figures part of Shiʿite memory and history as both opponents and as converts.

The dialogues of conquest and conversion also have value for contemporary scholars. The texts have preserved literary examples of popular medieval Christian and Muslim intra-religious and inter-religious apologetics. While scholars know of a significant number of these texts composed in Syriac and Christian Arabic, presenting some of the texts from the Islamic side is the first step toward answering the question of whether such texts are literary fabrications or literary constructions based on real encounters. Second, the accounts are valuable on a social-historical level for their presentations of the historical situation in the wake of the Islamic conquest and the early Believers' communities, including personalities such as ʿAli. To what extent did these authors construct their dialogues with written material? Do parts of them belong to earlier oral traditions? Is there some kernel of historical truth located in the dialogues? Third, the narratives preserved popular portrayals of discussion partners. The depiction of the emir, monk, patriarch, and bishop reveals that the construction of identity in Christian and

Muslim communities internalized the ideas of others, making them part of their own identity. In the Syriac dialogue between John of Sedra and the Muslim emir, there was an interest in the biblical foundations of both Christians and Believers and how those biblical interpretations would determine the relationship between the communities. In the Shi'ite dialogues, the authors conceived of a religious worldview in which their terms, definitions, and oral traditions would be intelligible and persuasive to an audience that had some resonance with Christianity, Christian figures, and the experience of conversion. Fourth, the dialogues had value in medieval discussions of historical memory. According to Shi'ite authors, Sunni communities had hidden and denied the conversions in order to sabotage 'Ali's right to leadership. The dialogue presents the "true" story – Shi'ite memory has preserved the sole candid narrative of 'Ali's intellectual conquests and conversions against competing Sunni narratives of history. Finally, the similarities between the dialogues suggest the widespread use of such texts in the early Islamic Middle East. The religious uses of the literary form belonged to the literary culture of such a time when conquest, conversion, and dialogue were not only part of a literary exercise in refutation, but a reality of the religious fabric of Middle Eastern societies.

4 Dialogue as Competing Historiographies

By the eighth and ninth centuries, Muslims were using the Qur'an and the interpretive framework of their communities to dialogue with others. Early Muslims distinguished their submission to God and the uniqueness of the Prophet Muhammad from the beliefs and observances of local Jews, Christians, and polytheists by means of literary forms that placed Islam at the center of world history.[237] By the beginning of the Abbasid period (750-1258), Muslim intellectuals employed dialogues as a model for new historiographies that envisioned the ascendency of the Islamic community as the culmination of history – a sacred history of salvation ordained and directed by God.[238] These dialogues utilized the Qur'an, its theological content, and their own creative capacities to support these historical interests.

The Qur'an's incisive critique of Christian faith and practice also encouraged the production of Islamic literature aimed at clarifying its ideas and defending its historical origins.[239] Early Muslims

---

[237] On the development of apologetic prophetic discourse, see Harald Motzki, ed., *The Biography of Muhammad: The Issue of the Sources* (Leiden: Brill, 2000).

[238] On medieval historians and their writing of history, see Chase Robinson, *Islamic Historiography* (Cambridge: Cambridge University Press, 2003).

[239] The genre of proofs for Muhammad's prophecy was a common literary form used to critique Christian faith and practice. For examples and studies of this theme, see Gabriel Said Reynolds, *A Muslim Theologian in a Sectarian Milieu: 'Abd Al-Jabbar and the Critique of Christian Origins* (Leiden: Brill, 2004); Gabriel Said Reynolds and Samir Khalil Samir, eds.,

assumed that the Qur'an was the normative standard for all discussion and their interpretations were the criteria according to which Christians were judged.[240] In response to Christian criticisms, a reliable historical account of the Qur'an's origins, the chronology of its revelation, and the biography of the Prophet all had important roles to play for Islamic communities in their dialogues with Christians. In constructing new histories, Muslims had a fundamental advantage over their Eastern Christian counterparts in the areas of language and religious terminology due to the hermeneutical world of the Qur'an: its discourse determined what was central or peripheral to interreligious discussions due to the widespread reception of its Arabic language, style, and thematic concepts in Islamic society. History was now in the service of faith and the development of the historical report (*khabar*) helped create a consensus on how to engage with other religious communities.

Muslim intellectuals were conscious and responsive to Christian methods of debate and their potential for exploiting scriptural interpretation and dialectical reasoning. As Christians began reading the Qur'an against the grain and critiquing perceived inconsistencies in Muslim doctrines as well as pointing out silences in Islamic texts, they played an important role in sharpening Islamic historical awareness.[241] According to the Muslim Mu'tazilite theologian of Basra, 'Amr Ibn Bahr al-Jahiz (d. 868), Christian polemic was

---

'Abd al-Jabbar: Critique of Christian Origins, A Parallel English-Arabic Text (Provo: Brigham Young University Press, 2010).

[240] On the qur'anic view of Christians, see Sidney Griffith, "Christians and Christianity"; David Marshall, "Christianity in the Qur'an"; and Jane Dammen McAuliffe, "Christians in the Qur'an and Tafsir."

[241] For some examples of Christians using the Qur'an and the Bible, see Sidney Griffith, "Arguing from Scripture: The Bible in the Christian/Muslim Encounter in the Middle Ages," in *Scripture and Pluralism: Reading the Bible in the Religiously Plural Worlds of the Middle Ages and Renaissance*, ed. T.J. Heffernan & T.E. Burman (Leiden: Brill, 2005), 29-58; Sidney Griffith, "The Qur'an in Arab Christian Texts; the Development of an Apologetical Argument: Abu Qurrah in the Maǧlis of Al-Ma'mun," *Parole de l'Orient*, 24 (1999), 203-233.

well-known to Muslims as they devised responses to its intellectual challenges:

> They hunt down what is contradictory in our traditions, our reports with a suspect line of transmission and the ambiguous verses of our scripture. Then they single out the weak-minded among us and question our common people concerning these things... and they will often address themselves to the learned and the powerful among us, causing dissension among the mighty and confusing the weak.[242]

Despite al-Jahiz's claim that Muslims were unprepared for Christian argumentation, several educated Muslims read Christian Arabic literary disputations, knew their arguments, and recognized the potential dangers involved in religious apologetics. For instance, the Muslim Mu'tazilite 'Isa Ibn Subayh al-Murdar (d. ca. 840) of Baghdad composed a now-lost response *Against the Christian Abu Qurra*, in response to a work by the Melkite bishop Theodore Abu Qurra. Another strategy employed by Muslim writers in response to these critiques was to use the literary form of dialogue, often in the form of a disputation. A number of educated Muslims were well-versed in real debates with Christians both in literary and oral form. It is not surprising that Muslim writers would choose the literary form of dialogue to respond to their opponents, given its popularity among other communities of the Middle East.[243]

---

[242] Quoted in Robert Hoyland's introduction to a collection of essays on formative Islam in Robert Hoyland, ed., *Muslims and Others in Early Islamic Society* (Aldershot, England: Ashgate Variorum, 2004), xiii-xxx, esp. xviii. An older and partial English translation was published by Joshua Finkel, "A Risala of Al-Jahiz," *Journal of the American Oriental Society*, 47 (1927), 311-334, see 331. For the Arabic, see A-S. M. Harun, *Rasa'il Al-Jahiz*, 4 vols. (Cairo: Maktabat al-Khanji, 1964-1979), 3:320.

[243] See the importance of the literary form in Ute Pietruschka, "Classical Heritage and New Literary Forms: Literary Activities of Christians during the Umayyad Period." On its value in history, see the book chapters in G. J. Reinink and H. L. J. Vanstiphout, eds. *Dispute Poems and Dialogues in the Ancient and Mediaeval Near East*.

Some of the earliest dialogue accounts, belonging to the eighth-century biographical literature about the Prophet, demonstrate Muslim interest in theological engagement. But employing the dialogue form in Arabic was feasible only at the advent of the Abbasid period for several reasons. Robert Hoyland summarizes the factors that generated such interreligious discussion in his introduction to *Muslims and Others in Early Islamic Society*:

> The cosmopolitan nature of Baghdad and its province, the caliphs' universal deployment of dialectical reasoning based upon categorical definitions, and the proliferation of converts and apostates, which meant that there were many with a genuine knowledge of two religions and with a real will to champion one over the other. But also, quite simply, there were matters that needed debating.[244]

The Abbasids constructed their new capital at Baghdad in 762, nearby the old Sasanian capital of Seleucia-Ctesiphon, providing the catalyst for participating in religious and scientific discussions of the time.[245] The translation movement, which brought literature from Greek and Syriac into Arabic, sparked an interest in Hellenistic thought and philosophical categories of knowledge.[246] Christians and Muslims came into close contact with one another as collaborators in the endeavor to translate ancient texts as a common enterprise. Arabic gradually became the dominant language of the administration during the eighth and ninth centuries. Arabic only became a convenient language for literary production when it was established as an administrative language for the caliphate and as the language for scholarship. These political and linguistic factors

---

[244] Robert Hoyland, "Introduction," in *Muslims and Others in Early Islamic Society*, xiii-xxxiv, esp. xviii-xix.

[245] For examples of genres from the period, see the chapters in M. J. L. Young, J. D. Latham, and R. B. Serjeant, eds., *Religion, Learning, and Science in the 'Abbasid Period* (Cambridge: Cambridge University Press, 1990).

[246] See Dimitri Gutas, *Greek Thought, Arabic Culture: The Graeco-Arabic Translation Movement in Baghdad and Early Abbasid Society (2nd-4th/8th-10th Centuries)* (London and New York: Routledge, 1998).

were significant reasons for the appearance of Muslim literary dialogues in Arabic.

Arab immigration and shifting demographics in the Middle East also contributed to the construction of literary dialogues. Because of Arab migration, Muslims in new territories had to govern not only Christians and Jews, but Zoroastrians, Mandaeans, and Manichaeans. Governance of the religiously plural caliphate required an acquaintance with such groups, and dialogue was a natural part of this effort. In addition, many converts brought new ideas to Islamic communities. Conversions were motivated by a desire for political power, a change in tax status, or a genuine spiritual commitment, but all converts shaped their Islamic practice according to their religious background.[247] Some Muslims converted to other religions or switched allegiance to different Islamic groups, necessitating each community to construct a sound defense within the pluralistic Abbasid society. Through the social and cultural realities of the Abbasid caliphate and the normative world of the Arabic Qur'an, scholarly Muslims began to compose dialogues as descriptions of their historical worldviews.

In the early Abbasid period, Muslims authors primarily used four sources to conduct encounters with Christians. First, they utilized the Qur'an as a source of authentication for their worldview. For instance, early biographical literature described Jesus Christ by using qur'anic stories rather than biblical accounts.[248] Second, they

---

[247] Yohanan Friedmann, *Tolerance and Coercion in Islam: Interfaith Relations in the Muslim Tradition* (Cambridge: Cambridge University Press, 2006).

[248] One example is his use of Q 3:43 and Q 19:21 as biblical stories about Jesus. These accounts have no parallel in the Bible, but in addition to the Qur'an they are located in the Infancy Gospel of Thomas and the Gospel of Pseudo-Matthew. For more on this topic, see Suleiman Mourad, "From Hellenism to Christianity and Islam: The Origin of the Palm Tree Story concerning Mary and Jesus in the Gospel of Pseudo-Matthew and the Qur'an," *Oriens Christianus* 86 (2002): 206-216; Suleiman Mourad, "Mary in the Qur'an: A Reexamination of Her Presentation," 163–174; and again: "On the Qur'anic Stories about Mary and Jesus," *Bulletin of the Royal Institute for Inter-Faith Studies* 1 (1999): 13–24.

used dependable traditions from Islamic literature (e.g., *hadith, tafsir, sira*) to verify their historical interpretations.²⁴⁹ Third, some employed dialectical reasoning (*kalam*) as a discourse for definite classifications of words and their meanings. Dialectical reasoning provided the technique by which they could discuss the character of rational knowledge and the true religion with Christians.²⁵⁰ Finally, some Muslim scholars turned to the Christian Bible as a resource for authenticating Islamic origins and for criticizing Christianity as a corruption of Jesus' message.²⁵¹ These four sources provided the forms with which Muslims would conduct their discussions with Christians about historical matters.

Muslim authors used dialogues to promote their strategies on six principal topics: the historical status of the Qur'an, the historical status of Muhammad as a prophet, the "real" history of Jesus, Christian doctrines and practices, the history of Jewish and Christian corruption of earlier scriptures, and an evaluation of the true religion. Such compositions found common grounds for discourse with Christians through dialectical reasoning as well as through reinterpreting Christian scriptures. However, the inspiration for

---

²⁴⁹ For instance, see Suleiman Mourad, "Christians and Christianity in the Sira of Muhammad," 57–71; Claude Gilliot, "Christians and Christianity in Islamic Exegesis," 31-56; David Cook, "Christians and Christianity in Hadith Works before 900," 73-82; and Marston Speight, "Christians in the Hadith Literature," 30-53.

²⁵⁰ For instance, see the three-volume collection by Richard Frank, *Texts and Studies on the Development and History of Kalam* (Aldershot, England: Ashgate Variorum, 2005-2008); and Josef van Ess, "Early Development of *Kalam*," 109-123.

²⁵¹ On Muslim interpretation of the Bible, see the table constructed by Martin Accad, "The Gospels in the Muslim Discourse of the Ninth to the Fourteenth Centuries: An Exegetical Inventorial Table," *Islam and Christian-Muslim Relations*, 14 (2003), 67-81, 205-220, 337-352, 459-479. See also Sidney Griffith, "Arguing from Scripture"; Hava Lazarus-Yafeh, *Intertwined Worlds*; Camilla Adang, *Muslim Writers on Judaism and the Hebrew Bible: From Ibn Rabban to Ibn Hazm* (Leiden: Brill, 1996); David Thomas, "The Bible in Early Muslim Anti-Christian Polemic," *Islam and Christian-Muslim Relations* 7 (1996): 29-38; Andrew Rippin, "Interpreting the Bible through the Qur'an."

such dialogues came chiefly from the Qur'an. For Muslim authors, the Qur'an and later biographical literature, including oral tradition and commentary writing, provided the inspiration for interreligious discourse, and supplied the necessary content according to which all Christian claims were to be judged. For those who used the literary form to communicate their historical vision, the Qur'an provided the necessary context for configuring the relationship between the ideal period of the Prophet and the contemporary Islamic community. The dialogue was used to create a historical link between the origins of the Islamic community and their current situation within the religiously plural Abbasid society, while criticizing alternative historical narratives from different Islamic and non-Islamic communities.[252]

MUHAMMAD AND THE CHRISTIANS OF NAJRAN

In biographical literature (*sira*) on Muhammad, John Wansbrough has argued that the production of these works signified the emergence of nostalgic and interpretive literature in the formation of Islamic memory in the following centuries.[253] The earliest known biography of Muhammad is attributed to Muhammad Ibn Ishaq (d. ca. 767) as transmitted through Ibn Hisham (d. ca. 833). It occasionally mentions Christians and Christianity. The biography historicizes qur'anic verses that mention Christians, using the Qur'an to create a framework of encounters, dialogues, sermons, and letters. Some of these encounters include a discussion of the rise of Christianity in Najran, the encounter with the monk Bahira, the alleged prediction of Muhammad in the Gospel, the story of the migration of Muhammad's followers to Ethiopia, the encounter with a delegation of Christians from Najran, and letters to Christian

---

[252] Dialogues were not the only way that Muslims engaged Christians. See editions and translations of four Muslim pieces from the Abbasid period concerning Christian faith and practice in David Thomas, ed., *Christian Doctrines in Islamic Theology* (Leiden: Brill, 2008).

[253] See the first chapter on historiography in John Wansbrough, *The Sectarian Milieu*.

kings.[254] Much like Christian hagiography, the biographer Ibn Ishaq depicts Muhammad with special knowledge and insight confirmed by outsiders. Muslim authors such as Ibn Ishaq used historical dialogues for discourse with Christian groups to answer later theological discussions, such as the proof of Muhammad's prophethood.[255]

Christians play a minimal but interesting part in the collection of Muslim oral traditions, most of which were collected in the ninth century.[256] These traditions represented a new effort on the part of Sunni Muslims to historicize their community's origins with authoritative and definitive collections of oral traditions. Among the authoritative collections, the oral traditions of al-Bukhari (d. 870) assert that Muhammad was aware of Christianity while he lived in Medina. Based on information also found in Ibn Ishaq's biography, Muhammad had a cousin named Waraqa ibn Nawfal, who had become a Christian and read the scriptures, mastering the Torah and the Gospel.[257] However, this reference is not a clear historical example of early Islamic discourse with Christians, but rather a symbol that Christians accept Muhammad's prophethood.

---

[254] For a summary of the accounts, see Suleiman Mourad, "Christians and Christianity in the Sira of Muhammad."

[255] While Muslim authors certainly developed hagiographical narratives of the heroes of their communities, their martyrdom accounts do not conform to the same form and content as found in Christian martyrdom stories, likely due to the political situation in which Islam was ascendant and the martyrs were inevitably those opposed to their rule, whether Christian, Jew, or heretical Muslim (*zindiq*).

[256] There are approximately five hundred oral traditions that deal with Christians or Christianity. See Marston Speight, "Christians in the Hadith Literature," 30; and also David Cook, "Christians and Christianity in Hadith Works before 900." Speight points out some affirmative verses, but most are critical of Christians for embellishing churches, reverence for clergy and monasticism, rejecting the Qur'an, and accepting Jesus as God. In particular, the oral traditions seek to distinguish Muslim Friday worship, prayer, and dress from Christian rituals, and restrict Christian freedom such as the traditions of expelling them from the Arabian Peninsula.

[257] The accounts are also found in Ibn Ishaq's biography in Alfred Guillaume, *The Life of Muhammad*, 83, 99, 107.

Waraqa confirms that Muhammad has been given the gift of prophecy from an angel, just like earlier prophets. Based on this reading, the dialogue seeks to historicize Islamic doctrine while subverting later Christian Arabic criticisms of Muhammad. In other words, the passage functions as historiography of the emerging Believers' community and their competition against Christian versions of their origins.

According to Ibn Ishaq's biography, Muhammad met with an Arab Christian delegation from Najran toward the end of his life.[258] Najran had long been a Christian stronghold in southwestern Arabia and was well connected with Ethiopian and Himyarite power.[259] Several scholars have argued that the encounter belongs to the genre of "salvation history" since the narrative is an attempt to contextualize and provide a chronology for the Qur'an and the occasions of its revelation (*asbab al-nuzul*), according to certain memorable events.[260] Other scholars of biographical literature have demonstrated that Muhammad's encounters with Christians in the biographies are utilized almost exclusively for the purpose of validating his prophethood and follow the biblical patterns established by earlier authors.[261] The characters in this particular dialogue reinforce these claims.

The story begins with a delegation from Najran traveling to Medina. The Christian leader in the group was a bishop named Abu Haritha Ibn 'Alqama. He is described as a respected leader,

---

[258] Alfred Guillaume, *The Life of Muhammad*, 270-272. For the Arabic text see Ibn Hisham, *Al-Sirat al-Nabawiyya*, 2:162-163.

[259] On the history of Christians in Najran and their identity, see Irfan Shahid, *Byzantium and the Arabs in the Sixth Century*, 1:33, 1:546-547; and Norbert Nebes, "The Martyrs of Najran and the End of the Himyar: On the Political History of South Arabia in the Early Sixth Century."

[260] See John Wansbrough, *The Sectarian Milieu: Content and Composition of Islamic Salvation History*; Reuven Firestone, "The Qur'an and the Bible: Some Modern Studies of Their Relationship," 1-22.

[261] See Uri Rubin, *The Eye of the Beholder: The Life of Muhammad as viewed by the Early Muslims*; Herbert Berg, "Context: Muhammad" in *The Blackwell Companion to the Qur'an*, 187-204; Harald Motzki, ed., *The Biography of Muhammad*.

scholar of Christianity, and Byzantine supporter. On his way to Medina, he tells his brother that Muhammad is the prophet for whom they have been waiting. Abu Haritha's only reason for remaining a Christian is because the leaders of the delegation would strip him of his wealth and honor if he converts to Islam.[262] This part of the dialogue reminds us to keep in mind the eighth-century motivations of the biographer Ibn Ishaq, who was responding to disputes about the historical origins of the Islamic community.

Ibn Ishaq tries to explain the Christological differences among the members of the delegation, although what he means is not clear. First, some of the Christians from Najran were saying that Jesus is God, while others said he was Son of God, still others said he was the third person of the Trinity – how this signified difference for Ibn Ishaq is ambiguous. The author reinforces this claim by explaining three aspects of their theologies: they affirm that Jesus Christ made clay birds and breathed life into them; they claim that Jesus spoke from the cradle on behalf of his mother Mary; and they call Jesus the "third of three."[263] Ibn Ishaq's description of Christian teaching in this section does not come from the Bible, but from qur'anic stories about Jesus Christ (Q 3:43; Q 19:21; and Q 5:73).[264] His Christology is qur'anic and acknowledges the presence of Christianity in seventh-century Najran. Second, the story mentions that the Christians are from the Byzantine rite. However,

---

[262] There are several other examples that follow the pattern of prophetic authentication, including the account of the monk Bahira and the narrative of the Ethiopian Negus (king) of Axum. On the dialogue with the king, see Alfred Guillaume, *The Life of Muhammad*, 146-153. For the Arabic, see Ibn Hisham, *Al-Sirat al-Nabawiyya*, 1:255-269.

[263] See Sidney Griffith, "Syriacisms in the "Arabic Qur'an": Who were "those who said 'Allah is third of three'" according to al-Ma'ida 73?"

[264] The accounts are not biblical but apocryphal Christian texts. In addition to the Qur'an the narratives are located in the Infancy Gospel of Thomas (clay birds), and the Arabic Infancy Gospel (although titled "Arabic" it was originally a Syriac document that mentions Jesus speaking in the cradle). See also Suleiman Mourad, "From Hellenism to Christianity and Islam: The Origin of the Palm Tree Story concerning Mary and Jesus in the Gospel of Pseudo-Matthew and the Qur'an."

the Arabic and Syriac-speaking Christians of Najran were more likely part of the West Syrian Jacobite communion and opponents to Byzantine bishops and their Christology. They followed a different liturgy (rite) that belonged to the Alexandrian tradition. He is less interested in reconstructing a historical event than in fashioning an interreligious literary encounter for his community's memory of the Qur'an.

The first exchange in the literary dialogue is a theological excursion on the Islamic understanding of monotheism in comparison with Jewish and Christian claims. After entering Medina and praying toward the east in the mosque, the Christian delegation sits down with Muhammad:

> When the two divines spoke to him the apostle of God said to them, "Submit yourselves." They said, "We have submitted." He said: "You have not submitted, so submit." They said, "Nay, but we submitted before you." He said, "You lie. Your assertion that God has a son, your worship of the cross, and your eating pork hold you back from submission." They said, "But who is his father, Muhammad?" The apostle of God was silent and did not answer them. So God sent down concerning their words and their incoherence the beginning of the sura of the Family of 'Imran up to more than eighty verses.[265]

The verbal exchange provides a context for the revelation of the beginning of the third sura and provides historical grounds for elaborating on Islamic qur'anic interpretation in light of an encounter with Christians. The story of a dialogue contextualizes the qur'anic verses with interpretations that fit Ibn Ishaq's theological view of Muhammad as a prophet and how Muslims should properly respond to Christians. Similarly, the qur'anic testimonies serve a polemical purpose in the way that the Qur'an engages its religious opponents. It has a didactic purpose in instructing and refuting, without completely sharing, the opponents' views. Truth is com-

---

[265] Alfred Guillaume, *The Life of Muhammad*, 272. For the Arabic text see Ibn Hisham, *Al-Sirat al-Nabawiyya*, 2:163.

municated through receptivity to the divine pronouncement in the Qur'an.

After Muhammad recites the testimonies from Q 3 on the Family of 'Imran as a response to the delegation from Najran, he believes that they are summoned to justice and divested from a reasonable argument. The dialogue is subsequently finished: the Christians must agree to a mutual invocation of a curse upon the false religion if they oppose Muhammad and his testimonies (Q 3:61). The delegation begs for an opportunity to consult with their chief advisor before coming to a decision. Once again, a Christian leader (this time the political leader) acknowledges Muhammad's prophecy rather than risk violence. The result is that the dialogue ends with the delegation informing Muhammad that they have decided not to offer up a curse and choose instead to leave him and his religion and return home.

As is evident from the biographical literature attributed to the early Believers' community, there is little concern for actual dialogue with Christian interlocutors. Rather, their characters are part of a literary device which constructs a historical context for the Qur'an and the prophetic qualities of Muhammad. The biographical literature reflects less dialogue with Christians than the Qur'an itself. In the Qur'an, such claims are alluded to and taken seriously, so that the prophetic voice acknowledges religious questions. Ibn Ishaq's dialogue between Muhammad and the Christian delegation of Najran does not consider the role of the Christian or other biblical literature as a source. Instead, the characters are typological figures for the truths that Ibn Ishaq seeks to impart to his audience. Composing a coherent historical framework for his community provided the necessary impetus for the reflective narrative.

THE ISLAMIC BAHIRA AND MUHAMMAD

The earliest biographical literature to deal with the question of the historical origins of Muhammad's prophethood and the origins of the Qur'an was also interested in Muslim-Christian relations.[266] In one narrative preserved by Ibn Ishaq and numerous other Islamic authors, a certain elderly Christian monk named Bahira (which is actually a Syriac honorific title designated for monks[267]) confirmed Muhammad's prophecy while he was a youth traveling in a caravan.[268] According to the story, the young Muhammad was traveling toward Syria with his uncle Abu Talib when the group stopped for water at a well. A monk named Bahira lived in a cell near the well and he was well-versed in Christianity and had gained much knowledge from a book he had in his cell. In contrast to the corrupt Christianity of the day, Bahira was one of the remnant followers of the "true" Christianity preached by Jesus in his Gospel, according to the novel historiography proposed by the story. Following a vision of Muhammad, he came out to the group, inviting them to feast with him. When Muhammad finally comes to see Bahira (he is initially left behind to care for the caravan), he calls for Muhammad to come to him and he predicts Muhammad's call to prophecy:

> When Bahira saw him he stared at him closely, looking at his body and finding traces of his description (in the Christian

---

[266] For the sources on Bahira, see Alfred Guillaume, *The Life of Muhammad*, 79-81. For the Arabic, see Ibn Hisham, *Al-Sirat al-Nabawiyya*, 1:147.

[267] The name Bahira is in fact a title for a monk who has proven himself, as shown by other Syriac texts. The Syriac root means "to prove" as in J. Payne Smith, *A Compendious Syriac Dictionary*, 41.

[268] For a discussion of the history of this story in Muslim and Christian traditions, see Sidney Griffith, "Muhammad and the Monk Bahira: Reflections on a Syriac and Arabic Text from Early Abbasid Times," *Oriens Christianus* 79 (1995): 146-174; Barbara Roggema, "A Christian Reading of the Qur'an: The Legend of Sergius-Bahira and Its Use of Qur'an and Sira," in *Syrian Christians under Islam: The First Thousand Years*, ed. David Thomas (Leiden: Brill, 2001), 57-73; Stephen Gero, "The Legend of the Monk Bahira, the Cult of the Cross, and Iconoclasm," in *La Syrie de Byzance à l'Islam, VIIe-VIIIe siècles: Actes du colloque international Lyon-Maison de l'Orient méditerranéen,* ed. Pierre Canivet and Jean-Paul Rey-Coquais (Damascus: Institut français de Damas, 1992), 47-58.

books)... Bahira said, "By God, answer me what I ask." He replied, "Ask me what you like." So he began to ask him about what happened in his sleep, and his habits, and his affairs generally, and what the apostle of God told him coincided with what Bahira knew of his description. Then he looked at his back and saw the seal of prophethood between his shoulders in the very place described in his book.[269]

When Bahira sees the mark, he visits with Muhammad's uncle Abu Talib, and warns him to go back to his land and to guard him carefully against the Jews. The exchange between the Christian monk Bahira ends with his warning that they will do great evil, but that Muhammad will have a great future.

This story claims that a Christian monk named Bahira, who read a certain prophetic book, had encountered Muhammad at one point in his life. The purpose of the story is to demonstrate that even Christians recognized Muhammad's prophethood during his lifetime. The story remained popular well into the medieval period, appearing in later biographies, histories, and commentaries written by Muslims.[270] On the other hand, Christians created a counter-history that recalled Sergius-Bahira as a heretical monk who had led Muhammad astray (it is unclear whether the Christian story or the Muslim story came first). Textual evidence suggests that later collectors of oral traditions were well-aware of an alternative Christian history that claimed Bahira did not recognize Muhammad's prophecy but provided him with biblical material for the Qur'an:

> There was a Christian who embraced Islam and read Surat al-Baqara and Al 'Imran, and he used to write (the revelations) for the Prophet. Later on he reverted to Christianity again, and he used to say: "Muhammad knows nothing except what I have written for him." Then God caused him to die and the people buried him, but in the morning they found that the

---

[269] Alfred Guillaume, *The Life of Muhammad*, 80-81; Ibn Hisham, *Al-Sirat al-Nabawiyya*, 1:147.

[270] For a discussion of the Islamic context of this account, see Barbara Roggema, *The Legend of Sergius Bahira*, 37-60, esp. 39 for sources.

earth had thrown his body out. They said, "This is the act of Muhammad and his Companions. They dug the grave of our companion and took his body out of it because he had run away from them."[271]

In this report, his body is thrown up out of the ground three times, presumably through divine fury at his claims that Muhammad had a human source for the Qur'an. What this tradition reveals is that Muslims were aware of polemical narratives composed by Christians, and the story acts as a historical response to these accounts of Sergius-Bahira.

Originally, the Islamic Bahira historical narrative was a literary instrument used to commend Islamic prophetology. It showed a lack of familiarity with Syriac Christian names, since Bahira is a title like 'venerable' given to a holy man. Its literary afterlife served multiple purposes for different Islamic communities. The structure of the story, including the account of Muhammad's committed monotheism, Bahira's miraculous foreknowledge, and the warning about the Jews, remained the core of the narrative. But some changes took place as well. First, some proto-Sunni versions included Abu Bakr affirming Muhammad in the account, making him the first Believer. This version was a clear attempt to provide a counter-history to Shi'ite claims that 'Ali was the first to follow Muhammad. Second, some versions made the marriage between Muhammad and his first wife Khadija a spiritual event rather than an economic decision, as his future role as a prophet was already known. Barbara Roggema argues that the Islamic Bahira narrative continued to fulfill the needs of different Islamic historiographies in the following centuries. Since the story confirmed the miraculous in Muhammad's life and revealed his prophethood, it became linked with the encounter with Bahira. Any new addition to the story came to be seen as enhancing its historicity, rather than undermin-

---

[271] See al-Bukhari, *Sahih al-Bukhari*, 9 vols. (Riyadh: Darussalam, 1997), 4:492.

ing its historical value.²⁷² This seems to be the first layer of the Bahira story.

In the second layer, an anonymous Christian author composed an apocalyptic dialogue in Syriac based on the assumption that the encounter happened.²⁷³ Christians disseminated the dialogue as a reconfigured historical event. This will be treated in the following section. In the third layer, later Islamic oral traditions tried to discount the Christian historical rewritings that Islam was a product of heretical Christian doctrine. In other words, some oral traditions about Christians reflect dialogues from the Abbasid period that indicate not only attentiveness to Christian arguments but familiarity with their responses to Islamic historiography.

THE CHRISTIAN SERGIUS-BAHIRA AND MUHAMMAD

The Christian Bahira Legend is a noteworthy literary dialogue due to its widespread diffusion, multiple recensions, and widely-varying content.²⁷⁴ The earliest mention of the Christian legend presupposes the historical setting of the Islamic Bahira story and the main structure. Indeed, it also presumes to offer a credible historiography that explains Q 25:5: "They say: 'Legends of the ancients that he has had written down, they are recited to him at dawn and in the evening.'"²⁷⁵ The Muslim version of the story mentioned above is a brief account of Bahira confirming Muhammad's prophethood without theological discussion between the two men. The Christian versions are quite different. For instance, the Christian legend assumes a detailed discussion took place and then uses the silence in the Islamic tradition to create a new "historical" event. The dialogue also adds the name Sergius, since Syriac authors recognized

---

²⁷² Barbara Roggema, *The Legend of Sergius Bahira*, 49, 51.
²⁷³ On the priority of the Syriac to the Arabic and the relationship of the recensions, see Ibid., 211-251.
²⁷⁴ For a comprehensive study, editions, and English translations of the four recensions, see Ibid.
²⁷⁵ See also Q 16:103 on the source of the Qur'an.

Bahira was a title (thus Sergius-Bahira means something equivalent to "the venerable Sergius").[276]

The legend recounts a series of discussions between the monk Sergius-Bahira and Muhammad, framed around an apocalyptic narrative concerning the future of the Islamic empire and the eschatological end of time.[277] The Christian version was circulating by the early eighth century and was likely based on earlier oral traditions. The work underwent many subsequent additions in the following centuries so that we now have Syriac recensions from the East Syrian (Church of the East) and West Syrian (Jacobite) churches, as well as two recensions in Arabic (Melkite). The dialogue took on a literary life of its own, and was subsequently translated into Armenian, Hebrew, and Latin.[278] These recensions incorporated additions into the texts, so that while the Syriac edition focused on the apocalyptic aspects of the text, the Arabic recension added more

---

[276] For more on the priority of the Islamic story based on the name Bahira, see Barbara Roggema, *The Legend of Sergius Bahira*, 58.

[277] On the formation of the apocalyptic portions of the text, see Ibid., 61-93.

[278] A study of the Latin text is available in J. Bignami-Odier and G. Levi della Vida, "Une version latine de l'Apocalypse syro-arabe de Serge-Bahira," *Mélanges d'archéologie et d'histoire* 62 (1950): 125-148. See also Barbara Roggema, "The Legend of Sergius-Bahira: Some Remarks on its Origin in the East and its Traces in the West," in *East and West in the Crusader States*, ed. Krijna Nelly Ciggaar and Herman Teule (Louvain: Peeters, 1999), 107-123; Krisztina Szilágyi, "Muhammad and the Monk: The Making of the Christian Bahira Legend," *Jerusalem Studies in Arabic and Islam* 34 (2008): 169-214; Sidney Griffith, "Muhammad and the Monk Bahira: Reflections on a Syriac and Arabic Text from Early Abbasid Times," and Robert Thomson, "Armenian Variations on the Bahira Legend," in *Eucharisterion: Essays Presented to Omeljian Pritsak*, 2 vols., ed. Ihor Ševčenko and Frank E. Sysyn (Cambridge, MA: Ukrainian Research Institute, 1979-80), 2:884-895. An older study was done by Richard J. H. Gottheil, "A Christian Bahira Legend," *Zeitschrift für Assyriologie* 13 (1898): 189-201, 252-268 (Arabic text); 14 (1899): 203-268; 15 (1900): 56-102; 17 (1903): 125-166 (English translation).

material about the conversations between Muhammad and Sergius-Bahira.²⁷⁹

The Sergius-Bahira account was pieced together from dialogue and apocalyptic material as an attempt to write a historical polemic of how Muhammad received his qur'anic revelations from a Christian monk. The story was a new historiography written in response to the Islamic story of Bahira composed in the biographical literature. Sidney Griffith has demonstrated the antiquity of the tradition among Christians based on an eighth-century literary dialogue between a monk of Bet Hale and a Muslim scholar, in which the monk specifically names Sergius-Bahira as the source of Muhammad's teachings on monotheism. During the late eighth century, the Syriac Christian Theodore Bar Koni alleged that Muhammad had received his information from a teacher who later denounced him.²⁸⁰ John of Damascus also claimed that Muhammad was influenced by an Arian monk in chapter 100 (or chapter 101) in his theological compendium *On Heresies*.²⁸¹ The Arabic letter written by 'Abd al-Masih al-Kindi includes the story of a monk (Nestorius) who fled to the region, instructed Muhammad in the Christian faith, only to have his teachings corrupted by the Jewish scribe Ka'b al-Ahbar.²⁸²

---

²⁷⁹ On the reception history, see Barbara Roggema, *The Legend of Sergius Bahira*, 151-201.

²⁸⁰ See Addai Scher, ed., *Liber Scholiorum: Textus; Theodore bar Konai* (Paris: E Typographeo Reipublicae, 1910-1912), 273.

²⁸¹ See the most recent English translation and theological study of the first part in Adelbert Davids and Pim Valkenberg, "John of Damascus: The Heresy of the Ishmaelites," in *The Three Rings: Textual Studies in the Historical Trialogue of Judaism, Christianity, and Islam*, ed. Barbara Roggema, Marcel Poorthuis, and Pim Valkenberg (Leuven: Peeters, 2005), 71-90. The critical editions of his works are found in P. Bonifatius Kotter, ed. *Die Schriften des Johannes von Damaskos*, vols. 7, 12, 17, 22, 29 (Berlin: de Gruyter, 1969-1988). For the full English translation, see Frederic Chase, ed., *Saint John of Damascus: Writings* (Washington, DC: The Catholic University of America Press, 1958), 153-160.

²⁸² See Anton Tien, ed., *Risalat 'Abdallah b. Isma'il al-Hashimi ila 'Abd al-Masih b. Ishaq al-Kindi yad'u-hu bi-ha ila l-Islam* (London: Society for

In the Christian narrative, Sergius-Bahira is an exiled monk who was sent away by his bishop for disagreeing about the proper veneration of the cross in a church.[283] The setting for the story takes place at his hermitage. In the Islamic narrative, Bahira simply recognizes the young Muhammad as a chosen man and nothing further is mentioned about the event. But in the Christian version, the young Muhammad regularly returns to visit the monk and he undergoes instruction on the basic doctrines of God and Jesus Christ. Following this introductory catechesis, Sergius-Bahira asks that the future prophet protect the Christian people. At first, Muhammad replies: "Everything you ask will be for you, but how will [my people] believe in me, not knowing a book?"[284] When Bahira explains how he should communicate his teachings, Muhammad asks how he can be accepted by the Arabs, to which he is told to claim prophethood. When Muhammad replies that he has no scriptural warrant, Sergius-Bahira responds:

> "I will teach you everything at night, and you teach them during the day." Muhammad said: "And if they say to me: 'From where did you receive this vision or teaching', what shall I say to them?" Sergius said: "Say to them 'The angel Gabriel has come to me at night and he has taught me all that will happen.'" Muhammad said: "And if they say to me: 'What is there in the other world?', what shall I say to them?" Sergius said:

Promoting Christian Knowledge, 1885, reprint, 1912); Georges Tartar, ed., *Dialogue islamo-chrétien sous le calife Al-Ma'mûn (813-834): Les épîtres d'Al-Hashimî et d'Al-Kindî* (Paris: Nouvelles Editions Latines, 1985). The English translation is in N. A. Newman, ed., *The Early Christian-Muslim Dialogue*, 355-545. An interesting parallel with al-Kindi's accusation is a later Islamic biography of the Prophet by Ibn Sa'd (d. 845), which says that the name of the monk was Nestorius. See also Barbara Roggema, "The Confession which Ka'b al-Ahbar handed down to the Ishmaelites," 403-405.

[283] On Bahira's iconoclasm, Christology, and conception of Paradise in the narrative, see Barbara Roggema, *The Legend of Sergius Bahira*, 95-128.

[284] Ibid., 278-279 (East Syrian); 348-349 (West Syrian); 404-405 (Short Arabic Recension); 458-459 (Long Arabic Recension).

"Say to them that there is a paradise and trees and that the best of all things are there."[285]

In the following sections, the anonymous author portrays Bahira as an instructor who gives Muhammad many of the verses in the Qur'an that commend the truth of Christianity and the moral good in general. Bahira offers guidance on instituting rules and practices for fasting, prayer, ablutions, and a description of Paradise. He tells him how to establish communal laws, the proof of his prophethood, the proof of his Scripture, and eschatological teachings. The work is therefore a Christian reading of the Qur'an that seeks to create a new historiography which challenges Muslim claims that their scriptures were corrupted. Instead, the dialogue claims the Qur'an was a text that echoed Christian teachings until it was subsequently changed and corrupted by the Muslim community and the Jewish scribe and early convert Ka'b al-Ahbar, who added a number of other teachings.[286]

During these conversations, the monk commends the proper interpretation of Christianity; the author's originality is to explain it through qur'anic idiom. The story sets the groundwork for contextualizing the Qur'an within a Christian hermeneutic, thereby removing the power of the verse from Muslim discourse. The qur'anic narrative is stripped of its authority through the literary dialogue, and the discursive space created by this critique allows Bahira's character to offer an alternative historiography for the Christian community which empowers their belief and secures their truth claims in the face of Islamic prophetology. According to the dialogue, Islam developed as a misinterpreted model of Christian faith and practice.

The historiography for Islamic origins in the Bahira dialogue reveals two striking features. First, a detailed yet bizarre portrait of the "historical" Muhammad materializes in the dialogue. He is described as an articulate and inquisitive young man. When he speaks

---

[285] Ibid.

[286] On the text as a Christian counter-history of the Qur'an, see Ibid., 129-149.

with Sergius-Bahira, he asks sharp questions about biblical prophecy, doctrines of God, and Christology. But as a disciple, his character is not confident, and he questions everything he is told, and worrying about Arab opposition to his ideas. Muhammad asks "How is this?" and demands "Teach me this!" so that even the detailed rules concerning prostration and ablutions come from Sergius-Bahira. Muhammad becomes a vessel through which the monk transmits his message. Muhammad collects their discussions and calls the book his *furqan* because it came from "scattered" (*mufarraq*) writings.[287] He is completely reliant on the monk, and Islamic traditions regarding Muhammad's illiteracy are reconfigured in a Christian story that gives him the proper interpretations of Scripture to convert his people. The "Christian" and Islamic portraits of Muhammad are similar only to the extent that they were both historical constructs by later communities competing for interpretive rights over the origins of Islam.

Second, the authors of the legends showed a remarkable knowledge of the Qur'an and its traditions (*ahadith*), the biographical narratives (*sira*), and commentaries (*tafasir*) that interpreted and contextualized qur'anic verses. For instance, in one story Muhammad tells his audience that he traveled to the Temple in Jerusalem. They ask him for details about its construction in order to confirm his experience. The Qur'an only makes a passing reference in Q 17:1 to a mystical experience: "Glory to the one who made his servant travel at night from the sacred mosque to the farthest mosque" (*al-masjid al-aqsa*). The author is clearly aware of the Islamic tradition in which some skeptics questioned Muhammad about the authenticity of his Temple experience.[288] The author's response to the situation demonstrates a level of comfort within the Islamic worldview and the writings that were circulating during the Abbasid period in the Middle East. Barbara Roggema and Sidney Griffith have highlighted other examples demonstrating the author's use of

---

[287] Although the writer connects these *furqan* with *mufarraq*, the word *furqan* is a calque on the Syriac cognate *purqana*, which means "salvation." See J. Payne Smith, *A Compendious Syriac Dictionary*, 439.

[288] See Alfred Guillaume, *The Life of Muhammad*, 182-183.

Muslim literature in re-creating a Christian narrative.[289] The work employs many of the same strategies as other literary dialogues in its use of Islamic material to commend the truth of Christianity and to construct a new historiography related to Muhammad and the rise of Islam.

CONCLUSION

The legacy of new historiographies in the eighth and ninth centuries had a lasting effect on Christian-Muslim relations. The attempts to historicize the origins of Islam through biographical traditions by Muslims writers and through the dialogue form by Christian authors shaped later communities and their attitudes toward each other.[290] Barbara Roggema argues that this counter-history was a product of the competitive historiographies being constructed by Christian and Muslim authors as a process of deconstructing the memory and identity of one's opponent. For Christians, the Sergius-Bahira legend was a way to defend their faith and re-shape Islamic traditions according to their ideals.[291] Indeed, the Christian retelling of the historical Muhammad, the origins of the Qur'an, and the origins of Islam were meant to challenge Islamic histories of the Bible and Christianity.

Four important features highlight how Muslims and Christians used the dialogue form in competitive narratives of the past. First, the dialogue was used to assess the "historical" Muhammad and the theological doctrines of prophetology. For Muslims, these traditions and biographies were meant to legitimize the Prophet's life and works and confirm the practice (*sunna*) of the community. For Christians, dialogues such as the Sergius-Bahira account were meant to offer a Christian reading of the life of Muhammad, and to challenge the historical narratives of Islamic tradition.

---

[289] Barbara Roggema, "A Christian Reading of the Qur'an: The Legend of Sergius-Bahira and Its Use of Qur'an and Sira"; Sidney Griffith, "The Qur'an in Arab Christian Texts."

[290] On Christian Arabic historiography, see Herman Teule, "Ta'rikh: Christian Arabic Historiography," 12:807-809.

[291] Barbara Roggema, *The Legend of Sergius Bahira*, 29-30.

Second, the literary form was influential in constructing histories of the Qur'an and its formation. For Muslims, the dialogues were meant to clarify the historical context of the revelations in the Qur'an, especially those involving Christian references. For Christians, the dialogue allowed for a Christian reading of the Qur'an, and even a Christian historical account of the Qur'an's origins. In the Sergius-Bahira dialogue, the Qur'an became a semi-Christian text with a reputable origin, only to be subsequently corrupted by the later community.

Third, the dialogues were used as apologetic and polemical tools to defend and refute religious others. Muslims used the literature to show Christian conversions to Islam, as well as condemnations for those who failed to grasp the truth. Christian authors used the dialogue to explain their faith and practice as well as criticize Islamic doctrines.

Fourth, Christians and Muslims employed the literary form of dialogue to imagine new historiographies for the emerging Islamic community and their respective place in the wider historical narrative. Muslims used dialogues in the biographical literature and the oral traditions to explain how Christians were part of a corrupt past, superseded by the monotheist community beloved by God. For these Muslim authors, all history was sacred history. In contrast, Christians re-read the origins of the Islamic communities to make sense of their role in world history. The Sergius-Bahira dialogue acknowledges that the Muslims have control over the land, but that their time will end according to apocalyptic prophecies. The new historical narratives of Muhammad, the Qur'an, and the Islamic community encouraged security among the Christian faithful, who knew that if only Muslims understood the "real" history, they would acknowledge their Christian origins and demonstrate greater respect for the Christian communities.

The dialogues surveyed in this chapter indicate that Christian and Islamic communities went to some effort to re-imagine the ideals of the other religious communities, making their own identity dependent upon the new constructed historiographies. In the competition to live with one another in the early Islamic Middle East, Christians and Muslims used dialogues to construct historical narratives that would have lasting effects upon their respective communities.

5 Dialogue as Theological Education and Dialectic

The medieval Eastern Christian education system was deeply tied to the religious structures of the Islamic Middle East. Following the collapse of secular education systems in the Byzantine Empire during the seventh century, Christian institutions took a substantial role in instructing students. In the Syriac and Christian Arab traditions, education was part of the monastic school and private education. Christian schools continued to encourage Greek learning during the Islamic period. The result was an education system that utilized oral debate and rhetoric to teach theology.[292]

For example, the East Syrian scholar-theologian Theodore Bar Koni composed a teaching manual for students in Syriac entitled the *Scholion*. The *Scholion* is an interpretation of texts and themes that are deemed crucial for students. As a monk from the Church of the East, Theodore Bar Koni was a teacher in Kashkar, Iraq sometime near the end of the eighth century.[293] In his book he included a chapter on how to respond to Muslim critiques of Christi-

---

[292] For more on Syriac Christian education in the Middle East, see Ute Pietruschka, "Classical Heritage and New Literary Forms: Literary Activities of Christians during the Umayyad Period" and Adam Becker, *Fear of God and the Beginning of Wisdom*.

[293] This information is based upon the studies done by Sidney Griffith, "Chapter Ten of the *Scholion*: Theodore Bar Kônî's Apology for Christianity," *Orientalia Christiana Periodica* 47 (1981): 158-188; and Sidney Griffith, "Theodore Bar Kônî's *Scholion*: A Nestorian *Summa Contra Gentiles* from the First Abbasid Century," in *East of Byzantium: Syria and Armenia in the Formative Period*, ed. N. G. Garsoïan, Thomas Mathews and Robert Thomson (Washington DC: Dumbarton Oaks, 1982), 53-72.

anity. The chapter is an apology for Christianity based on a series of questions and answers related to scriptures, prophecies, apologetics, faith, and reason.[294]

Theodore presents a dialogue between a teacher and student in which the student represents the Muslim and the teacher responds to him as the Christian representative. The work is supposed to instruct students about proper interpretation of Scripture in light of Islamic challenges. Over the course of the chapter, the teacher explains the correct interpretation of Scripture in relation to Jesus Christ, Baptism, Eucharist, veneration of the Cross, the Sacraments, the title Son of God, and other controversial matters. Theodore portrays his conversation partner's arguments in an authentic fashion. For instance, he faithfully adheres to qur'anic doctrines about God not having a son, and accuses the Christian teacher of worshipping three gods. Theodore produces an accurate Muslim Christology through his understanding of Islamic doctrine:

> I believe that Christ was born of a virgin woman and that he was sent by the one who gave the Law, and that he will bring about the resurrection and the judgment, and that he is now in heaven. But that I should call him the Son of God, as you blaspheme; that God has a connatural son, born of him, perfect like him in everything, I cannot accept.[295]

Although question-and-answer literature differs from dialogues in their lack of a historical setting, writings such as Theodore Bar Koni's *Scholion* provided a useful resource for writers who wished to use educated arguments in their literary dialogues. Stories in which Christian interlocutors displayed knowledge of Muslim beliefs added to the drama of the narrative.[296] Others question-and-

---

[294] Quoted in Sidney Griffith, "Chapter Ten of the *Scholion*: Theodore Bar Kônî's Apology for Christianity," 168. See the Syriac text in Addai Scher, ed., *Liber Scholiorum*.

[295] Quoted in Ibid., 181.

[296] For another example of Christian-Muslim discussion in question-and-answer format, see Sidney Griffith, "*Answers for the Shaykh*: A 'Melkite' Arabic Text from Sinai and the Doctrines of the Trinity and the

answer dialogues focused on apologetics for Christian doctrines.[297] Muslims also used the genre effectively for their own interests.[298]

Many Muslim scholars were interested in Greek learning and dialectical reasoning through oral debate. Beginning in the eighth century and continuing for centuries afterward, Muslim leaders supported a comprehensive translation movement to bring the knowledge of other cultures into the Arabic language.[299] Syriac and Arabic-speaking Christians, including the East-Syrian Church of the East, the West-Syrian Jacobites, and the Orthodox Melkites, contributed the majority of translations that were used in education during the medieval period in the Islamic Middle East. For their part, Muslim patrons encouraged the religiously plural societies to participate in acquiring and applying this knowledge. For example, the Islamic interest in grammar began a debate about its place alongside logic as a scientific endeavor. One dialogue recalls the tenth-century Muslim grammarian Abu Sa'id al-Sirafi discussing

---

Incarnation in 'Arab Orthodox' Apologetics," 277-309; and Eid Salah and Mark Swanson, "Masa'il wa-ajwiba 'aqliyya wa-ilahiyya," 661-663. On a Greek question-and-answer disputation, see Peter Schadler, "The Dialogue between a Saracen and a Christian," 367-370.

[297] For instance, see Georg Graf, "Christlich-arabische Texte: Zwei Disputationem zwischen Muslimen und Christen," in *Veröffentlichungen aus den badischen Papyrus-Sammlungen: Griechische, Koptische und Arabische Texte zur Religion und religiösen Literatur in Ägyptens Spätzeit*, eds. Friedrich Bilabel and Adolf Grohmann (Heidelberg: Universitätsbibliothek Verlag, 1934), 1-31; and Mark Swanson, "A Christian Arabic Disputation (PSR 438)," and "Vienna, Papyrus Erzherzog Rainer – Inv. Ar. Pap. Nr. 10.000," 386-387, 654-655. See also Harald Suermann, "Une Controverse de Johannan de Litarb," *Parole de l'Orient* 15 (1988-1989): 197-213; and Harald Suermann, "John the Stylite of Mar Z'ura at Sarug," 314-316. See also A. Binggeli, "Anastasius of Sinai," 193-202; and Sidney Griffith, "Anastasios of Sinai, the Hodegos, and the Muslims," *Greek Orthodox Theological Review* 32 (1987): 341-358. Also, see some of the works in Michel Hayek, ed., *'Ammar al-Basri, apologie et controversies* (Beirut: Dar al-Machriq, 1977); and Mark Beaumont, "'Ammar al-Basri," 604-610.

[298] Hans Daiber, "Masa'il wa-ajwiba," 6:636-639.

[299] For a comprehensive survey, see Dimitri Gutas, *Greek Thought, Arabic Culture*.

this topic with the Christian philosopher Matta ibn Yunus.[300] In another instance, the Spanish Muslim scholar Ahmad ibn Muhammad ibn Sa'di visited Baghdad during the tenth century, where he witnessed a type of interreligious dialogue that encouraged the use of reason:

> At the first session I attended I witnessed a meeting which included every kind of group: Sunni Muslims and heretics [Shi'ite groups], and all kinds of infidels: Majus [Zoroastrians], materialists, atheists, Jews and Christians. Each group had a leader who would speak on its doctrine and debate about it. Whenever one of these leaders arrived, from whichever of the groups he came, the assembly rose up for him, standing on their feet until he would sit down, then they would take their seats after he was seated. When the meeting was jammed with its participants, and they saw that no one else was expected, one of the infidels said, "You have all agreed to the debate, so the Muslims should not argue against us on the basis of their scripture, nor on the basis of the sayings of their prophet, since we put no credence in these things, and we do not acknowledge him. Let us dispute with one another only on the basis of arguments from reason, and what observation and deduction will support." Then they would all say, "Agreed." Abu Umar said, "When I heard that, I did not return to that meeting. Later someone told me there was to be another meeting for discussion, so I went to it and I found them engaging in the same practices as their colleagues. So I stopped going to the meetings of the disputants, and I never went back.[301]

Several dialogues from the eighth and ninth centuries involve Christians and Muslims in discussions that use dialectical reasoning

---

[300] See David Margoliouth, "The Discussion between Abu Bishr Matta and Abu Sa'id al-Sirafi on the Merits of Logic and Grammar," *Journal of the Royal Asiatic Society* 37 (1905): 79-129.

[301] Quoted in Sidney Griffith, *The Church in the Shadow of the Mosque*, 64. See Abu 'Abd Allah al-Humaydi, *Jadhwat al-Muqtabis*, ed. Muhammad ibn Tawit al-Tanji (Cairo: Dar al-Misriyya, 1953), 101-102.

and other philosophical arguments to demonstrate the reasonableness of their religion. They were inspired by the real debates sponsored by Muslim rulers, such as the one mentioned above. One of the main goals of such dialogues was instruction. Although question-and-answer literature has an explicitly didactic goal, authors also used the literary dialogue form to provide a theological education to their audience. Indeed, the readers were mostly monks, clergy, and well-educated people who would have studied at the religious schools of instruction. Since most Christian manuscripts are preserved in these centers of learning in the Middle East, it is reasonable to conjecture that dialogues were composed with this student audience in mind. Second, the dialogues were meant to reveal one's own knowledge and capacity for dialectic (or its Arabic counterpart, *kalam*). This was the art of contradiction making, so that one asks a series of questions until one's conversation partner is unable to respond and must submit to the questioner's viewpoint. This method became one of the most popular ways of discussing religion in medieval Islam among the dialectical theologians (*mutakallimun*).[302] A third goal was to use a balance of faith and reason to explain one's religion. Through scriptural reasoning, theologians used analogies from the Bible to explain their logic, and likewise used reasoning from nature to discover knowledge of divine matters. A fourth goal was the use of inductive and deductive reasoning, especially in the form of analogy. By arguing from particular examples in nature, disputants argued for general conclusions about their theological doctrines. Exploring how Christians and Muslims made these arguments will clarify their commitments to theological education and dialectical reasoning.

---

[302] For more on dialectical method in this period, see Michael Cook, "The Origins of 'Kalam'," *Bulletin of the School of Oriental and African Studies* 43 (1980): 32-43. See also the collected works of Richard Frank, *Texts and Studies on the Development and History of Kalam*.

A CHRISTIAN MONK OF BET HALE AND AN ARAB NOTABLE

Sometime after 720, a Syriac Christian composed a dialogue between a monk of Bet Hale and a notable Arab Muslim.[303] The dialogue is written in the form of a letter to a certain Father Jacob, who asked the author to offer an account of Christianity ("the Apostolic Faith") based on a conversation with a "son of Ishmael" set in the form of question and answer.[304] The thirteenth-century author 'Abdisho mentions a dialogue with the Arabs belonging to an Abraham of Bet Hale in his catalogue of Church writers. According to scholars, the author is likely Abraham a monk of Dayr Mar 'Abda, an East Syrian monastery located near Kufa and Hira in southern Iraq.[305] Gerrit Reinink and other scholars accept the historicity of such an event, but deny the content of the dialogue reflects what actually took place during this encounter.[306]

The setting for the story begins when the emir Maslama ibn 'Abd al-Malik (d. 738), the governor of Iraq at the time, made a stop at the monastery. One of the Muslim Arabs in his company had developed an illness, and needed to stay at the monastery for a period of ten days. According to the author, the Arab notable was

---

[303] There is no published edition of the text available. For studies of the dialogue, see Gerrit Reinink, "Bible and Qur'an in Early Syriac Christian-Islamic Disputation"; Gerrit Reinink, "Political Power and Right Religion in the East Syrian Disputation between a Monk of Bet Hale and an Arab Notable"; Sidney Griffith, "Disputing with Islam in Syriac: The Case of the Monk of Bet Hale and a Muslim Emir"; Sidney Griffith, *Syriac Writers on Muslims and the Religious Challenge of Islam*, 26-37; and Robert Hoyland, *Seeing Islam as Others Saw It*, 465-472.

[304] There are three manuscripts mentioned in various catalogues: MS Diyarbakir syr. 95 (early 18th c.), MS Mardin 82 (1890), and MS Siirt 112 (15th c.).

[305] Sidney Griffith, *Syriac Writers on Muslims and the Religious Challenge of Islam*, 27.

[306] Gerrit Reinink, "Bible and Qur'an in Early Syriac Christian-Islamic Disputation," 57-58; Gerrit Reinink, "Political Power and Right Religion in the East Syrian Disputation between a Monk of Bet Hale and an Arab Notable," 160.

knowledgeable in both the Qur'an and the Bible (something rare among Muslims). He talked with the Syriac-speaking monks through an interpreter, indicating that he spoke only Arabic, while the monks were bilingual. Due to the earnestness of the monks, the Muslim became interested in their actions and initiated a dialogue:

> When he saw our rites performed at the appropriate seven times, in accordance with what the blessed David said: "Seven times a day I praise you for your judgments, O righteous one," he called me to him. And because he had acted as steward in the government for a long time and because of his exaltedness and our lowliness, he would speak with us via an interpreter. He began by reproving us for our faith, saying: "You make prayers much, night and day you are not silent, and you outdo us in prayer and fasting and in your petitions to God. However, in my own opinion, your faith rules out that your prayers will be accepted."[307]

When the monk heard the Arab Muslim's critical words, he responded that they could only have a fair discussion by speaking respectfully without an interpreter. Presumably, the monk spoke in Arabic so that the discussion could take place, although the dialogue is recorded in Syriac. For the monk, God loved what was true, and that should be the criteria by which they could discuss some of the Muslim's questions. The ground rules for the dialogue show an attention to theological instruction and the willingness to argue using faith and reason. The monk insists that the Arab may ask whatever he likes, and that he will respond using the scriptures, human reason, and arguments from nature.

The Arab notable begins the dialogue by arguing that Islamic political authority and their observances of Abrahamic faith demonstrate God's approval of their faith. The monk uses the argument from nature, pointing out that in history there have been a number of rulers. In fact, he argues, the Arabs are not even world rulers for there are kings in the Far East, the Byzantines in the West, and others to the south. For him, political power was not an

---

[307] Quoted in Robert Hoyland, *Seeing Islam as Others Saw It*, 466.

indication of divine love, and creation was not subject to Islamic authority.

Next, the Muslim asks why Christians do not observe the commands of Abraham, such as circumcision, even when Scripture commands it. According to the monk, the laws of Abraham are to be interpreted typologically through Jesus Christ, whose new covenant fulfilled those laws and provided a new model for life. In this section, the monk uses testimonies from the scriptures to argue that Abraham's life and actions prefigured Jesus Christ in history. Abraham's plan to sacrifice Isaac was a type revealed by God in the passion, death, and resurrection of Jesus Christ. Now that he has come, the monk argues, salvation history has been fulfilled.

The third question revolved around the problem of how God could suffer and die as Jesus Christ. For the Arab Muslim, Jesus was neither God, nor was he crucified. Using the Christology of the Church of the East, the monk argues that the divinity was with Christ, but it was not mixed or intermingled with the human, "It was by way of the will, in such a way as not to be harmed or to suffer."[308] He supports his argument with examples from nature:

> Listen to two examples, which are very trustworthy for the friends of God. Just as when the sun stands on a wall, and you take an axe and ruin the wall, the sun is not harmed and does not suffer, so the body, that [is] from us, died and was buried and rose, whereas the Divinity did not suffer. And just as iron that one leaves in the fire, if one does not throw it into the water how long it may be when one want it [so], increases its working, so the eternal Son, who sojourned in the temple which [is] from us, was with him on the cross and in the tomb and in His resurrection and showed His working.[309]

---

[308] Quoted in Sidney Griffith, *Syriac Writers on Muslims and the Religious Challenge of Islam*, 30.

[309] Quoted in Gerrit Reinink, "Bible and Qur'an in Early Syriac Christian-Islamic Disputation," 71. Reinink points out that the second example means that the longer one leaves iron in fire, the more its

Next, the Arab notable asks him to explain the doctrine of the Trinity as the Father, Son, and Holy Spirit. In response, the monk gives a number of examples from the Old and New Testaments as well as examples from nature to show that God is one and yet known in three hypostases (*qnome*). He uses the argument from nature that we should understand the Trinity just as we see the Sun emitting light and heat – all three are distinct and yet part of the one Sun.

The monk then asks the Arab to explain his understanding of 'Isa son of Maryam, whom Christians call Jesus Christ. The Arab notable replies that they follow Muhammad in calling him the word of God and his spirit (quoting Q 4:171).[310] The monk replies: if the Arab agrees to this statement, then he essentially agrees with the Annunciation story in Luke 1:28-36. If Jesus is God's Word and Spirit, the monk reasons, "I ask from you now one thing of two: either you remove the 'Word of God and His Spirit' from him, or you proclaim him straightforwardly [to be] the Son of God."[311]

The Arab notable changes the topic to the monk's view of Muhammad. For the monk, Muhammad was important for two reasons: he was wise and he was able to move his people from idolatry to recognition of the one God. Then the Arab asks why Muhammad did not teach the Trinity to Muslims. The monk responds:

> Know, o man, that when a child is born, because it has no solid sense yet which can take in solid food, they feed it milk for two years, and after that they give it bread to eat, likewise Muhammad, because he was aware of your childishness and the paucity of your knowledge, has first made the One True God known to you, a teaching which he had received from Sergius

---

strength increases, and in this way the divinity was not weakened in the death and resurrection of Jesus Christ.

[310] The author of the dialogue must have been familiar with Q 4:171 and its Christological statement regarding Jesus. In fact, this dialogue is perhaps the earliest Christian document to explicitly discuss the Qur'an.

[311] Quoted in Gerrit Reinink, "Bible and Qur'an in Early Syriac Christian-Islamic Disputation," 63.

Bahira. Because you were still children in knowledge, he did not teach you about the mystery of the Trinity, lest you erred [by worshipping] a large number of Gods, because you might have said: "If Muhammad proclaims three, we will make seven others, because when there will be ten, they will become even more powerful." And you would have pursued idolatry, just as before.[312]

This passage is valuable for its scriptural testimonies alluding to 1 Cor. 3:2 and Heb. 5:12-13. Also, it makes the earliest reference to Sergius-Bahira as a teacher who explained Christian doctrine to Muhammad (mentioned in chapter 4 above).[313]

The following three questions from the Arab notable all concern Christian practice – why do they venerate things other than God? Using the testimonies from Scripture and typological interpretation, the monk explains that Christians venerate icons as prototypes which point to the one real God. They are images that remind the faithful of the original figure. Then the Arab acknowledges that he has heard of the icon made by Jesus Christ and sent to Abgar of Edessa during the first century.[314]

When the notable asks why they venerate the cross when it is not explicitly mentioned in the Bible, the monk explains the Christian tripartite understanding of authority as Scripture, Apostolicity,

---

[312] Quoted in Barbara Roggema, *The Legend of Sergius Bahira*, 158.

[313] The reference to Sergius-Bahira means that Christians already had an established legend of a renegade monk being the source of Muhammad's teaching by the early eighth century. This may seem late, but it predates the earliest biography of Muhammad (mid-eighth century) in the Islamic tradition.

[314] This apocryphal account, which can be found as early as the fourth century in the *Doctrine of Addai*, states that Jesus received a letter from King Abgar of Edessa who was ill. Jesus dictated a letter back that he would heal him by faith without coming to Edessa and he would send an apostle to Abgar after his ascension to heaven. According to tradition, the apostle Thaddeus (Addai) evangelized Edessa and the portrait of Jesus also came to Edessa.

and the Church. For example, he argues, Muslims also use different sources of authority:

> I think that even in your case, Muhammad did not teach all your laws and commandments in the Qur'an, but you learned some of them from the Qur'an; some of them are in surat al-Baqara, and in G-y-g-y, and in T-w-r-h.[315]

His comments seem to indicate that surat al-Baqara, the second chapter in today's Qur'an, appeared to be a separate law code. The early Christian writer John of Damascus also made this same statement in his work *On Heresies*.[316] The other words (gygy and twrh) are most likely the Gospel and the Torah. For our purposes, it demonstrates that Christians in the early eighth century were using human reason, historical argument, and scriptural critique to respond to the challenge of Islam.

In the next question on the veneration of martyrs' relics, the monk reminds his interlocutor that Christians ask for their intercession through prayers on their behalf. For example, he argues, we ask counselors and leaders to work on our behalf. In the same way, the martyrs and saints in heaven are capable of praying on our behalf to God.

Then the Arab asks why Christians pray facing the east. According to the monk, Scripture and precedent are the criteria which verify Christian practice. Since Paradise was located in the east, and that is where Christians hope to return, and since Jesus Christ and his apostles prayed facing east, all churches worship toward the east. At this point in the dialogue, the Arab notable acknowledges that his argument has validity and he states, "Even Muhammad our prophet said about the inhabitants of the monasteries and the mountain dwellers that they will enjoy the kingdom."[317]

---

[315] Quoted in Sidney Griffith, *Syriac Writers on Muslims and the Religious Challenge of Islam*, 33.

[316] See Frederic Chase, ed., *Saint John of Damascus*, 159.

[317] Quoted in Sidney Griffith, *Syriac Writers on Muslims and the Religious Challenge of Islam*, 35. Whether this was an oral tradition circulating at the

Following this positive statement, the Arab notable asks the monk why God allowed Christians to be conquered, persecuted, and killed, if they are in fact his chosen people. In response to his question about the conquest, the monk replies that the Arabs were given authority by God only on account of the Christian communities' sins, citing Deut. 9:5 as an example. The monk argues that God chastises those whom he loves.

The final question from the Arab notable concerns the ultimate fate of Muslims in the Christian view: will they enter God's kingdom or not? Using the scriptural proof text of John 3:5, he quotes Jesus' words to Nicodemus: "Truly, truly I say to you, unless one is born of water and the Spirit, he cannot enter the kingdom of God." But the monk acknowledges that despite the need for Baptism and Christian faith, someone with good deeds will live in grace like a hired servant, evoking an allusion to the parable of the Prodigal Son (Luke 15:11-32).

At the conclusion of the dialogue, the Arab notable tells the Christian monk:

> I testify that were it not for the fear of the government and of shame before men, many would become Christians. But you are blessed of God to have given me satisfaction by your conversation with me.[318]

Scholars tend to view the text as a representation of the types of arguments that Christians and Muslims were having in the early eighth century, rather than a transcription of a particular conversation that occurred at the monastery. Indeed, the author mentions that he has composed the letter to be of use for his correspondent. Robert Hoyland has linked the dialogue with similar motifs in Jewish-Christian debates, and Gerrit Reinink has also highlighted the similarities with other Christian apologists.[319] In their arguments,

---

time or a literary creation of the author is unclear, since no other record of this specific statement is found in Islamic tradition other than Q 5:82-85.

[318] Quoted in Ibid., 36-37.

[319] See Gerrit Reinink, "Bible and Qur'an in Early Syriac Christian-Islamic Disputation," 63-65; and "Political Power and Right Religion in

they highlight the importance of its didactic use for an educated and theologically-inclined audience.

The dialogue highlights several features of Christian-Muslim encounter in the eighth century. First, the story reveals their interest in the true religion. The Arab notable notes that monks pray well but their confession is wrong, the monk defends and explains the Christian understanding of the true religion with Scripture, reason, and examples from nature. Second, the dialogue teaches East Syrian Christology and Trinitarian doctrine. For instance, the monk uses examples about the sun and its heat and light to clarify the Trinity to his Muslim conversation partner. Third, the dialogue's author did not have direct knowledge of the Qur'an, but was familiar with Islamic traditions, including some allusions to the Qur'an (4:171) Q and oral traditions. Fourth, the dialogue makes abundant use of biblical citations to commend the Trinity, Jesus Christ, and Christian practice. The Bible and its role in early testimony collections were likely significant for East Syrian theological education. Fifth, while the arguments from reason are important to the dialogue's narrative, they are not as systematic as one finds in a treatise or in later more-developed dialogues. Instead, it reflects an early stage of Christian-Muslim engagement using the human intellect and examples from nature. Later dialogues, such as the one between Patriarch Timothy and Caliph al-Mahdi would present more complex forms of argumentation.

PATRIARCH TIMOTHY AND CALIPH AL-MAHDI

By the later eighth century, the East Syrian Church of the East had an established educational system for the preservation of their intellectual heritage in the areas of secular and religious knowledge. Patriarch Timothy (d. 823), the head of the Church of the East for forty-three years, is an outstanding example. Timothy was born in the region of Adiabene in Iraq. As a boy, Timothy began his studies at a monastery in Bashosh, about sixty miles north of Mosul in

---

the East Syrian Disputation between a Monk of Bet Hale and an Arab Notable," 159; Robert Hoyland, *Seeing Islam as Others Saw It*, 469-470.

Iraq. Utilizing his educational background and contacts, Timothy refined the standards for Christian education related to school formation, approaches to the Bible, jurisdictional authority, theological orthodoxy, canon law, and boundaries for relations with religious others. Timothy was also influential in the frontiers of missionary work. He helped members of the Church of the East adapt to roles in the administrative and economic life of the caliphate as court scribes, physicians, and translators. Most important for our purposes, Timothy was concerned with education through dialogue with Islamic leaders. Timothy composed several letters recounting dialogues with Muslims, and these represent his attentiveness to dialectic and rational argumentation in interreligious dialogue.[320]

In Syriac education, the Syriac Bible (Peshitta) served as the source for all areas of learning. Progressing through Syriac grammar, prose, and poetic works, students were taught to speak through the medium of the scriptures. The Bible functioned as the literature of common discourse for medieval Eastern Christians. Students studied the Psalms to learn how to read and pronounce words. Then they moved on to the study of the Old Testament, and then the New Testament using "literary, historical, philological, and lexical resources."[321] Syriac Christians were also shaped by the East Syrian liturgy (*qurbana*) and daily prayers, which were suffused

---

[320] Besides the focus of this section on Timothy's dialogue with the caliph al-Mahdi, he wrote another letter recalling his dialogue with a Muslim Aristotelian philosopher. See Thomas Hurst, "Letter 40 of the Nestorian Patriarch Timothy I (727-823): An Edition and Translation" (Master's Thesis, The Catholic University of America, 1981). For an analysis of these other dialogues, see Sidney Griffith, "The Syriac Letters of Patriarch Timothy I and the Birth of Christian Kalam in the Mu'tazilite Milieu of Baghdad and Basrah in Early Islamic Times," in *Syriac Polemics: Studies in Honour of Gerrit Jan Reinink*, ed. W. J. van Beekum, J. W. Drijvers, and A. C. Klugkist (Leuven: Peeters, 2007), 103-132; and Martin Heimgartner, "Timothy I," 515-519.

[321] Thomas Hurst, "The Syriac Letters of Timothy I (727-823): A Study in Christian-Muslim Controversy" (PhD diss., The Catholic University of America, 1986), 7.

with Scripture. Following their study and use of the Bible, East Syrian Christians moved toward interpretive methods of analysis. They utilized the exegetical commentaries of Ephrem and Theodore of Mopsuestia from the Syriac tradition. Timothy's letters show that his education included the study of John Chrysostom, Diodore, Nestorius, Justin Martyr, Hippolytus of Rome, Methodius of Olympus, Athanasius, Basil of Caesarea, Gregory of Nyssa, Gregory of Nazianzus, Amphilochius of Iconium, and Ambrose of Milan.[322]

Students were also initiated into the philosophical works of Aristotle. Their work involved reading the texts in Greek and learning to translate from Greek into Syriac. This method of learning was crucial for Syriac-speaking people who sought positions within the Abbasid government as translators and secretaries. The study of languages in the schools was not only limited to Syriac and Greek, but included Arabic and Pahlavi. The system of theological education in the early Islamic Middle East prepared Timothy well for his discussions with Muslims.

Timothy was named patriarch in 780 and ruled until his death in 823. Only one year into his reign, Timothy recorded a dialogue that took place between him and the Abbasid caliph al-Mahdi (d. 785) over the course of two days at the ruler's court in Baghdad. The dialogue took place in Arabic, although Timothy recorded the discussion in Syriac, in the form of a letter, suggesting that its narrative can be placed around 781.[323] Timothy's composition was originally sent to his friend Sergius, the headmaster of the school at Bashosh. But he expected the composition to be disseminated for a wider reading audience, including the students of the school, as a catechetical instruction for the Church of the East in response to

---

[322] See Lucas van Rompay, "Past and Present Perceptions of the Syriac Literary Tradition," *Hugoye: Journal of Syriac Studies* 3 (2000): http://syrcom.cua.edu/Hugoye/Vol3No1/HV3N1VanRompay.html.

[323] For a comprehensive study of Timothy, see especially Hans Putman, *L'église et l'islam sous Timothée I (780-823)*.

the challenge of Islam.³²⁴ Although the document likely reflects an encounter between the patriarch and the caliph, the dialogue represents a literary composition rather than a documentary transcription of the event.³²⁵

The story begins when Timothy has an audience with al-Mahdi at his court, where he praises God and the caliph. Usually, Timothy only had a limited amount of time before al-Mahdi would speak with different people about other concerns across the Abbasid Empire. But this time, al-Mahdi took time to respond to Timothy: "O Catholicos, a man like you who possesses all this knowledge and utters such sublime words concerning God is not justified in saying about God that he married a woman from whom he begat a son."³²⁶ When al-Mahdi presses Timothy to explain the Christian concept of Jesus Christ as the Son of God apart from a literal understanding, he clarifies what was already predicted in the prophets:

> O our King, that [Jesus Christ] is a son and one that is born, we learn it and believe in it, but we dare not investigate how he was born before the times, and we are not able to understand the fact at all, as God is incomprehensible and inexplicable in all things; but we may say in an imperfect simile that as light is

---

³²⁴ For more on Timothy and theological education, see Harald Suermann, "Timothy and his Concern for the School of Basos," *The Harp* 10 (1997): 51-58.

³²⁵ See the studies by Sidney Griffith, "Disputes with Muslims in Syriac Christian Texts: from Patriarch John (d. 648) to Bar Hebraeus (d. 1286)," 251-273; reprinted in Sidney Griffith, *The Beginnings of Christian Theology in Arabic*, Chapter 5; Robert Hoyland, *Seeing Islam as Others saw It*, 472-475. On Timothy's letters and his treatise-style presentation, see Oskar Braun, "Der Katholikos Timotheos I und seine Briefe," *Oriens Christianus* 1 (1901): 138-152; Oskar Braun, ed., *Epistulae Timothei patriarchae I* (Paris: E Typographeo Reipublicae, 1914; reprint, Louvain: L. Durbecq, 1953); Erica Hunter, "Interfaith Dialogues: The Church of the East and the Abbasids," in *Der Christliche Orient und seine Umwelt*, ed. S.G. Vashalomidze and L. Greisiger (Wiesbaden: Harrassowitz, 2007), 289-302.

³²⁶ Alphonse Mingana, ed., "The Apology of Timothy the Patriarch before the Caliph Mahdi," 153.

born of the sun and word of the soul, so also Christ who is Word, is born of God, high above the times and before all the worlds.[327]

After Timothy explains Jesus' birth, al-Mahdi then asks how Mary could remain a virgin. For him, there is no proof in the scriptures or in nature. Timothy responds with particular examples in nature to draw general conclusions about the nature of this birth. First, Timothy argues that Eve is an example from the book of Genesis, and says,

> All fruits are born of trees without breaking or tearing them, and sight is born of the eye while the latter is not broken or torn, and the perfume of apples and all aromatic substances is born of their respective trees or plants without breaking or tearing them, and the rays are born of the sun without tearing or breaking its spheric form. As all these are born of their generators without tearing them or rending them, so also Christ was born of Mary without breaking her virginal seals.[328]

Following this line of thought, al-Mahdi declares that if Jesus is divine and human, then Christians have a duality of persons. He argues that John 20:17 ("I am going to my God and your God") shows that Jesus cannot be God if he is Son, for as God he would also be Father, which would be incomprehensible.[329] In response, Timothy confirms the Christian understanding of the Father and the Son in comparison with a letter. Jesus is Son and Word of God the Father, just as a letter written by the caliph might be said to represent his Word and he is said to be its father.[330]

---

[327] Ibid.

[328] Ibid., 154.

[329] See Martin Accad, "The Ultimate Proof-Text: The Interpretation of John 20.17 in Muslim-Christian Dialogue (second/eighth-eighth/fourteenth centuries)," in *Christians at the Heart of Islamic Rule: Church Life and Scholarship in 'Abbasid Iraq*, ed. David R. Thomas (Leiden: Brill, 2003), 199-215.

[330] Alphonse Mingana, ed., "The Apology of Timothy the Patriarch before the Caliph Mahdi," 157.

The caliph decides to change the focus of the discussion from the Incarnation of Jesus Christ to the topic of the Trinity. He demands that Timothy explain to him how the Word and Spirit can be with God eternally, without mixing and without confusion. Timothy responds with a comprehensive list of verses from the Old and New Testaments. For Timothy, these confirm that Jesus operates in the Trinitarian relationship as life and light to the world, working in conjunction with the Father. He points out that the Trinitarian relationship is equivalent to one who does not mix pearl, gold, or brass, but keeps three pearls together which are similar in nature and resemble one another perfectly in everything.

Following more questions, al-Mahdi returns the discussion to Jesus Christ and his earthly life. He asks if Jesus is the enemy of the Mosaic Law since he fulfilled it through his Gospel. Timothy responds with three analogies to illustrate how Jesus fulfilled the Law. The stars are not the enemies of the sun when it rises and their light disappears, men are not enemies of their childhood when they leave it behind, and this world is not the enemy of the Kingdom of God when it will be abolished.[331]

Continuing their discussion of Jesus' ministry, the caliph al-Mahdi asks Timothy how Jesus could be the Word of God if he prayed to God:

> And our King said to me: "There is no creature that has no need of worship and prayer." And I replied: "Has Jesus Christ, the Word of God, sinned or not?" And our King said: "May God preserve me from saying such a thing!" And I then asked: "Has God created the worlds with his Word or not?" And our King replied in the affirmative and said "Yes." And I then asked: "Is the one who is neither a sinner nor in need of anything in need of worship and prayer?" And our King answered "No." And then I said to him: "If Christ is a Word from God, and a man from Mary, and if as a Word of God he is the Lord of everything, and as a man he did not commit any sin as the Book [Qur'an] and our King testify, and if he who is the Lord

---

[331] Ibid., 164-165.

of everything and a creator is not in need, and he who is not a sinner is pure, it follows that Jesus Christ worshipped and prayed to God neither as one in need nor as a sinner, but He worshipped and prayed in order to teach worship and prayer to his disciples, and through them to every human being."[332]

After they change the subject, Timothy and al-Mahdi discuss the relationship between Muhammad's prophethood and Christianity. Al-Mahdi argues that when Jesus spoke about the Paraclete, he was making reference to Muhammad. But Timothy combines John 15:26, 16:14, and 14:26 to demonstrate that the Paraclete is part of the Trinity and was already manifested soon after Jesus' ascension. Timothy paraphrases other verses to show that the Paraclete knows the depth of God and Muhammad does not claim this knowledge. Indeed, the Paraclete was with the apostles and the Church based on the descent of the Paraclete at Pentecost in Acts 2:1-4. Timothy paraphrases John 16:13-15 to show that the Paraclete taught the apostles that God is in three persons. He asserts that the Paraclete brought forth great miracles and numerous signs through the apostles. Finally, Timothy quotes Ps. 32/33:6 to demonstrate that the Spirit is part of the active Trinity.[333]

At several points later in the dialogue, Timothy employs verses from the Qur'an to support his Christian claims. The dialogue has preserved some of the oldest extant quotations from the Qur'an; it is one of the first instances of knowledge of the Qur'an by a group other than Muslims themselves. Timothy uses the Qur'an to argue for Jesus' crucifixion and resurrection. First he quotes Q 19:34 as proof of Jesus' death: "Peace be upon the day I

---

[332] Ibid., 167.
[333] Ibid., 169-172. This evidence suggests that the question of Muhammad's relationship to Jewish and Christian scriptures engendered a new search for proof texts to counter Muslim scriptural interpretation. It also demonstrates that the Islamic Paraclete argument was already prevalent among Muslim disputants by the late eighth century.

was born and the day I die and the day I am raised alive."[334] Then he cites Q 3:48: "God said to Jesus, 'I will make you die and I will raise you up to me." Timothy even postulates a Christian reading into the mysterious letters that are at the heading of several suras in the Qur'an. He surmises that the headings "such as A. L. R. and T. S. M. and Y. S. M. and others which are three in number, refer also in your Book to God, His Word and His Spirit."[335]

In a later section, al-Mahdi charges: if Jesus Christ was crucified, then was he willing to be crucified or not? If he was willing to be crucified, then the Jews were simply following his will. If he was not willing to be crucified, then he was unable to save himself and thus cannot be God. This dialectical question was one of the common arguments used by Muslims throughout the period. In response, Timothy uses an analogy about God. When God created Satan as one of the angels, did he want him to be an angel or not? If he wanted him to be Satan, then Satan was merely following God's will by turning against him. But if he did not want him to become Satan, then God is weaker than Satan. Timothy argues that Jesus was accomplishing the divine will, since his crucifixion and death led to our salvation.

Next, al-Mahdi asks if Jesus Christ is good or not. Timothy replies that Jesus is the Word of God, and since God is good, Jesus Christ is good, for "he is one nature with God like light is one with the sun."[336] Then the king uses his scriptural challenge: did not Jesus say that no one is good but God (Mark 10:18)? In response, Timothy asks al-Mahdi if King David the prophet was just, as the Qur'an teaches. After al-Mahdi agrees, then Timothy points out one of his Psalms that declares none are just. In the same way, Timothy argues, each case excludes the speaker from the statement. At the conclusion of his explanation al-Mahdi replies: "If

---

[334] Ibid., 177. Timothy refers to this chapter in the Qur'an as surat 'Isa (Jesus). The title of sura 19 today is sura Maryam. However, in late eighth-century Baghdad, that title had not yet gained currency.
[335] Ibid., 203-204.
[336] Ibid., 189.

you accepted Muhammad as a prophet your words would be beautiful and your meanings fine."[337]

Later al-Mahdi claims that Christians and Jews have changed and corrupted their scriptures over time and they cannot be used as evidence. Timothy replies that if the scriptures were changed by either Jews or Christians, then the text would be different in each community. By virtue of their identical wording and the lack of evidence for an uncorrupted manuscript, the scriptures cannot be corrupt. Timothy shows that even though the Old Testament points to the Messiah as Jesus, the Jews retained those verses. Christians have not corrupted Scripture to make Jesus divine, since it is found even in Ps. 72:17 and in Isa. 7:14: "Behold, the virgin will conceive and give birth to a son, and his name shall be called Emmanuel."[338] Timothy discounts the possibility that the scriptures could have been corrupted by either community. This argument closed the discussion for the first day.

During the next day, al-Mahdi continued their conversation by asking Timothy for his opinion about Muhammad. If Timothy declared him a prophet, he would become a Muslim, but if he denied his prophethood, he could be charged with blasphemy. In response, Timothy claims that Muhammad did things similar to the prophets, such as teaching monotheism, forbidding idols, encouraging good works and teaching about God's Word and Spirit. Thus Timothy says that "Muhammad walked in the way of the prophets" but he does not intend this to mean that Muhammad was a prophet.

After this topic, al-Mahdi asks for further clarification of the Trinitarian doctrine, since Christians appear to profess three different gods. Timothy explains that Christians find the royal "We" referring to the Godhead as confirmation of their Trinitarian doctrine. How can three be one and one be three, al-Mahdi asks. Timothy explains:

---

[337] Ibid., 190.
[338] Ibid., 191-195.

The sun is also one, O our victorious King, in its spheric globe, its light and its heat, and the very same sun is also three, one sun in three powers. In the same way the soul has the powers of reason and intelligence, and the very same soul is one in one thing and three in another thing. In the same way also a piece of three gold denarii, is called one and three, one in its gold (that is to say its nature), and three in its persons (that is to say in the number of denarii). The fact that the above objects are one does not contradict and annul the other fact — that they are also three, and the fact that they are three does not contradict or annul the fact that they are also one.[339]

After discussing Christian Trinitarian doctrine further, the caliph al-Mahdi replies that reasoning from nature cannot be used to demonstrate any knowledge of God who is completely other. Timothy disagrees, pointing out that Christian and Muslim scriptures are dependent upon nature and language and use it constantly in their descriptions of God as King, Lord, and the Almighty. For Timothy, the use of logical reasoning is an essential way for humans to learn about their creator, for "as it is impossible to conceive a pearl without luster, or a sun without light, or a soul without reason and mind, so it is never possible that God should be without Word and Spirit."[340]

As they continue to argue about the relationship between the Father, Son, and Holy Spirit in the Trinity, al-Mahdi becomes increasingly skeptical about Timothy's rational argumentation. So Timothy offers a defense of arguments from nature as an essential part of Christian-Muslim discourse:

And the King said: "You will not go very far with God in your bodily comparisons and similes." And I said: "O King, because I am a bodily man I made use of bodily metaphors, and not of those that are without any body and any composition. Because I am a bodily man, and not a spiritual being, I make use of bodily comparisons in speaking of God. How could I or any

---

[339] Ibid., 205.
[340] Ibid., 211.

other human being speak of God as he is with a tongue of flesh, with lips fashioned of mud, and with a soul and mind closely united to body? This is far beyond the power of men and angels to do. God himself speaks with the prophets about himself not as he is, because they cannot know and hear about him as he is, but simply in the way that fits in with their own nature, a way they are able to understand."[341]

Following a discussion of Jesus Christ's status as Word or servant, and a conversation about the differences between the Christology of the Church of the East in comparison with the Jacobites and Melkites, Timothy closes with the analogy of the pearl. All religious people are in a dark location, and the precious pearl is on the ground for only one of them to find. When light comes, he continues, we will see the true possessor of the pearl. While it is dark and we cannot see in the fog, Timothy reasons, we can know something of the pearl in our world through good works and miracles of the true religion. These lights of truth, Timothy suggests, belong to Christianity. At this point, Timothy wishes caliph al-Mahdi and his children good health, and he returns to his patriarchal office.

Patriarch Timothy has a clear methodology in the dialogue. First, he utilized the Socratic method of question and answer. At other times, he also used dialectic as a process of question and answer. Second, Timothy used dialectical reasoning and its philosophical basis as a technique to explain his theology. In particular, Timothy favored the syllogism and inductive logic by means of analogy for his arguments. For Timothy, these methods allowed him to propose sustained arguments and conclusions about theological truths.

In his portrayal of the caliph al-Mahdi, Timothy highlights the active spirit of Christian-Muslim encounters during the eighth century. He praises him throughout the dialogue by calling him "our victorious king/caliph," "Commander of the Believers," "God-loving king," "powerful," "wise," "benevolent and gracious,"

---

[341] Ibid., 215.

"King of Kings," and "intelligent sovereign." At the beginning of the second day of discussion, Timothy writes of the caliph: "He is a lovable man, and loves also learning when he finds it in other people."[342] These compliments are not only literary devices; the dialogue's language exemplifies the proper courtesy that is to be shown in a work of learned literature. Because of the length of the conversation, the caliph speaks more than fifty times throughout the discussion, playing host to a range of theological topics. While Timothy is the master of the discourse in his answers, the caliph is the master of the topic of conversation. Al-Mahdi initiates the discussion. He is comfortable in his faith; there is no change of heart as happens in other more polemical dialogues. Instead, he probes Timothy with brief questions, but often interjects with clarifications or rebuttals. Timothy has the last word on each point in these discussions, but he is confined to the Islamic terms of debate in al-Mahdi's court.

In this respect, al-Mahdi is a powerful figure indeed since the Qur'an is the ultimate arbiter for him and Timothy during the discussion. Since the discourse is within his own court, al-Mahdi acts as judge over Timothy's reasoning. When Timothy describes humanity's knowledge of God, al-Mahdi objects to the fact that a demonstration through analogy between creature and Creator could be permitted. When Timothy replies that this would leave humans in ignorance concerning God, the caliph explains the Islamic concept of the attributes:

> We call God by these names, not because we understand Him to resemble things that we have with us, but in order to show that He is far above them, without comparison. In this way, we do not attribute to God things that are with us, we rather ascribe to ourselves things that are His, with great mercy from Him and great imperfection from us. Words such as: kingdom, life, power, greatness, honour, wisdom, sight, knowledge, and justice, etc., belong truly naturally and eternally to God, and they only belong to us in an unnatural, imperfect, and temporal

---

[342] Ibid., 196.

way. With God they have not begun and they will not end, but with us children of men they began and they will end.[343]

In his analysis, the caliph echoes many of Timothy's thoughts about humanity's knowledge of God. But the caliph also cautions applying created particulars to the uncreated God. In this respect, al-Mahdi is somewhat skeptical of analogical reasoning in its ability to explain God's nature and attributes.

When Timothy explains the eternality of the Trinity, he gets caliph al-Mahdi to explain how God can eternally perceive before creation without having something to perceive:

> The nature of the subject will not compel us, therefore, to believe that if the perceiver is eternal, then the perceived should also be eternal, because the fact that God is an eternal perceiver of the creature does not carry with it the necessity that the creature which is perceived by Him is also eternal, and the fact that the creature is perceived does not carry with it the necessity that He also is the perceived object like it. As such a necessity as that you were mentioning in the case of the creature has been vitiated, so also is the case with regard to the word and the spirit.[344]

Even after Timothy's clarification of the Christian doctrine, the caliph remains unconvinced that the Word and Spirit could be uncreated. Further on, he skeptically declares that Timothy cannot describe much of God through the use of bodily comparisons and metaphors. Near the end of the discussion, al-Mahdi advocates the acquisition of rational knowledge by means of natural theology and Scripture. Therefore, the literary dialogue portrays al-Mahdi as a man willing to consider inductive reasoning, albeit cautiously, in conjunction with faith.[345]

At other times in the discussion al-Mahdi is the aggressor in the encounter. He asks Timothy if Jesus Christ is his leader. Al-

---

[343] Ibid., 206.
[344] Ibid., 212.
[345] Ibid., 217.

Mahdi declares that Timothy doesn't follow Jesus since he is not circumcised in imitation of him.[346] This forthright style of argumentation was likely to have been the caliph's preferred method of dialogue.

Yet the caliph is cordial with his Christian interlocutor. At the close of their first day of conversation Timothy writes about the caliph's kind words. The following day Timothy mentions that he converses in a "sweet and benevolent way." When al-Mahdi hears of the Christological doctrines of the Melkites, Jacobites, and Church of the East, he judges that Timothy's belief is more correct than the others since it is impossible that God could die. Finally, the relationship between the two men concludes on a positive note with Timothy's commendation of the caliph, his sons, and his kingdom.

Al-Mahdi's character is quite developed within the dialogue. Timothy consistently praises him in his conduct and his disposition. The caliph controls the session in a confident fashion. He is the judge of the entire affair which he decides according to his own knowledge of the Qur'an, which ultimately regulates the discourse. He allows Timothy to employ scriptural and dialectical reasoning for his argumentation, but he is somewhat skeptical of Timothy's methodology in light of his own knowledge of Islamic theology and qur'anic interpretation. At times, al-Mahdi is quite aggressive in his questioning, even using dialectical methods to criticize Christian doctrines. These methods allowed Timothy to propose a positive method of dialogical encounter between Christianity and Islam.

Timothy likely composed his literary dialogue with caliph al-Mahdi in order to train students to answer questions about their faith. His dialogue educated in the scriptures, dialectical reasoning, apologetics, and intellectual thought. Timothy encouraged educated people to examine Islam not only through the Arabic language, but through knowledge of the Qur'an. For Timothy, the literary dialogue genre was an essential part of catechesis and a way to promote positive encounters with Muslims on the basis of Scripture and reason. At the same time, the dialogue provided a means of

---

[346] Ibid., 163-164.

authority in the literary realm that increased the influence of Timothy's ideas. Through the responses of its readers and audience, the literary dialogue was a form of intellectual empowerment in the face of a dominant Muslim majority.

IMAM AL-RIDA AND THE ARAB CHRISTIANS

'Ali ibn Musa al-Rida (d. 818), the eighth imam in Twelver Shi'ite Islam, was among the most well-known leaders of the Shi'ite community in the Abbasid period. He was made the heir apparent to the caliph al-Ma'mun in 816, likely as a way for the caliph to gain support among the Shi'ite communities. 'Ali al-Rida was also known as a transmitter of oral traditions and remembered among proto-Sunni groups and Sufis. According to historical sources, he was more interested in religious learning than political activism, and many of the accounts of al-Rida in dialogue concern religious matters.[347]

Most of the dialogues attributed to 'Ali al-Rida belong to intra-Islamic dispute and are concerned with the merits of Twelver Shi'ite Islam in relation to Sunni traditionists, dialectical theologians, and philosophers. There are two other short dialogues between al-Rida and Christians still extant that were recorded in Arabic sometime during or after 817. The first dialogue includes a short discussion between al-Rida and a friend of the Patriarch named John Abu Qurra. The text addresses the question of a religion's authenticity in relation to other religions' testimonies. The second text is a brief discussion between al-Rida and a Christian named Ibn Qurra concerning Christian Christological vocabulary about Christ. The length of each discussion is brief and the trans-

---

[347] For more on 'Ali al-Rida, see Michael Cooperson, *Classical Arabic Biography: The Heirs of the Prophet in the Age of al-Ma'mun* (Cambridge: Cambridge University Press, 2000), 24-32, 70-106, 193-196; Tamima Bayhom-Daou, "'Ali al-Rida," in *The Encyclopaedia of Islam, Third Edition*, ed. Gudrun Krämer, Denis Matringe, John Nawas, and Everett Rowson (Leiden: Brill, 2009), 2:69-74.

mission of these encounters may indicate that they represent authentic reports of Muslim-Christian dialogues.[348]

One dialogue recalls an encounter between al-Rida and John Abu Qurra, a companion of the Catholicos (*jathaliq*). The report is transmitted through Safwan ibn Yahya (d. 825), a traveling companion and secretary of Imam al-Rida.[349] According to his biographers, Safwan ibn Yahya was remembered as an agent and defender of the Imamate against the claims of the Sunni caliphs and their cohorts. He was also known as a secretary for their encounters with opponents, and as a respected companion and transmitter of oral tradition in the Twelver Shi'ite historiographical tradition.[350] The dialogue is preserved in a later text where it is attributed to

---

[348] See David Bertaina, "Safwan ibn Yahya," 535-539.

[349] According to the catalogue of Ibn al-Nadim (d. 995 or 998) and the biography of al-Najashi, he composed thirty books, though only portions of these writings remain today. Most important for our purposes is the reference in al-Tusi's catalogue to Safwan's accounts of Muslim discussions with Christians. The biographer notes he composed a book of questions and narratives given by the imam 'Ali al-Rida (*Masa'il 'an Abi l-Hasan Musa wa-l-riwayat*). It is likely that the latter work was preserved in sections by later Shi'ite compilers, thus making such dialogue encounters traceable to the early ninth century.

[350] The biographical references to Safwan's life do not offer many chronological certainties. As an agent for the Shi'ite leadership in the region of Kufa, he would have collected alms for the imam and carried out important tasks for the leadership. As a merchant, Safwan was well-traveled but also closely connected to the family of the imams. According to the biographer al-Kashshi, Safwan recorded sayings from the seventh, eighth, and ninth imams: Musa al-Kazim (d. 799), 'Ali al-Rida, and Muhammad al-Jawad (d. 835). One chronological assurance is that Safwan was present with Imam al-Rida during his stay with the caliph al-Ma'mun in 817-818. He also recorded some of al-Rida's conversations during his stay in Khurasan. Safwan died in 825 in Medina. For biographical information on Safwan ibn Yahya, see especially al-Najashi, *Rijal Al-Najashi* (Beirut: Dar al-Adwa', 1408/1988), 439-440; and Muhammad ibn al-Hasan al-Tusi, *Al-Fihrist Al-Tusi* (Najaf: al-Matba'a al-Hadariyya, 1356/1937), 83-84.

Safwan ibn Yahya.[351] The verbal exchange highlights the importance of rhetorical skill and proper conduct. The entire text follows in translation:

> Safwan ibn Yahya, a fine-clothing merchant, said: Abu Qurra, the companion of the Patriarch, asked me to escort him to al-Rida, so I asked for his permission regarding the matter. So [al-Rida] said: "Have him come to me." When he came to him, he kissed the carpet and said: "In this manner for us in our religion we greet honored ones among our colleagues." Then [Abu Qurra] said to him: "May God be good to you, what would you say about a sect appealing to a claim for which another sect equally testifies?" He replied to him: "They have a legitimate claim." [Abu Qurra] said: "What if another sect appeals to a claim for which there is no testimony other than their own?" He said: "They have nothing." [Abu Qurra] said: "As for us, we claim that Jesus is the Spirit of God and His Word, so we concur with the Muslims about that. But Muslims claim that Muhammad is a prophet, and we do not agree with them about this. What we agree about is better than what we disagree about." Then al-Rida said to him: "What is your name?" He replied, "John." He said: "John, we believe in Jesus the Spirit of God and His Word, who believed in Muhammad and proclaimed him and confessed himself that he was a mastered servant. So if Jesus is the one who is Spirit of God and His Word according to you, he is not the one who believed in Muhammad and proclaimed him, nor is he the one who confessed servitude and ownership to God. We are free of it, so how do we agree?" Then he arose and said to Safwan ibn Yahya: "Get up! How have we benefited from this discussion?"[352]

---

[351] Muhammad ibn 'Ali Ibn Babawayh al-Qummi (d. 991/2), *'Uyun akhbar al-Rida* (Najaf: al-Matba'a al-Haydariya, 1390/1970), 232. See also Muhammad Baqir al-Majlisi, *Bihar al-Anwar*, 4:428.

[352] Ibid.

Using the dialectical method and analogical reasoning, John Abu Qurra argues that since Christians and Muslims both testify that Jesus Christ is Word and Spirit, this claim is more truthful than the claim that Muhammad is a prophet, since they do not agree about this assertion. However, al-Rida points out that when Christians and Muslims use the same terms, they are referring to a different set of signifiers and ideas. For al-Rida, the term "Spirit and Word of God" connotes a different set of principles based upon qur'anic interpretation that is incompatible with John Abu Qurra's ideas. His response demonstrates that Muslims were aware of Christian claims that the Qur'an could be interpreted within a Christian context to affirm the divinity of Jesus Christ.

The second dialogue attributed to al-Rida is also transmitted via Safwan ibn Yahya.[353] The text revolves around the Christian definition of Christ as being of God (*min Allah*). During this encounter, al-Rida challenges Ibn Qurra in the form of a series of questions to argue that his words regarding the relationship between Christ and God are imprecise. The complete dialogue follows:

> Al-Rida said to the Christian Ibn Qurra: "What do you say about Christ?" He replied: "My lord, He is of God." So [al-Rida] said: "What do you mean by your phrase 'of'? 'Of' four persons, not five of them? Do you mean by your word 'of' like the part of a whole, so he would be a part? Or like the vinegar of wine as in the way of transmutation? Or like the offspring of a child, as in the manner of marriage? Or like the work of a craftsman as in the way of being created from a creator? Or do

---

[353] The dialogue was preserved by the Twelver Shi'ite Muhammad ibn 'Ali Ibn Shahrashub (d. 1192), who took it from the *Kitab al-Safwani*. See Muhammad ibn 'Ali Ibn Shahrashub, *Manaqib Al Abi Talib*, 3 vols. (Najaf: al-Matba'a al-Haydariya, 1376/1956), 3:462. The title *Kitab al-Safwani* is ambiguous, and may refer generically to a work of Safwan ibn Yahya, or it may have been preserved from another unknown account.

you have another sense that you might present to us about him?" But he refrained.[354]

Similar to the dialogue with John Abu Qurra, al-Rida emphasizes the differences in meaning behind words that his interlocutors take for granted. He does not approach the argument through methods of dialectical reasoning; rather he responds to the questions as an Arab grammarian who confronts, objects, and disputes Christian claims in light of the Islamic worldview. For al-Rida, all discourse is analyzed through proper understanding of "clear Arabic speech" (Q 16:103) based upon the Qur'an.

Both dialogues also indicate that the Imam al-Rida had some knowledge of Christological doctrines, but only to the extent which the Qur'an explained Christian failures to properly express Jesus' relationship to God. The hermeneutical world of the Qur'an determined the way in which al-Rida argued against his Christian opponents; it provided the framework for his religious discussions based upon the guarantee of God's oneness (*tawhid*).

The two brief dialogues portray John Abu Qurra and Ibn Qurra as real historical figures that questioned al-Rida about Muslim-Christian matters. While the details of the discussions may be the product of a stylized composition, this does not change the fact that they could represent simple reminiscences of brief exchanges about religious topics. The rhetorical champion in each encounter is al-Rida, but some of the specific elements of the debates exhibit a sense of authenticity.

John Abu Qurra is portrayed as a companion of the patriarch who seeks an audience with al-Rida. If the dialogue occurred while al-Rida was staying with the caliph al-Ma'mun in Merv in Khurasan, then John Abu Qurra most likely belonged to the Church of the East, which was the only community in that region. Even if the dialogue took place in Baghdad, that was the location of the East Syrian patriarchate. John shows due reverence for al-Rida's position by kissing the carpet before him. He addresses him as a colleague rather than an adversary. The author of the accounts, Safwan ibn

---

[354] Ibid.

Yahya, portrays John Abu Qurra before the heir to the caliphate in the same way that the Patriarch Timothy portrays himself in his literary dialogue with the caliph al-Mahdi. The conduct within the discussion is polite, and the speakers enter into a discussion of a particular theological matter. John Abu Qurra's questions use dialectical reasoning to show that what Christians believe about Jesus is more important than their differences with Muslims. John never has a chance to further the debate because al-Rida abruptly ends the discussion in irritation.[355] Thus the literary dialogue does not have a theological lens through which it determines John's character, but it allows him to utilize the dialectical method for his argument.

The second dialogue is really only a brief exchange so little can be said of Ibn Qurra as a literary figure in the encounter. We know nothing of his first name, profession, or confessional identity. He is described as a Christian who is presumably present at a court discussion with al-Rida. He offers a polite response to al-Rida, calling him "my lord." Much like the other short dialogue, al-Rida has the last word and the Christian does not engage in further debate. Ibn Qurra's response to the question about Christ and al-Rida's discourse on the grammatical meanings of the Arabic word for "from/of" indicate that such discussions were transpiring during the Abbasid period.

The two brief literary dialogues are a helpful contribution to our knowledge of Muslim-Christian discourse during the ninth century and the topics and methods which interested those who engaged in interreligious disputations. The texts are significant as indicators of Shi'ite knowledge of Christian argumentation during the early ninth century under the caliphate of al-Ma'mun. Moreover, they have intrinsic value as one of the few popular Muslim literary dialogues from this historical period pertaining to Christian-Muslim

---

[355] For more on such behavior in the *majlis*, see Sarah Stroumsa, "Ibn Al-Rawandi's *Su Adab Al-Mujadala*: The Role of Bad Manners in Medieval Disputations," in *The Majlis: Interreligious Encounters in Medieval Islam*, ed. Hava Lazarus-Yafeh, Mark R. Cohen, Sasson Somekh and Sidney Griffith (Wiesbaden: Harrassowitz, 1999), 66-83.

relations, in contrast to the more prevalent intellectual treatises. The narratives are also valuable for historical and biographical information. They depict al-Rida as an adept theologian, a refuter of a Christian theology, and a rhetorician who responds to others' questions and challenges them with his method of logic. The dialogues do not show any extravagance in language or depiction. The encounters have an authentic quality in the Christian argumentation, the Muslim rebuttal, and the abrupt ending to the conversation, even while the focus of the story is still upon the intellectual acumen of Imam al-Rida.

CONCLUSION

By the end of the eighth century, the dialogue form had important pedagogical value for Muslims and Christians. First, the dialogues recorded the ways in which they argued using Scripture, dialectical reasoning, inductive reasoning, and combinations of revelation and rational knowledge. The literary form preserves the patterns, assumptions, and interests of these participants in the Muslim-Christian dialogue in the early Islamic Middle East. Second, the dialogues were often meant for a wider audience to be used as resources for instruction in apologetic technique and religious debate. The Christian and Islamic education systems encouraged the literary form of dialogue as a teaching tool on how debates would proceed in real life. Medieval Christians and Muslims appropriated the literary form to strengthen the theological education of their local communities and to instruct them in logical ways of reasoning.

6 Dialogue as Hagiography

A common theme in medieval dialogues is the presentation of a hagiographical hero who emerges victorious despite the difficulties of the situation. As the word "hagiography" implies, such a hero was extolled for his holiness. Many authors chose to write about the saints/imams, as well as martyrdom, using a mixture of biography and dialogue. For the authors of dialogues, hagiography made use of memory as a tool for creating a reason for their worldview. In the literary realm, memory offered a means of empowerment for communities that were always challenged, sometimes persecuted, and occasionally martyred. Responding to challenge, persecution, and martyrdom was a primary goal of such dialogues. For instance, Christians used hagiography effectively in response to pagan persecutions before the rise of Islam. Authors adapted the classical traditions and set them within the world of Islam, such as the Georgian martyrdom of Abo of Tiflis.[356] Others used the genre to demonstrate the miraculous works of their members, such as the Melkite hagiographic work on John of Edessa.[357] Writers employed the literary form to meet the contemporary needs of the community through memorable religious encounters.[358]

---

[356] See the introduction and translation in David Marshall Lang, *Lives and Legends of the Georgian Saints* (Crestwood, NY: St. Vladimir's Seminary Press, 1976), 115-133.

[357] See John Lamoreaux and H. Khairallah, "The Arabic Version of the Life of John of Edessa," *Le Muséon* 113 (2000): 439-460.

[358] See for instance Elizabeth Castelli, *Martyrdom and Memory*.

Memory was a tool in the hands of the author. In its literary form, memory was shaped according to the will of the composer. In this way, literary dialogues internalized the memory of a conversation and made the religious other a part of one's own religious identity. The literary dialogue was a vehicle for historiography that empowered the community; its text was a testimony of the ways things should be ideally. The dialogues also offered the memory of a hagiographical hero, who offers meaning to the reader and a message that faith and logic are truthful. For instance, in the ninth-century dialogue between Israel of Kashkar and al-Sarakhsi, the bishop-hero uses philosophical demonstrations to prove the coherency of Trinitarian doctrine. At the same time, the dialogue may have served as a hagiography for Israel of Kashkar among his supporters in the Church of the East.[359] By participating in the reading of such a dialogue, the reader takes the author's memory of the event and makes it their own.

There are many hagiographies that include theological debates and conclude with the martyrdom of the saint, such as that of the monk Michael of Mar Sabas monastery.[360] Because hagiographic literature is so vast and diverse, this chapter focuses exclusively on the disputation-style dialogues where no one's life is at stake. In each of the following dialogues, a champion overcomes his adversaries through rhetorical flourish, quick wit, sharp dialectic, and a charismatic personality. Unlike saints' lives and the martyrs' stories, these people are remembered not only because of their holiness. Rather, they exhibited special characteristics and were able to command respect and represent their particular communities in a memorable fashion.

---

[359] See Barbara Roggema, "The Debate between Israel of Kashkar and al-Sarakhsi," 840-843; and Matti Moosa, "A New Source on Ahmad ibn al-Tayyib al-Sarakhsi: Florentine MS Arabic 299," *Journal of the American Oriental Society* 92 (1972): 19-24.

[360] For the text, see Monica Blanchard, "The Georgian Version of the Martyrdom of Saint Michael, Monk of Mar Sabas Monastery," *ARAM* 6 (1994): 149-163.

WASIL OF DAMASCUS AND THE BYZANTINE LEADERS

One of the earliest texts to seriously address the merits of Christian argumentation using the dialogue form is a Sunni account between the Muslim Shaykh Wasil of Damascus and his four Christian discussion partners: the patrician Bashir (d. c. 742), an Orthodox priest, the patriarch, and the Byzantine emperor. The event purportedly took place in the early eighth century, based on the fact that it refers to an iconoclast emperor who may have been the emperor Leo III (d. 741). The text specifically mentions a companion of Leo named Bashir, who is mentioned elsewhere by historians.[361] However, since the text mentions that the encounter took place "during the rule of the Umayyads" it presupposes that the composition of the dialogue took place during the Abbasid period, most likely in the ninth century according to Sidney Griffith, who has done a study, edition, and translation of the text.[362]

The dialogue begins with a background story about the Byzantine patrician Bashir.[363] Originally he had been a young Christian who was enslaved and raised as a Muslim, learning poetry, oral traditions, reading, and recitation of the Qur'an. However, as he grew older, he returned to the Byzantine Empire and embraced Christianity again. For his reconversion, the Byzantine emperor made him a patrician.

---

[361] There are both Christian and Muslim recensions of the life of Bashir, with the Christian accounts based on the authority of the Byzantine historian Theophanes (d. 818). Other Syriac accounts in Michael the Syrian and the chronicle *Ad Annum Pertinens 1234* also mention an account of a historical figure that may be Bashir. For the Christians, he is a betrayer of Christian iconography and a collaborator with the iconoclastic policies of the emperor Leo. According to the Muslim recension, Bashir was an apostate Muslim who returned to Christianity and impressed the king enough to be made a patrician.

[362] Sidney Griffith, "Bashir/Beser: Boon Companion of the Byzantine Emperor Leo III," 293-327; reprinted as the eleventh chapter in Sidney Griffith, *The Beginnings of Christian Theology in Arabic*.

[363] Sidney Griffith, "Bashir/Beser: Boon Companion of the Byzantine Emperor Leo III," 326-327.

Following this biographical account, the story recalls a time when thirty Muslims were captured and brought to Constantinople. Among them was a prisoner named Wasil of Damascus, whom Bashir questioned regarding his religion. During this first encounter Wasil refused to speak with Bashir.[364]

On the second day, Bashir returns to speak with Wasil. He begins the conversation by reciting Q 3:59, about Jesus being a created servant. Wasil refuses to comment on account of the potential to be persecuted for his words. So Bashir grants him immunity to speak freely without fear of retribution. At this point, Wasil challenges Bashir on the Christian understanding of Jesus' human and divine natures – does the dominant nature acknowledge the weaker or not? Wasil tells the Christian Bashir:

> If you say it does know, I say, how could its own power be independent of it, since it could not dispel these disabilities without it? And if you say it does not know, I say, how could it know the secret things, and not know the position of a spirit with it in a single body?[365]

Wasil is remembered in the dialogue as a remarkable figure for his use of dialectical reasoning, or *kalam* argumentation, as his primary method of discourse. In contrast to other works that used the Qur'an as the only source for interreligious discussion, Wasil dis-

---

[364] Ibid., 302-303. Due to the author's lack of explicit references, we do not know the exact time that this is supposed to have occurred, nor do we know of any historical figure named Wasil of Damascus. Sidney Griffith conjectures that the author may have used the famous Mu'tazilite dialectical theologian Wasil ibn 'Ata (c. 700-c. 749) as a model when he composed the work. Griffith connects a reference in the work to Wasil as an Arab "the sea has thrown up to you" with an Arab naval attack upon Constantinople in 717-718, in which the Arab fleet was destroyed and there would have been Muslim prisoners in the city. This would have made Wasil ibn 'Ata a young man during his participation in the war. However, Griffith acknowledges that the disputation text claims its main character is from Damascus; Wasil ibn 'Ata was a native of Medina and spent much of his life in Basra.

[365] Ibid., 318-319.

plays a willingness to engage his opponents on issues of Christian faith and practice, advancing beyond scriptural proof texts. For instance, he continues along this line of dialectical argumentation:

> The Shaykh said, "I am going to ask you a question, my son. Do you worship the cross as a likeness for Jesus, Mary's son, because he was crucified?" Bashir said, "Yes." The Shaykh said, "Was it with approval on his part, or resentment?" Bashir said, "This point is the same as the previous one. What do you want to say? If I say with approval on his part, you say, 'How blessed you are! They got what they asked for and wanted.' If I say with resentment, you say, 'Why do you worship what he himself could not stop?'"[366]

Wasil's overall tone in the text is more polemical than apologetic since he criticizes Christian doctrines and practice and does not focus on defending Islamic doctrines from Christian polemical attacks. Nevertheless, his assumptions are still permeated with the hermeneutical thought of the Qur'an. For instance, Wasil's main argument concentrates on Jesus' identity in the same way that the Qur'an is preoccupied with negating the claims of Jesus' divinity. Wasil argues that Jesus is human like Adam, he had a human will, he participated in all human activities including prayer to God, he was not "the third of three" gods (Q 5:73), and he would have been unjust toward his mother Mary by being crucified. In short, Wasil creates an intellectually and theologically coherent account of how Jesus fits into the Islamic prophetic framework.

Such arguments were part of the stock of Muslim polemicists who were familiar with debating Christians in oral and written forms. However, this knowledge can only be ascertained because this text furnishes scholars with extant proof that intellectuals were using such arguments in their interreligious encounters. The dialogue is valuable not only for its use of dialectical reasoning, but as confirmation that such disputes were part of the oral and literary

---

[366] Ibid. This same question is asked by a Muslim in Jerusalem in a work by the Christian theologian Theodore Abu Qurra called *Against the Outsiders*, mentioned later in the chapter.

tradition of Muslims during the early Abbasid period. Wasil is therefore the ideal rhetorician, as acknowledged by Bashir. Following their exchange, Bashir tells an Orthodox priest to engage Wasil in dialectic until he converts him.

On the third day, the Orthodox priest enters the discussion along with Bashir. Wasil holds the real power over the priest since he acts in the role of questioner. This role was often given to the one who was at a disadvantage, often because they were in the court of a person from another religious or sectarian perspective. Utilizing dialectical methods, he frames each issue in such a way as to provoke silence from his opponent. For instance, the priest tells Wasil that he will baptize him soon. Then the priest tries to explain the history and theology of Baptism to Wasil but he fails miserably. At first he claims to sanctify the water of Baptism, and then reneges on his comment and acknowledges he does not make it holy, but rather than it is a practice from Jesus. Wasil then replies that if Baptism is a blessing through the hands of someone else, then Christians should worship John, who anointed Jesus' head and called for a blessing upon him. The author portrays the priest as misunderstanding baptismal theology. He is unable to explain the relationship between God's sanctifying action and the act of the one who baptizes. The exchange in the dialogue may have been intended as an insult to Christian clerics, or the result of the author's own lack of knowledge concerning Christian Baptism. While such an argument would not be compelling for an educated audience, popular readers would have found Wasil's intellectual criticisms entertaining. Even the Christian patrician Bashir tells the priest: "Stand up, God shame you, I summoned you to convert him to Christianity, and now you have become a Muslim!"[367]

After this exchange ends, Wasil is brought before the Byzantine emperor. He suggests that the "Head of the Christians" speak with him. In this discussion with the patriarch, Wasil is also aware of Christian practices, such as priestly celibacy, the veneration of the cross, prayer, and the controversy surrounding iconography. Wasil uses his sharp mind and dialectic to criticize both Christian

---

[367] Ibid., 320-321.

faith and particular practices in his argument.³⁶⁸ Wasil asks the patriarch why a Christian leader cannot have a wife or children on account of maintaining purity while the patriarch claims that Jesus Christ, the Lord of the Worlds, resided in the womb "and sullied himself with menstruation."³⁶⁹

When the patriarch hears his words he simply asks for Wasil to be taken away. But Wasil has a long monologue in which he uses a series of dialectical arguments to criticize the Incarnation and Trinitarian doctrine. At this, Wasil is brought away to a church, with the expectation that he would be made a Christian. Instead, Wasil offers the Islamic call to prayer in the church, and so he is beaten and brought out to the emperor. Wasil tells him that if Christians attack people for praying to God, then their religion is worthless. The Byzantine emperor agrees with Wasil.

In the final scene, Wasil identifies the veneration of icons in churches with idolatry, challenging the patriarch to find verification for the practice in the Gospel or otherwise acknowledge that Christians imitate what idol worshippers practice. When the Byzantine emperor hears the priest unable to give a response, he declares:

> "Why do you make my religion like the religion of the people of the idols?" And he gave orders for the destruction of the churches, and they began to destroy them, and they were weeping… And the King set his hand to the killing of priests and bishops and patricians to the point that they fled into Syria, because they did not find anyone who could give him an argument.³⁷⁰

---

³⁶⁸ The notable exception to this case is the work by the Mu'tazilite theologian 'Abd al-Jabbar in his work on the *Confirmation of the Proofs of Prophethood (Tathbit dala'il al-nubuwwa)*. See Gabriel Said Reynolds and Samir Khalil Samir, eds., *'Abd al-Jabbar: Critique of Christian Origins*, and Gabriel Said Reynolds, *A Muslim Theologian in a Sectarian Milieu*.

³⁶⁹ Sidney Griffith, "Bashir/Beser: Boon Companion of the Byzantine Emperor Leo III," 322-323.

³⁷⁰ Ibid., 326-327.

The story of Wasil demonstrates how Muslims in the Abbasid period were interested in defining their communities within the context of a religiously plural society. For the author, the literary genre was able to convey his knowledge of Christians and their claims while simultaneously using Wasil as a hero of Islamic dialectical reasoning. The dialogue constructs an Islamic hero who teaches that only Islam provides a sensible and rational account for theology and history. Only the Islamic historiography of Christian faith and history is authentic, for Christian claims have become corrupt over time.

The dialogue has two heroes in its narrative: Wasil and the Byzantine emperor. The emperor defends Wasil for making the Islamic call to prayer in a church since he was remembering the one God. He also supports Wasil's arguments against icons, finding no reference in the Gospel and thus orders the destruction of icons across the empire.[371] The story is not unlike some Christian apologetic dialogues in which a Muslim leader secretly becomes a Christian. The author depicts the Christian emperor as the complement to Wasil. Since Wasil offers the best dialectical reasoning among the disputants, the emperor acknowledges the merits of his conclusions.

The dialogue is meant to represent a victory for Islam and Wasil of Damascus in particular. At the same time, the author acknowledges that Islam must confront Christianity and its claims in order to assert priority in matters of faith and reason. By defeating the most learned men in Christendom, Wasil of Damascus is the ideal Muslim: one skilled in dialectic, scriptural training, and theology. The literary form of dialogue becomes the means by which an Islamic identity is constructed. This identity presupposes a plural society in which truth claims must first be met with skepticism and subject to imagined critique before they can be confirmed. Wasil is the hagiographic hero who provides this portrait for his readers and audience.

---

[371] Ibid., 326-327.

HISHAM IBN AL-HAKAM AND THE PATRIARCH BARIHA

In contrast to the Wasil of Damascus dialogue, the Shi'ite tradition has historically employed the dialogue genre to confirm the authority of the imams against external opponents (Christians) and internal opponents (proto-Sunni traditionists). The dialogue between Hisham ibn al-Hakam (d. ca. 796) and the patriarch Bariha, which reputedly took place in the eighth century Baghdad, fits the criteria. The story contains a hagiographical portrait that extols the sixth and seventh Twelver Shi'ite imams, Ja'far al-Sadiq (d. 765) and Musa al-Kazim (d. c. 799). While the dialogue begins with a debate about Christianity, it concludes by commending the truth of Shi'ism. The dialogue is concerned with constructing a comprehensive identity for the Twelver Shi'ite community, their authority, and leadership in particular. It presents a theological vision of Shi'ite Islam, shaped by qur'anic interpretation, prophetic tradition, and other communal traditions, in order to construct a hagiographic narrative about the preeminent place of the imams in Islam.[372]

The dialogue between Hisham ibn al-Hakam, who was a well-known dialectical theologian, and the patriarch Bariha, is included among the historical recollections meant to honor the imams.[373]

---

[372] The text is embedded in the work of the tenth-century Shi'ite author Muhammad ibn 'Ali ibn Babawayh al-Qummi (d. 991-992), although the original text may date back to a disciple of Hisham ibn al-Hakam. On Hisham ibn al-Hakam, see Hossein Modarressi, *Tradition and Survival: A Bibliographical Survey of Early Shi'ite Literature, Volume 1* (Oxford: Oneworld, 2003), 259-268. The text may belong to his ninth-century disciple Yunus ibn 'Abd al-Rahman according to Modarressi, 196. For more on Ibn Babawayh al-Qummi, see A. A. A. Fyzee, "Ibn Babawayh," *Encyclopaedia of Islam, Second Edition*, 3:726-727.

[373] David Thomas has done a study and translation of this debate; therefore my work will summarize his findings and consider some thematic issues not explored within his article. See David Thomas, "Two Muslim-Christian Debates from the Early Shi'ite Tradition." See also the critique by David Wasserstein, "The Majlis of al-Rida: A Religious Debate in the Court of the Caliph al-Ma'mun as Represented in a Shi'i Hagiographical Work about the Eighth Imam 'Ali ibn Musa Al-Rida," 108-119.

The other Muslim characters in the dialogue are the sixth imam, Ja'far al-Sadiq, and his son Musa ibn Ja'far al-Kazim, who was the seventh imam among the Twelver Shi'ites.[374] Thus, the dialogue claims to trace back to the later eighth century.

On the other hand, a number of details demonstrate that the work was intended for internal consumption to verify the historical truth of Shi'ite Islam and to invite its readers to acknowledge the charisma and authority of the imams. The patriarch Bariha represents a literary type rather than a real figure. He is a patriarch who has reigned for more than seventy years and is depicted as an inept theologian and debater, despite suggestions to the contrary that he was skilled in apologetics. Furthermore, there is no Christian or Muslim historical record of this figure as head of the Church of the East. Even the name Bariha is unknown among Syriac Christian names from the period.[375] In addition, there are many features of the dialogue which suggest the literary creativity of the writer was the inspiration for the narrative. Bariha's inner turmoil is described in dramatic detail and characters' clothes and emotional responses are meticulously described. Based on the purpose of the literary dialogue, the evidence suggests that the composition belongs with other literary dialogues from the ninth and tenth centuries, when the genre was at its height. In other words, aggrandizing the imams was a driving force behind its composition in this literary form.

The dialogue introduces the Christian patriarch Bariha, who has studied Islam and the characteristics of Christ. His study of Christ's attributes is important to the story, as they lead him to see these same qualities in the imams. Through Bariha's studies, he has

---

[374] Abu Musa ibn Ja'far al-Kazim was the seventh imam according to Twelver Shi'ism, while the Ismailis recognized his brother Ismail ibn Ja'far as the rightful leader and consequently a split developed between these communities.

[375] David Thomas has suggested the name is a corruption of the name Bahriz. Another possibility is that Bariha could be altered from Barih (brh), which means "to leave" or "to turn from the left to face (a group) at the right." In this case, his name could signify the action of someone who converts to Islam.

become skeptical of Christianity, and he begins to seek other alternatives. Unconvinced by Sunni arguments for Islam, Bariha seeks out the Shi'ite scholar Hisham ibn al-Hakam. The dialogue setting is presented in dramatic form by Hisham:

> While I was seated in my shop in Karkh with people around me reading out the Qur'an for me, suddenly there appeared a crowd of Christians, both priests and others, about a hundred men all in black with hooded cloaks, and among them was the chief patriarch Bariha. They stopped around my shop and my chair was offered to Bariha. He sat on it and the bishops and monks stood around leaning on their staffs, their hooded cloaks over their heads.[376]

At this display of strength, Bariha declares that he wishes to debate Islam with Hisham. First, Hisham links Muhammad with Jesus Christ as extended family, since Jesus was descended from Isaac and Muhammad from Ishmael. Then he explains to Bariha that the Christian description of the Father and the Son is inconsistent, challenging him to think about the justice of the Father and Son if they are each capable of all things: then the Son could be the father of the Father, and the Father could be the son of the Son. This paradox distresses Bariha and he leaves confused. The next day he returns alone and asks about the qualities and attributes of the one from whom Hisham derived his religion. In particular, Hisham focuses on the personal holiness of the leader of the true religion:

> He is sinless since he commits no sin, generous since he has no avarice, brave since he has no fear, without need of more knowledge since he is not ignorant, a guardian of religion standing by its injunctions; he is from the stock of the prophets, the collector of the prophets' wisdom; he is gentle where there is anger, and acts justly where there is wrong; he helps secure agreement, and establishes right before friend and ene-

---

[376] David Thomas, "Two Muslim-Christian Debates from the Early Shi'ite Tradition," 55.

my; he makes no excessive demands in respect of his enemy and does not impede advantage to his friend. He acts according to the revealed teaching and talks about miraculous things; he is one of the pious. He relates the sayings of the imams, sincere friends, and no argument ever confounds him; he is never ignorant of a question, gives opinions on every religious practice, and reveals all that is dark.[377]

After Hisham describes the features of a Shi'ite imam, Bariha concludes this charismatic leader must be a source of truth and he travels to Medina to visit with the imam Ja'far al-Sadiq and his son Musa al-Kazim. When Musa recites the Christian Gospel from memory for Bariha, he becomes his disciple. At Bariha's death a few years later, Musa buried Bariha himself and hoped that more Christians would be like him.

The author makes some use of dialectical reasoning in order to argue about the relationship between the Father and the Son in the Godhead. His argument is based upon a passing knowledge of Christological ideas. He structures the dialectical presentation of his questions without scriptural references from the Bible or the Qur'an. Rather, the argument is subordinated to the author's main intent of presenting a conversion story that exalts the theological characteristics of Shi'ite leadership. In this way, the literary form is used to promote an intra-faith apologetic argument against Sunni Islam even while the story recounts a polemical Christian encounter.

More importantly, the purpose of the dialogue is to commend the Shi'ite faith through a presentation of memorable heroes. The evidence suggests it was created as a historical memory to support the Shi'ite community and provide an authoritative example of the community's enduring authority and divine power, even in the face of other Muslim and Christian challenges. The work seeks not so much to denigrate Christian faith as to endorse a Shi'ite worldview of history that would empower and demonstrate the superiority and holiness of their leaders.

---

[377] Ibid., 59.

The patriarch Bariha represents the audience who is willing to hear the claims of Shiʿite Islam. His character makes the dialogue text a conversion story and also confirms the hagiographical heroes of the narrative. The dialogue begins with dialectical reasoning, but it does not remain the focus of the story. Rather, the narrative is interested in how the dialogue can be used in the service of its own theological endeavor to promote Shiʿite identity. The truth is communicated not through dialectical reasoning nor through scriptural argumentation, but through personal holiness.

IMAM MUSA AL-KAZIM AND THE MONK AND NUN OF NAJRAN

The seventh Twelver Shiʿite imam, the eighth-century figure Musa al-Kazim, was also remembered through hagiographic portraits of his encounters with Christians.[378] One dialogue in particular recounts the story of a Christian monk and nun from Najran in southern Arabia who came to discuss religious matters with him. The names of the monk and nun are never mentioned in the dialogue, and many of the individual arguments are glossed over. The attention to personality over religious argumentation is a prominent feature of medieval Shiʿite hagiography.

The day after their arrival in Medina, the monk and nun are seated outside with Musa al-Kazim and a number of his followers. At first, the nun begins asking a number of questions, all of which are answered by the imam. But when the nun is unable to answer any of his questions in kind, she accepts Islam (the story does not explain the content of any of these questions from either character).

---

[378] Muhammad ibn Yaʿqub al-Kulayni, *al-Kafi*, 8 vols., ed. ʿAli Akbar Ghaffari (Tehran: 1957-1961), 1:481-484. See also pp. 479-481 for another dialogue between a Christian monk and Musa al-Kazim that is similar in style to the dialogue analyzed here. For more on the tenth-century author of the account, see Christoph Marcinkowski, "A Glance on the First of Four Canonical Hadith Collections of the Twelver Shiʿites: *al-Kafi* by al-Kulayni (d. 328 or 329 A.H./940 or 941 C.E.)," *Hamdard Islamicus* 24 (2001): 13-29.

Following her conversion, the nun disappears from the story, which now focuses on the special knowledge of Musa al-Kazim during his conversation with the monk. Following some undisclosed questions, the monk shares his reason for coming to visit Musa. Initially, he was strong in his Christian faith and believed himself the most knowledgeable Christian in the world. But one day, he heard of a man from India who was able to make pilgrimage to the "Holy House" (*Bayt al-maqdis*) in one day and night and then he would return to his home in Sibdhan, India. According to the monk, he had heard that the Indian monk even knew how Sheba's throne was brought before Solomon during their encounter (a story found in the Qur'an, Islamic commentaries, and Jewish folklore).

At this point, Musa al-Kazim seemingly changes the topic by asking the Christian monk if he knows the special names of God, which achieve one's desired result if they are invoked. The monk answers that there are seven, but the actual names are one of the reasons that he has traveled to see the imam:

> By God who brought down the Torah to Moses and appointed Jesus as an example for the world, and a trial for the gratitude of those of understanding, who granted Muhammad as a blessing and mercy and granted 'Ali as an example and source of insight, and who appointed a regent from his descendents and Muhammad's descendents, I do not know. If I was aware of them you would not have asked me and I would not have come to you or asked you questions.[379]

The Christian monk continues the dialogue by explaining his encounter with the Indian monk. Since he had heard about these special divine names but did not know their hidden meanings or explanations, he set out from Najran until he arrived in Sibdhan in India. He discovered from the locals that the monk had built a monastery in a nearby mountain where God had given the monk a water source and caused food to be produced for him. When the monk went to the monastery, he finally met the Indian Christian

---

[379] Ibid., 481-482.

monk who was praying in a standing position, looking and weeping at the sky, earth, and mountains.

The Christian of Najran asked him about the stories he had heard: "I was told that you know certain names of God through which you can reach the "Holy house" that is in Syria every day and night. Is it true?" But instead of answering the question, the Indian monk asks him if he knows the features of the "Holy House." At first, the monk of Najran assumes it must be Jerusalem, the holy city, known by its title (*Bayt al-maqdis*). However, the Indian monk confides in him that the "Holy House" is actually the family of Muhammad. In fact, the seven special names of God have only been preserved through the successors of Muhammad's family, the imams. Since the family holds this knowledge, the Indian monk admonishes the monk of Najran to go to Medina. This brings the monk's story up to the present discussion with Musa al-Kazim.

As a confirmation of his special knowledge, Musa reveals the identity of the Indian monk. According to the imam, the monk was a Persian named Mutammim ibn Fayruz. He had acknowledged that God had no partners, and had left the Christian community for his monastery in India because of his belief. Despite the distance, he would visit Mecca for the pilgrimage each year. Astounded at this miracle, the Christian monk continued to ask Musa more questions, including a riddle. He had heard of eight letters that were revealed, four to be manifested on earth, and another four in heaven. The monk asks Musa about the recipient of the heavenly ones. In response to the riddle, Musa explains that the righteous one, sent as the final imam, will interpret the last four.[380] Not even these are known to the messengers and prophets. When the monk asks about the four on earth, Musa reveals his knowledge of divine things:

---

[380] The author of the story seems to confirm that Musa was not the final imam. Some Shi'ite followers believed that Musa was the Mahdi who would return at the end of time. For more information, see M. Ali Buyukkara, "The Schism in the Party of Musa al-Kazim and the Emergence of the Waqifa," *Arabica* 47 (2000): 78-99.

I will tell you about all four. The first one is "there is no god except God" who is one and has no partners; he is eternal. The second is "Muhammad is the messenger of God" purely. The third one is we are the "Family of the House" (*Ahl al-bayt*). The fourth one is our party (*Shi'a*) among us, and we are from the messenger of God and the messenger of God is from God through reason.[381]

Upon receiving this divinely-inspired response, the monk gives the testimony of faith in God and Muhammad as the prophet, along with a commitment to the imams. For the Christian monk of Najran, Musa al-Kazim has demonstrated that God chose them and purified them from evil. Upon his conversion, Musa asks that a gown, shirt, scarf, shoes, and a hat be brought for the new convert, as he may now wear the clothes of a Muslim rather than a Christian monk. The dialogue ends with the miraculous knowledge and generosity of the imam Musa al-Kazim.

This dialogue confirms the motifs of the imams found in the previous account: the power of dialectic is not so important as the miraculous knowledge and wonderful virtues of the descendents of Muhammad. Like his predecessors 'Ali and Ja'far, the seventh imam Musa al-Kazim is capable of moving hearts and minds to the truth of Islam via his words as much as his actions.

THEODORE ABU QURRA AGAINST THE OUTSIDERS

Among the most well-known Christian theologians of the Abbasid period is Theodore Abu Qurra, the Melkite bishop of Harran (ca. 755-ca. 830).[382] Approximately twenty-three of Theodore's authen-

---

[381] Ibid., 483.

[382] Several scholars have attempted to reconstruct Theodore Abu Qurra's biography based on accessible historical data. See Ignace Dick, "Un continuateur arabe de saint Jean Damascène, Theodore Abuqurra, évêque melkite de Harran; la personne et son milieu," *Proche-Orient Chrétien* 12 (1962): 209-223; 319-332; 13 (1963): 114-129; Georg Graf, ed., *Die Arabischen Schriften des Theodor Abû Qurra, Bischofs von Harrân (ca. 740-820): Literarhistorische Untersuchungen und Übersetzung* (Paderborn: Ferdinand Schöningh, 1910); Sidney Griffith, *Theodore Abu Qurrah: the intellectual profile*

tic Arabic works and forty-three Greek works attributed to him have passed down to the contemporary period. Medieval historical memory recalls Theodore Abu Qurra as the bishop of Harran in the province of Edessa (present-day southeastern Turkey), and as one of the first Christian theologians and dialecticians (*mutakallimun*) to compose in Arabic.[383] Theodore was a defender of Melkite Arab Orthodoxy against the claims of the East Syrians and West Syrian Jacobites, and a spokesman closely connected with the Jerusalem patriarchate and its monasteries. He was best known as a remarkable apologist in response to the challenge of Islam.

While no ancient writer composed a biography of Theodore Abu Qurra, one of his Melkite contemporaries recognized him as "the most blessed and most philosophical bishop."[384] Theodore studied medicine, logic, and philosophy during his formation, as

---

of an Arab Christian writer of the first Abbasid century (Tel Aviv: Tel Aviv University, 1992); Sidney Griffith, "Reflections on the biography of Theodore Abu Qurrah," *Parole de l'Orient* 18 (1993): 143-170; John Lamoreaux, "The Biography of Theodore Abu Qurrah Revisited," *Dumbarton Oaks Papers* 56 (2002): 25-40; John Lamoreaux, transl., *Theodore Abu Qurrah*, xi-xxxv; Joseph Nasrallah, ed., *Histoire du mouvement littéraire dans l'Église Melchite du Ve au XXe Siècle; contribution à l'étude de la littérature arabe chrétienne* (Louvain: Peeters, 1987), 2/2:104-134; Samir Khalil Samir, "Al-jadid fi sira Thawudurus Abi Qurra wa atharihi," *al-Machriq* 73 (1999): 417-449; Samir Khalil Samir and Juan Pedro Monferrer-Sala, eds., *Abú Qurrah: vida, bibliografía y obras* (Córdoba: Universidad de Córdoba, 2005).

[383] Harran is first mentioned in Genesis 11:31. In the tenth century, the bishop of Harran was one of approximately eleven bishops who were suffragans in the province of Edessa under the Antiochian patriarchate. For more information see Cyril Charon (Korolevsky), *History of the Melkite Patriarchates*, ed. Bishop Nicholas Samra (Fairfax, VA: Eastern Christian Publications, 2000), 3/1:255-262. On his birthplace, see Ignace Dick, ed., *Maymar fi ikram al-ayqunat; li-Thawdhurus Abi Qurrah (Théodore Abuqurra, traité du culte des icons)* (Juniyah, Lebanon: Librarie Saint-Paul, 1986), 208. See Sidney Griffith, ed., *A Treatise on the Veneration of the Holy Icons; Written in Arabic by Theodore Abu Qurrah* (Louvain: Peeters, 1997), 91.

[384] This reference by John the Deacon in the ninth century is included in his preface to Abu Qurra's Greek *Refutations of the Saracens*, in John Lamoreaux, transl., *Theodore Abu Qurrah*, 212.

well as the languages of Syriac (presumably his native tongue), Greek, and Arabic.[385] There is no indication of the exact date of his birth, which can only be estimated on the basis of a few sources that show he was Bishop of Harran around the turn of the ninth century; that he participated in a debate in Armenia in 814, and possibly entered into a debate with Muslims in 829.[386] Besides these significant events in Theodore's historical record, there are some references to his life and works in external sources.[387]

Theodore Abu Qurra was also known among Muslim scholars as a translator, apologist and dialectical theologian. He made an Arabic translation of the work *On the Virtues of the Soul*, a pseudo-Aristotelian treatise, for Tahir Ibn al-Husayn, who was a military leader under caliph al-Ma'mun.[388] The catalogue of Ibn al-Nadim

---

[385] Samir Khalil Samir, "Al-jadid fi sira Thawudurus Abi Qurra wa atharihi," 418. In his Syriac chronicle, the twelfth-century Jacobite, Michael the Syrian, also refers to Abu Qurra as "a Chalcedonian of Edessa." See Jean-Baptiste Chabot, ed., *Chronique de Michel le Syrien*, 3:32.

[386] Based on this chronology, Abu Qurra would have been thirty years old when Theodoret became patriarch of Antioch, and seventy-four years old at the time of his debate before al-Ma'mun. This seems reasonable now that there is no reason to connect Theodore Abu Qurra with St. John of Damascus (d. c. 755) as a personal associate.

[387] The twelfth-century Syriac chronicle of the Jacobite patriarch of Antioch, Michael the Syrian, presents the most extensive reference to historical events in Theodore's life, albeit late and in an antagonistic manner. Thus his account must be read with a certain amount of caution and skepticism regarding his claims about Theodore's life and activities. See Jean-Baptiste Chabot, ed., *Chronique de Michel le Syrien*, 3:32-34 (French), 4:496 (Syriac). The Jacobite theologian Habib Ibn Khidma Abu Ra'ita, a dialectical theologian (*mutakallim*) and opponent of Theodore Abu Qurra, describes him as a "scholar," a "sage," and a "philosopher," but also as a "Melkite Chalcedonian, Maximimist" who deceives naïve Christians into Nestorian ways of thinking. See Griffith, *Theodore Abu Qurrah: the intellectual profile of an Arab Christian writer of the first Abbasid century*, 22.

[388] Mechthild Kellermann, "Ein pseudoaristotelischer Traktat über die Tugend: Edition und Übersetzung der arabischen Fassungen des Abu Qurra und des Ibn at-Tayyib" (Ph.D. diss., Friedrich-Alexander-

(d. ca. 995) mentions that Abu Qurra composed a book against the "Nestorians."[389] The catalogue also notes a polemical text written against Theodore Abu Qurra by the Mu'tazilite author 'Isa ibn Subayh al-Murdar (d. ca. 840 AD), entitled *Against Abu Qurra the Christian*.[390] However, the work is lost. Other Muslim polemicists seem to have been aware of Theodore's arguments for Christianity since they take them into account, although his name is not specifically cited.[391]

In subsequent historiography, Theodore was commemorated as a learned Christian scholar connected to Mar Sabas monastery in the environs of Jerusalem. The purpose was to frame his message of Orthodoxy as part of the education that came from this monastic center. Regardless of whether we can know more about his activities, it is possible to make some conclusions about Theodore Abu Qurra's identity. First, his theological labors manifest a robust Melkite identity and a close alliance between the Orthodox Melkites of Mesopotamia and the Jerusalem patriarchate in spiritual, jurisdictional and monastic affairs, as well as a shared concept of apostolic tradition. Secondly, the theological and social background of Mesopotamia and northern Syria consisted of a broad assortment of Christians, Jews, pagans and Muslims, thus providing the stimulus and motivation for Theodore Abu Qurra's commitment to religious dialogue, though it was not only of local importance,

---

Universität zu Erlangen-Nürnberg, 1965), 13; Jean-Baptiste Chabot ed., *Chronique de Michel le Syrien*, 3:36.

[389] Rizza Tajaddud, ed., *Kitab al-Fihrist lil-Nadim* (Tehran, 1971), 36; Bayard Dodge, ed., *The Fihrist of Al-Nadim: A Tenth-Century Survey of Muslim Culture*, 2 vols. (New York: Columbia University Press, 1970), 1:46.

[390] Rizza Tajaddud, ed., *Kitab al-Fihrist lil-Nadim*, 207; Dodge, ed. *The Fihrist of Al-Nadim*, 1:394.

[391] The author 'Abd al-Jabbar (d. 1025 AD) mentioned Abu Qurra's work as a source for his knowledge of Melkite doctrines. See 'Abd al-Jabbar al-Hamadhani, *Al-Mughni fi-abwab al-tawhid wa-l-'adl*, ed. Taha Husayn (Cairo: Al-Dar al-Misriyya lil-ta'lif wa al-tarjama, 1958), 5:144. See also the Zaydi Shi'ite theologian al-Qasim Ibn Ibrahim (d. 860) in Wilferd Madelung, "Al-Qasim ibn Ibrahim and Christian Theology," *ARAM* 3 (1991): 35-44.

but held a universal significance for him, as is verified by his travels to Alexandria, Jerusalem, and Armenia. Thirdly, the proliferation of Theodore Abu Qurra's works and the memory of his identity as a debater and dialectical theologian demonstrate that he was a popular figure in the early Abbasid period, and he would have been an admired personality to have associated with Arab Christianity and the Orthodox theological tradition. It is this focus on hagiographic portraits that is preserved in his memorable encounters with Muslims.

One collection of writings attributed to Theodore Abu Qurra is entitled *Against the Outsiders*.[392] John Lamoreaux has prepared an edition and translation of the work.[393] The text comprises a series of eight encounters between Theodore Abu Qurra and other religious interlocutors. The initial two sections in the text belong to the genre of literary dialogues, while the remaining six sections belong to the genre of question-and-answer literature (i.e., the questions lack characters). For the purpose of this work, the first and second sections will be examined for their use of dialectical reasoning, along with their hagiographic portrait of Theodore as the ideal rhetorician.

The first dialogue answers the question of whether Christ was willingly crucified by the Jews. According to the setting, Theodore was making a pilgrimage to Jerusalem with other Christians. While he was at the Church of the Resurrection (Holy Sepulchre), Theo-

---

[392] The work also demonstrates remarkable similarities with some Greek literary disputations attributed to Theodore in a number of texts found in his Greek writings. See the English translations done by Lamoreaux, transl., *Theodore Abu Qurrah*, 211-254. Also, J.-P. Migne, ed., *Patrologiæ Græca*, 97:1462-1610.

[393] Damascus, Greek Orthodox Patriarchate, codex 181 [olim 1616]. I would like to especially thank John Lamoreaux not only for bringing this unpublished work to my attention but also for supplying me with his preliminary work for the edition and translation of Theodore's dialogues. When I cite from the text, I will offer the numbering system used by Lamoreaux to divide up the dialogues. For all of Theodore's works related to Christian-Muslim topics, see John Lamoreaux, "Theodore Abu Qurra," 439-491.

dore was accosted by a Muslim and some of his friends who sought to convert him from Christianity. In the form of a syllogism, a Muslim suggests that if the Jews crucified Jesus in accordance with his will, then they should be blameless, but if it was done against Jesus' will, then the Christian God is weak. Theodore responds with a syllogism of his own to demonstrate a flaw in his premise: by the same token, the Christian claims about a Trinitarian God are made either in accordance with God's will, which commends Christian doctrine, or against the Muslim's God's will, which would make their God weak. Thus the tone of the entire conversation is based on dialectical reasoning without the use of biblical or qur'anic scriptures. At the same time, Theodore's sharp mind and use of rational argumentation are highlighted for the dialogue's readers and audience.

Following this initial exchange, Theodore employs inductive reasoning through the use of analogy to further his point and refute the accusations of his Muslim interlocutor. Theodore demonstrates to his adversary that it is the intent of the actor and not the act alone which determines the excellence or depravity of the person. For instance, if a Byzantine kills a Muslim who desires paradise in battle, he won't be congratulated by other Muslims for his act, but he would be killed in retaliation.[394] Theodore uses another analogy to highlight that his Muslim opponent's premise is faulty because it judges according to the act without considering the intent of the one who acts.

Theodore is the hero of the debate and has the greater speaking part during the encounter; however the unnamed Muslim and his friends also play a prominent role in the debate, which is described in a lively manner. They all gather around Theodore and speak together. After setting forth the syllogism, the main speaker

---

[394] This same encounter occurs in Greek *Opuscula* 9, demonstrating that some of Theodore's Greek works indeed have Arabic antecedents. This is based on the study of John Lamoreaux which suggests that the Arabic composition preceded the Greek dialogue. See the translation of this dialogue, with minor differences, in Lamoreaux, transl., *Theodore Abu Qurrah*, 240-241.

declares: "There is no escape for you from it. It demolishes your religion."[395] Theodore asks the Muslim's friends if they agree that premises in the argument are valid. But after Theodore points out the flaw in its reasoning, they exclaim: "By God, our friend has been put to shame!"[396] The Muslim group acts as a chorus and impartial judge between the two interlocutors; their presence verifies the truth of Theodore's argument by virtue of his dialectical reasoning. In other words, the dialogue purports to recall that Muslims themselves acknowledged Theodore's intellectual abilities as well as his formidable character.

In the second half of the argument, Theodore Abu Qurra employs two analogies to prove that the Islamic argument is untenable. At the end of the first analogy, the Muslim arbiters declare their defeat and the effectiveness of his response. When the conversation is finished, the group agrees with his argument and they depart. The dialogue does not give detailed characteristics about the Muslims due to the brevity of the encounter. Just like Theodore, they are concerned with the merit of his argument rather than scriptural proof texting. Their responses follow in the manner of a philosophical disputation rather than a religious argument. When they accede to his reasoning they represent a fair and honest group of Muslims. Theodore's apologetic in response to their polemic portrays both sides in the manner of a real encounter between religious opponents.

The second literary dispute takes place somewhere in Syria, where Theodore and a friend were participating in a wedding celebration. At their table are two Muslims who are mocking other Christians with the question, "What do you think about a man who kills his mother?" in reference to Jesus and Mary. The Muslim argues that Jesus was unjust in allowing his mother to see his suffering and allowing her to die like any other mortal. The Christians avoid answering the question because of the wedding feast, and so too does Theodore, so as not to draw attention to himself. But his friend encourages him to engage the Muslim antagonist with the

---

[395] 1.3
[396] 1.7

use of analogical reasoning from Scripture. Theodore uses the biblical story of Abraham, his son, and his relationship to God as an analogy to rationally demonstrate the imperfect assumptions in the Muslim's reasoning. If God caused Abraham suffering by asking him to sacrifice his son, then the Muslim's argument would be an indictment against his own God, if carried out to its logical conclusion (cf. Q 37:99-111). Theodore offers an analogy to prove God's justice concerning the relationship between Jesus Christ and Mary:

> "Tell me, is God not just?" He said, "Yes." I then said, "If I were a king and accused you, my father, and a close friend, of one and the same crime, one for which all of you merited death, but I were then to remit the penalty of death for my father and my friend, would you not consider me to have contravened the limits of justice?" He said, "Yes. And what of it?" I then said to him, "Do you not know that God sentenced Adam and the whole of his seed to death?" He said, "Yes." I then said to him, "If he were to go ahead and kill everyone, but exempt those he loves, would this not make void his prior just sentence? Far be it from him that he contradict himself, for otherwise he will be an object of derision! May he be exalted above that!"[397]

When the Muslim acknowledges his reasoning, Theodore is vindicated as a hero by the wedding party and subsequently in the memory of the Melkite Church.

As for his depiction of his Muslim discussion partner in this exchange, it seems to draw upon a real experience. Theodore's focus is upon the argument itself, and not the development of character; it is a sign of attention to the merit of the argument. The Muslim is the aggressor in the encounter, even harassing other people with his polemics. Theodore's goal is not a polemical attack; it is an apologetic response that demonstrates how Muslim arguments against Christianity contain invalid assumptions. After Theodore boldly tells his adversary to ask him the question, "fear then came on his heart and his tongue began to tremble, and he wanted

---

[397] 2.20-21.

to take back his question."³⁹⁸ The verbal exchange continues in the form of question-and-answer between Theodore and his opponent, with Theodore in the position of master and the Muslim as his disciple. At the conclusion of the dialogue, Theodore's scriptural and analogical arguments persuade his conversation partner.

The dialogues attributed to Theodore Abu Qurra in *Against the Outsiders* appear to be polished literary accounts that record certain memorable events that occurred during his lifetime. Theodore's brief dialogues belong to the popular form of the literary genre. The focus of each dialogue is a precise question at a specific time and location; the exchanges between the speakers are much more brief and colloquial. At the same time that Theodore's dialogues exhibit the popular aspects of disputation, they retain the technical parts of intellectual reasoning that lend verisimilitude to the arguments and the encounters. Theodore's argumentation moves from the particular to the universal – he uses particular examples to corroborate generalized conclusions. Combining this inductive reasoning with Scripture, Theodore's method was apologetic as well as polemical. It is thematically driven in application, instructive in teaching orthodox Christian doctrine, and innovative in defending Christianity. The literary form aggrandizes not only Theodore Abu Qurra as the hero of the story, but it also magnifies his intellectual capabilities in response to Islamic theological claims.

CONCLUSION

In the question-and-answer genre, the focus of the exchange is upon the methods and arguments in the text. But the popularity of the literary dialogue genre was such that it created memorable figures for those arguments as well. The dialogue form did not always dispense with rational argumentation, but it transformed the encounter into a story about people rather than ideas alone. In this process, famous figures of Muslim and Christian communities were commemorated for their words and actions. For instance, the rhetorical abilities of Wasil of Damascus depicted a heroic figure over-

---

[398] 2.7

coming his circumstances in the very heart of hostile Byzantine Christianity. The patriarch Bariha provides the ideal prototype for the faithful convert and believer in the imams, while Hisham ibn al-Hakam exemplifies the virtues and intellectual acumen of the Shi'ite believer. The eighth-century imam Musa al-Kazim and his esoteric knowledge reveal the divine character of the imams, while the dialogue creates a consistent historiography of the imams' moral and intellectual virtues. For Theodore Abu Qurra, his encounters confirmed his reputation as defender of the Melkite Arab Orthodox faith. In each case, the dialogue form is a tool to construct the hagiographic encounter and memorialize the hero of the community. The hagiographic feature of dialogue literature was that it supported the community's memory and commitment to emulate that person. Although martyrdom literature and lives of holy people were the predominant forms of hagiographic writing, authors also considered the theme of holiness when composing interreligious dialogues.

Figure 3. A Hagiographical Portrait of Theodore Abu Qurra. Illustrated by the Rt. Rev. Mark Melone.

7 Dialogue as Scriptural Reinterpretation

Throughout their respective histories, many Muslims and Christians have been concerned with biblical and qur'anic interpretation. In the early Islamic Middle East, Christians continued to comment on biblical texts, while Muslim commentators focused on the Qur'an. Some began to engage in scriptural reinterpretation of their own holy books and the religious texts of other communities. One of the key ideas behind this interpretive move was the concept of Scripture.

For both Muslims and Christians, their holy books were part of their central authority, along with the authority of the community. Through the interpretive rights of the commentators, one could explore the possibilities of scriptural interpretation and apply those possible meanings to the contemporary context. Scripture can be a dynamic, ever-present, fruitful source for understanding the place of one's community in the world through readings of it. We must remember that while contemporary society is interested in historical-critical methods and historicizing texts, medieval readings of Scripture had few qualms about their ability to access divine truth.

Muslims and Christians shared a number of ideas regarding holy books. For Jews, Christians, and Muslims, the Torah was accepted as a book from God. Likewise, Christians and Muslims accepted the Gospel as a divine source. For Muslims, the Torah and Gospel texts of the Jews and Christians had been corrupted. Some Muslim authors argued that the corruption was complete and there was no benefit to examining the scriptures of the People of the Book. Others said that the later communities had changed particular verses in their scriptures so that some original portions agreed with Islamic doctrine, proving the truth of God's revelation to them. Others said that Jews and Christians simply misinterpreted their scriptures and they needed to be read in light of the Qur'an.

Along with the authority of the Qur'an, medieval Muslims used theoretical and textual criticism from pre-Islamic literature by non-Christian critics, such as Samaritan, Gnostic, pagan, and Manichaean texts, as sources for biblical criticism. Among the prominent Islamic biblical critics of the period were 'Ali ibn Rabban al-Tabari (d. ca. 864) and Ibn Hazm of Cordoba (d. 1064).[399]

For some Christian interpreters, the Qur'an contained no truth, while others acknowledged that it brought the Arabs out of idolatry. Other theologians argued that it must have had a semi-Christian origin and was corrupted by the later Islamic communities. Sidney Griffith notes:

> In Arab Christian apologetical texts generally one finds a certain ambivalence about the Qur'an. On the one hand, some authors argue that it cannot possibly be a book of divine revelation, citing in evidence its composite and, as they see the matter, its all too human origins. But on the other hand, given the progressive inculturation of Christianity into the Arabic-speaking world of Islam from the eighth century onward, most Arab Christian writers themselves commonly quoted words and phrases from the Qur'an. Inevitably its language suffused their religious consciousness. Some of them even built their apologetical arguments in behalf of Christianity on a certain interpretation of particular verses from the Islamic scripture. In short, while Christian apologists argued that the Qur'an is a flawed scripture, they nevertheless also often quoted from it as a testimony of truth.[400]

Based on their assumptions about Scripture, their legacies of interpretation, and their opportunities for fruitful commentary, Muslims and Christians began to read one another's scriptures against the grain, pointing out silences in the text, and examining the books for verses confirming certain theological convictions present in the local community. Through scriptural analysis, interpreters sought to discover new defenses and new critiques that

---

[399] See Hava Lazarus-Yafeh, *Intertwined Worlds*, 130-141.
[400] Sidney Griffith, ""The Qur'an in Arab Christian Texts," 204.

subsequently contributed to the formation of doctrine in their respective communities. By reading Scripture from a new focus point – the outsider's community – the text gained novel interpretive possibilities and offered new insights for the historical imaginations of medieval Christians and Muslims. The following sections highlight how Muslims and Christians employed the dialogue form to reinterpret the holy books of other communities. By engaging in scriptural reinterpretation, they gave implicit authority to books that did not belong to their own community. In the process of reinterpretation they made religious others and their scriptures part of their own identity.

IMAM AL-RIDA AND THE PATRIARCH

Shi'ite authorities have transmitted a significant number of dialogues attributed to the ninth-century imam 'Ali ibn Musa al-Rida. Included among these dialogues are accounts where al-Rida argues with Christians, Jews, Zoroastrians, Sunni dialectical theologians, philosophers, grammarians, and other opponents. Several of his encounters with Christian interlocutors were mentioned in the fifth chapter.[401] One dialogue in particular commemorates Imam al-Rida at the court of al-Ma'mun where he debates with a Christian patriarch. This dialogue is particularly significant for its use of Muslim biblical interpretation.[402]

According to a report, the caliph al-Ma'mun called for an assembly of religious representatives to debate al-Rida, including a patriarch, a Jewish leader, a Sabaean, a Zoroastrian leader, and other Muslim intellectuals. The goal of the debate, according to the story, was to humiliate al-Rida. However, in a conversation the night before the debate, al-Rida tells his confidant that he will argue

---

[401] For a brief introduction to the Muslim literary genre of disputation, see Bo Holmberg, "The Public Debate as a Literary Genre in Arabic Literature," *Orientalia Suecana*, 38-39 (1989-1990): 45-58.

[402] See David Thomas, "Two Muslim-Christian Debates from the Early Shi'ite Tradition," 65-80; Steven Wasserstrom, *Between Muslim and Jew: The Problem of Symbiosis under Early Islam* (Princeton: Princeton University Press, 1995), 113-116.

with everyone according to their own texts and terminologies, silencing and refuting them to demonstrate God's divine favor for him.

The next day after the group was gathered, al-Ma'mun asks the Christian patriarch to debate al-Rida in a fair manner. But the patriarch balks at the idea since he rejects both the Qur'an and the prophet as a source of authority in debate. Al-Rida agrees to dispute with the unnamed patriarch using only the Gospel. The patriarch agrees that since the Bible is God's true word, he will accept al-Rida's arguments. The dialogue suggests a calculated effort by the author to construct a framework for biblical interpretation based on traditional qur'anic polemic and historical criticism of early Christianity. For the author, Imam al-Rida's extraordinary abilities in analysis and interpretation of Christian material are more important than the composition of a convincing dialectic (*kalam*). As they begin their conversation, the narrative emphasizes al-Rida's impeccable religious knowledge and theological acumen.[403]

Al-Rida argues that Jesus, his Gospel, and his disciples acknowledged the prophethood of Muhammad. But the patriarch requires two witnesses for this claim. In response, al-Rida refers to the Gospel according to John, in which he claims that Jesus refers to Muhammad, his family, and community:[404]

> "I entreat you to say whether the Gospel relates that Yuhanna [John] said, 'The Messiah told me about the religion of Muhammad the Arab, and informed me that he would come after him; I informed the disciples about him and they believed in

---

[403] These abilities are mentioned in al-Rida's description of his ancestor 'Ali ibn Abi Talib, who through the power of Muhammad revives the dead. See Muhammad Baqir al-Majlisi, *Bihar al-Anwar* 4:407; David Thomas, "Two Muslim-Christian Debates from the Early Shi'ite Tradition," 71.

[404] However, the author mistakenly confuses John the Evangelist with the seventh-century Syriac missionary John of Daylam and the text does not quote the verse, leaving the argument rather vague. It is presumably the references to the Paraclete in John 16:7-11 which the author has in mind, and its association with Ahmad in Q 61:6.

him'?" The Patriarch: "John did say this about the Messiah, and gave news about the prophethood of a man, his house, and his deputed agent. But he did not stipulate when this man would come, and did not name to us the people so that we might recognize them."[405]

Then al-Rida tells the patriarch that he can prove the Bible points to Muhammad as the promised figure. He asks a Greek Christian and an exilarch if they know the third Gospel, which they affirm. Al-Rida reads out the Gospel until he reaches the reference to Muhammad (although the dialogue never mentions the text itself or where it is located in the Gospel). When al-Rida challenges the patriarch to confirm that Jesus made reference to the prophet and the authority of his family, the patriarch acknowledges his claim.

The next question demonstrates al-Rida's knowledge of the disciples and early Christian leaders. When the patriarch asks the imam al-Rida to give the number of disciples and experts on the Gospel, he replies quickly:

> You have encountered one who knows. As for the disciples, they were twelve men, and the best and most knowledgeable was Aluqa; as for the experts of the Christians they were three men, Yuhanna the Great in Aj, Yuhanna in Qarqisiya, and Yuhanna al-Daylami in Zajan who gave the reference to the Prophet, his house, and his community, and who informed Jesus' community and the people of Israel about him.[406]

Then al-Rida responds to the patriarch with the traditional Islamic polemic against Jesus' divinity because he prayed and fasted. He argues that Jesus' miracles cannot verify his divinity since the biblical prophets such as Elisha and Ezekiel performed similar deeds, as did the Muslim prophet Muhammad. After a Jew present at the debate reads the Torah to confirm these miracles, al-Rida

---

[405] David Thomas, "Two Muslim-Christian Debates from the Early Shi'ite Tradition," 68.

[406] Ibid., 69-70. The name Aluqa likely refers to Luke, and the third John (Yuhanna of Daylam) is the only known historical figure of the other three.

offers further examples, taken from the Qur'an and the oral traditions, such as the miracles of reviving the dead performed by 'Ali ibn Abi Talib. The Christian leader is reduced to silence and makes the profession there is no god but God.

In each case, Imam al-Rida is depicted as a keen reader of biblical scriptures. He employs scriptural interpretation from a qur'anic perspective as his method of debate. Yet he also displays a passing knowledge of Christian history and makes a critique of Christian origins. Thus, dialogue has a twofold purpose: critique Christianity and the Bible through the hermeneutical thought of the Qur'an and praise the aptitude of 'Ali al-Rida.

In the next section, al-Rida employs Islamic biblical exegesis to interpret the two riders mentioned in Isa. 21:7 as Jesus and Muhammad. This traditional Islamic argument, also found in Patriarch Timothy's dialogue with the caliph al-Mahdi, shows that the author had either been instructed in Muslim biblical polemic, heard such arguments during oral debate, or had access to a text that used such arguments.[407] The text reinforces the dichotomy between a Muslim reading of the Bible and Christian exegesis. Al-Rida quotes from John 20:17, 14:26, 15:26, and 16:5-8 together to argue that they were part of Jesus' authentic Gospel, while other portions of the Bible are not reliable. The patriarch maintains that Christians lost the Gospel for only one day.[408] But for al-Rida the resulting corruptions came through the later works of Luke, Mark, John, and Matthew.[409] While the patriarch is not aware of this story, he surprisingly acknowledges it, setting the way for al-Rida to list further

---

[407] It is unlikely that the material came from a Christian convert, since the text employs typical arguments that would have been part of a Muslim apologist's education. On Timothy's dialogue text, see Alphonse Mingana, ed., "The Apology of Timothy the Patriarch before the Caliph Mahdi," 173-174.

[408] There are no details about Christians losing the Gospel for a day in the dialogue. Presumably, the argument is that after Jesus' death, his message was recorded imperfectly by his followers, who had lost the Gospel brought by Jesus.

[409] Muhammad Baqir al-Majlisi, *Bihar al-Anwar*, 4:408; David Thomas, "Two Muslim-Christian Debates from the Early Shi'ite Tradition," 74.

biblical verses in support of his claims about Jesus' humanity and Jesus' predictions of Muhammad's prophethood. As they close their discussion, the patriarch offers his astonishment at the biblical expertise of Imam al-Rida.

Like other Islamic dialogues, the qur'anic worldview determines the process by which all categories are defined and evaluated. The dialogue is concerned with presenting convincing Muslim readings of the Bible based upon polemical topics found in the Qur'an. The internal framework of the debate exhibits close attention to the merits of its interpretive arguments, even if they are typical of Muslim polemic against Christianity. The dialogue's use of scriptural reinterpretation offers a Muslim reading of the Bible and early Christianity as a method of commending Imam al-Rida.

The literary form is the vehicle by which the text demonstrates interest in Shi'ite doctrinal matters of the imamate even to the exclusion of plausible critiques of Christianity. For instance, the patriarch congratulates the imam for properly instructing him about the formation of the gospels and decides that the Gospel authors lied about Jesus.[410] Since the point of the discussion is to magnify al-Rida, the author does not need the patriarch's conversion to Islam. Rather, it is his capitulation to the Shi'ite vision of history (and its vision of the history of Christianity) which confirms al-Rida's victory and the power of the imams. The literary form is a crafted piece of dramatic historical fiction that demonstrates the author's hagiographic tendencies and interest in Islamic reinterpretations of the Bible.

ABRAHAM OF TIBERIAS AND 'ABD AL-RAHMAN AL-HASHIMI

The dialogue between Abraham of Tiberias and 'Abd al-Rahman al-Hashimi was one of the most popular dialogues among Christian communities of the Middle East.[411] There are at least thirty-three

---

[410] Ibid.

[411] For a study, critical edition and French translation, see Giacinto Bulus Marcuzzo, *Le Dialogue d'Abraham de Tibériade avec 'Abd al-Rahman al-Hashimi à Jérusalem vers 820*. For an English translation of a longer East

manuscripts still extant, and they are found in the Melkite, Coptic, Jacobite, and Church of the East communities.[412] It is unclear if the monk Abraham of Tiberias is the author of the text. Most likely, the author belonged to the Melkite community and was a monk who was comfortable using biblical and qur'anic citations. The editor of the critical edition of the dialogue argues that these characteristics demonstrate that Abraham of Tiberias was the author or reported his account when he was present at a debate in Jerusalem around 820.[413] As for the Muslim emir 'Abd al-Rahman al-Hashimi, he is a known historical figure of the same period.[414] The work could be a literary improvement upon what happened at a historical debate that took place in the early ninth century. During the dialogue, Abraham mentions that the Muslims have assassinated seven of their own caliphs in less than two hundred years (Caliph al-Amin was the seventh in 813). To arrive at a date just under two hundred years from the rise of Islam, it is likely that the dialogue was composed around 820.

The story begins with the Muslim emir 'Abd al-Rahman al-Hashimi, who wants to understand more about the confusing doctrines of the Christians. How can they claim that God is three hypostases and Christ is the Son of God? So he calls in an Orthodox (Melkite) patriarch, an East Syrian bishop, two members of his entourage that had converted to Islam from Christianity, one Jewish convert to Islam, two Jews, and a physician. But the speakers are suspicious of 'Abd al-Rahman's intentions and they refuse to offer

---

Syrian version of the dialogue, see N. A. Newman, ed., *The Early Christian-Muslim Dialogue*, 269-353.

[412] For scholarly attention to the work, see Mark Swanson, "The Disputation of the Monk Ibrahim al-Tabarani," 876-881.

[413] For his argument on the historicity of the account, see Giacinto Bulus Marcuzzo, *Le Dialogue d'Abraham de Tibériade avec 'Abd al-Rahman al-Hashimi à Jérusalem vers 820*, 97-133. For a different opinion, see Sidney Griffith, "The Monk in the Emir's *Majlis*: Reflections on a Popular Genre of Christian Literary Apologetics in Arabic in the Early Islamic Period," 13-65.

[414] See Giacinto Bulus Marcuzzo, *Le Dialogue d'Abraham de Tibériade avec 'Abd al-Rahman al-Hashimi à Jérusalem vers 820*, 120-127.

specific details to the emir for fear of being punished. According to the story, 'Abd al-Rahman saw Abraham walking by while he was on pilgrimage in Jerusalem. The emir brought Abraham in to discuss Christianity. This sets up the background for the dialogue.

The dialogue between Abraham of Tiberias and 'Abd al-Rahman is significant for its cultural comfort within the linguistic world of Islam. In particular, Abraham uses the Qur'an as a source of truth, while simultaneously offering a historical-critical account for its origins and relationship to Middle Eastern culture. While the participants make more than eighty biblical citations during the course of the dialogue, there are also more than ninety qur'anic references. Examining how Abraham uses the Qur'an will reveal how Eastern Christians made use of scriptural reinterpretation to fit the Qur'an within their biblical worldview.

After the Muslim emir 'Abd al-Rahman promises Abraham protection and liberty to speak, the monk explains the true religion by evoking several qur'anic allusions in the style of Islamic language:

> The religion most pleasing to God is the religion which he chose for his glory, in which his angels delight, which he wants for his servants (Q 5:3), with which he has endowed his friends, and the people obedient to him. His prophets announced it; his messengers put the seal on it, and his choice friends have preserved it in his pure treasuries. He has led peoples and nations into it without sword, or constraint, or false deceit. He has purified its ordinances from uncleanness, and has adorned it with every good quality. He has made it a sign and a safeguard, a guide and a light for the people in every land (Q 4:49, 46:12, 5:44, 5:46). The best community is those who devote themselves to fasting, who perform prayer, who give the most alms, and who read the verses of the truth night and day. They give liberally of themselves and their wealth, en-

dure severe wrong, and shed their blood in various kinds of torment out of loyalty for their master and love for him.[415]

The emir assumes that Abraham is speaking about Islam, and asks him why he is still Christian. However, Abraham says that his description applies only to Christianity. 'Abd al-Rahman protests that Christians have misunderstood Jesus who was a Word and Spirit from God, quoting several qur'anic passages (Q 3:67, 4:171, and 3:85 among others). When Abraham responds, the emir replies, "How good are your words, O monk, but how ignorant are your actions."[416] At this point, Abraham seeks another promise to speak freely in the emir's presence while not accepting his invitation to Islam. Abraham agrees to discuss Christian theological issues, but refuses to discuss Islam for fear of being persecuted. Nevertheless, the Muslim emir 'Abd al-Rahman requires him to enter into debate the following day before he will allow him to leave.

The next day, Abraham returns with a book which offers several Christian readings of the Qur'an and historical interpretations of formative Islam. Since no mention is made of the book's author, it is unclear if it was a literary device to protect Abraham's polemical statements about Islam or part of the actual narrative. Regardless, the section provides several insights on Christian interpretations of Islam:

> As for your statement about your prophet that he was the "seal of the prophets" (Q 33:40), he is not a prophet but he is a king approved by God, in which and by means of whom God fulfilled his promise to Abraham regarding Ishmael.

---

[415] Ibid., 283, 285. See also the insights in Sidney Griffith, "The Monk in the Emir's Majlis," 30-32. Griffith shows that the dialogue uses qur'anic phrases, such as *Ansar Allah* ("helpers of God" Q 3:52), revealing the author's interest in accommodating Christian concepts with scriptural reinterpretations of the Qur'an.

[416] Giacinto Bulus Marcuzzo, *Le Dialogue d'Abraham de Tibériade avec 'Abd al-Rahman al-Hashimi à Jérusalem vers 820*, 299.

As for your statement "the community upon which there is mercy," know that the mercy of God is abundant upon all creation, for "he makes his sun rise and rain fall upon the believers and the unbelievers" (Matt. 5:45) without showing preference for one of them over his companion.

As for your statement "the community who loves its prophet and his family" (*ahl al-bayt*), well see, if you want, then I will tell you the truth: by God, they spilled the blood of his family ['Ali ibn Abi Talib and his sons Hasan and Husayn], they destroyed their homes, and they pillaged their goods. And you are aware of that. So what community is worse than this? When a man comes to them and he gives them authority over the world, and by his intercession he promises them paradise, and then they do to his family what they did to him?[417]

This book from which Abraham reads highlights three themes. First, Abraham argues that Muhammad was used by God to fulfill his promise to Ishmael – a very striking acceptance of his role in the divine plan. Nevertheless, this did not qualify him as a prophet but rather emphasizes his status as a political ruler. Second, the monk Abraham claims that salvation is contingent upon God's mercy, and not the criteria of the Islamic community. In fact, the divisions among the Islamic communities and their actions in history against one another contradict their supposed status as the only elect community of God. Third, Abraham argues that the divisions between proto-Sunni traditionists and Shi'ite followers reflects poorly upon the community, which has corrupted any valuable truths taught during the life of Muhammad. For example, the Commander of the Believers lives in fear of his own children and family, and in less than two hundred years, seven leaders had already been assassinated by their fellow Muslims. Abraham continues his reinterpretation of some qur'anic verses, highlighting the fact that the Islamic community does not live up to the standards professed in the Qur'an (Q 34:24, 46:9, 6:70, 3:200, and 49:13).

---

[417] Ibid., 321, 323, 325.

Abraham shifts his approach in the following section, dealing with the origins and canonization of the Qur'an. He points out that Muhammad is not the composer of the text, but later collators who worked on creating a cohesive text:

> As for your statement about the Qur'an, I will explain to you that Muhammad brought this Qur'an, but his companions wrote it down after his death. These are some of their names: Abu Bakr, 'Umar, 'Uthman, 'Ali, 'Abdullah ibn al-'Abbas, Mu'awiya ibn Abi Sufyan, the scribe of the revelation. After these ones, al-Hajjaj ibn Yusuf compiled it and organized it.[418]

For Abraham, a historical-critical approach to the formation and canonization of the Qur'an confirmed that it did not have divine origins, but rather it was a creation from diverse communities that could not agree with one another, even on the content and revelation of the Qur'an itself. For instance, Abraham argues that competing Shi'ite and proto-Sunni traditionist claims have only led to hatred, condemnation, and destruction of the original qur'anic message:

> Let me tell you what you know with certainty. A group of you claim that prophethood did not properly belong to Muhammad, but only to 'Ali, and Gabriel made a mistake. He wanted to present it to 'Ali, but he presented it to Muhammad. The proof of that is in this: they call the children of 'Ali the children of the Messenger of God. Who are the people whose ancestry is traced to their mothers, if you are of those who say that prophethood belonged to 'Ali? A group of you curse 'Ali and 'Uthman in the pulpits. A group of you claim that authority belonged to Abu Bakr, 'Ali, 'Umar, and 'Uthman. A group of you see the killing of the children of al-'Abbas as like a sacrifice. Three-fourths of you think the curse against Mu'awiya is justified. And all of you testify against al-Hajjaj, that he is of the people of Gehenna. What just judge could testify that this Scripture belongs to this community, when this is your claim

---

[418] Ibid., 330.

about your prophet and his family and his companions? As for your profession of faith "there is no god but God," God revealed these words to Moses his prophet and his blessed pure one.[419]

At this point, Abraham closes the book and finishes his reading, but 'Abd al-Rahman is already deeply upset. Abraham insists that he did not intend to denigrate Islam but only offer the facts – nothing he said was wrong about the Islamic communities. So the Muslim emir calls for the lawyer al-Manzur ibn Ghatafan al-'Absi to debate Abraham.

The dialogue continues with a discussion of Scripture and the status of Christ. In this section, Abraham quotes Q 4:171 back to his Muslim conversation partner, asking him to acknowledge that "Christ is the Word of God and his Spirit," born of the virgin Mary, and that he performed miracles, ascended to heaven, and will come again to destroy the anti-Christ at the end of time. When Manzur al-'Absi agrees with Abraham, he points out that Christians do not agree about Muhammad's prophethood, thereby showing the greater reliability of the Christian claim in comparison.

A little later, Manzur al-'Absi asks Abraham about the Incarnation: how could Jesus fulfill the definition of God as infinite, impassable, and indescribable as a human being? Indeed, how can he remain upon the throne of God (Q 7:53)? Abraham responds with Christological teachings about Jesus Christ, asserting that through his salvific death, he saved them from error and unbelief, which they had in worshipping the devil Iblis. Showing his familiarity with Islamic terminology and the Qur'an, Abraham uses the qur'anic word Iblis (from the Greek word *diabolos*) for the devil, rather than the Christian term Satan. But Manzur argues that from the Christian view, Christ was humiliated through the cross. For the Muslim Manzur, the crucifixion was a curse which God would not have allowed to happen to one of the prophets. Abraham responds that Jesus permitted the crucifixion precisely because it was

---

[419] Ibid., 331, 333.

in accordance with God's will. It was not on account of God's weakness or the power of the Jews that the crucifixion took place.

Next, Manzur argues that Christians worship Christ because he raised people from the dead, but other prophets did so like Elijah and Ezekiel. For him, raising the dead is a sign of God's permission, not of Christ's lordship. Abraham says that while they may do similar things, only Christ says he is the Son of God. Abraham declares that Jesus is superior to the prophets, for "he walked in the markets and among men" while he revealed signs and miracles by means of his authority. Here, the dialogue alludes to Q 25:7, where Muhammad's critics also said that he walked in the markets like a human being, while he claimed angelic sources for his revelation. Abraham creatively uses the qur'anic defense of Muhammad to defend his account of Jesus' humanity. Abraham also uses the qur'anic language of the "unseen" (*ghayb*) to describe Christ's ability to know the hearts of men while the prophets and other humans could not do so.

The Muslim emir 'Abd al-Rahman interjects, challenging Abraham: Christians claim Jesus was crucified, but in truth "it was made to appear so to them" (Q 4:157). Following the gospel accounts, Abraham argues that the apostolic eyewitnesses are reliable sources, and in fact God would have been doing a disservice in hiding the fact that he wasn't crucified. After all, Abraham claims, the Qur'an agrees that the disciples were faithful witnesses to Jesus' message. In Q 3:52, Jesus asks who are my supporters (*ansar*)? The disciples respond: "We are God's supporters, we believe in God, so bear witness that we submit." Abraham's reinterpretation of the qur'anic narrative supports his biblical arguments about the disciples' witness to the crucifixion and resurrection. While Manzur may protest that Christ is not the Son of God, Scripture bears witness to it clearly.

When Abraham mentions Scripture, Manzur attacks the reliability of Jewish and Christian writings. The Gospel has been corrupted, Manzur claims, just as the other scriptures. The only true and original Gospel belongs to the Muslims, who received it from the prophet. But John and his fellow gospel authors, having lost the Gospel after the ascension of Christ into heaven, composed whatever they liked.[420] In response, Abraham offers a detailed argument for the authenticity of the Gospel sources. He includes the witness of the apostles and the fact that Christian poverty seems more realistic than a message of wealth and power as evidence. This would have been more convincing to potential converts.

Next the emir interjects, arguing that Muhammad was greater and nobler than Christ before God. The monk Abraham replies:

> No, by God, I did not know that. But I know that heaven is more honorable and noble than the earth according to God, and that the inhabitants of heaven are more honorable and noble than humans according to God. I know that Christ is in the highest heaven, and that Muhammad and all of the prophets are beneath the earth. [I know] that in heaven is the throne and seat of God, and that Christ sits upon the throne in power at the right hand of the Father above the angels and servants. How can someone beneath the earth be nobler according to God than someone who is in heaven upon a throne in power?[421]

In the following encounter, the Muslim emir introduces another Muslim figure to the debate. The Bedouin Arab al-Bahili is asked to converse with the monk about matters related to Christianity and Islam. Early in their exchange, the Muslim al-Bahili asks Abraham why Christians do not ritually purify themselves from sexual impurity before each prayer (Q 4:43). Abraham replies that God told the believers that their community is holy before God, so there is no sin or blame on account of sexual impurity. Instead, it is spiritual purification rather than ritual purification which God desires. Abraham continues:

> "For you Muslim, what is nobler, faith or Islam?" The Muslim said: "Faith is Islam and Islam is faith." The monk replied:

---

[420] Ibid., 395.
[421] Ibid., 405, 407.

"Your book refutes this statement of yours, because in a passage it says to you: 'Fear God with genuine fear of him, and do not die except as believers'. But you said, 'Prophet of God, who is capable of this?' So he said to you, 'Fear God as you are able, and do not die except as Muslims' (Q 3:102). You see that faith is greater and nobler than Islam. Since you were not capable of faith, he gave you Islam. Since you were not capable of the purification of faith, he gave you water."[422]

Then Abraham says that Muslims have no argument against Christians with regard to ritual purification using water, since Q 4:43 expressly acknowledges there are instances when it is permissible to do prayers without water ("If you are sick or on a journey, or if any one of you has relieved himself, or you have touched women and could not find water, you can rub yourselves with clean earth, wiping your faces and hands with it").

When al-Bahili asks whether Christ is created or uncreated, the monk replies that Christ is creator through the essence of his Father, while he is created by the substance of his mother. When al-Bahili declares a created being cannot be worshipped, Abraham uses a verse from the Qur'an to demonstrate the contrary: "Isn't it in your Scripture that your Lord said to the angels, 'Prostrate to Adam' and they prostrated, except for Iblis who refused and was prideful and among the disbelievers?" (Q 2:34) For Abraham, the same situation pertains to Christ, only as the Son of God.

Following this exchange, the monk Abraham debates with a Muslim pilgrim from the city of Basra. Their dialogue focuses on the divinity of Christ. Why did Jesus pay the tax to Caesar? This narrative is in Matt. 17:24-27, when Peter is asked if Jesus will pay the temple tax. Jesus tells Peter to catch a fish and in its mouth will be coins for the tax. For al-Basri, this proved that Jesus Christ could not be God, since he paid a tax to his own servants. But for Abraham, Christ used the opportunity to demonstrate his call to people through his kindness and humility. Abraham uses qur'anic language to refer to the tax as the *jizya* (Q 9:29), which was the poll

---

[422] Ibid., 433.

tax that Christians paid to their Muslim rulers. Indeed, Peter testified to Christ as one of his helpers (Q 3:52). Since Christians and Muslims acknowledge Christ is "the Word of God and his Spirit" (Q 4:171), the Qur'an supports Abraham's argument for Jesus' divinity in the question. He even quotes the Qur'an's words about Jesus in closing, saying that Jesus had changed some Jews into apes and pigs (Q 5:60) and that Jesus had blown his breath into clay birds giving them life so that they flew away (Q 3:49). Abraham's creative reinterpretation demonstrates how the dialogue intertwined biblical and qur'anic interpretation into a narrative and logical whole.

In his next question, al-Basri asks Abraham what would have happened to Jesus if Mary had fallen and died while pregnant. Using analogical reasoning and the Qur'an, Abraham replies:

> Do you not believe this verse in your Qur'an, that God is "in the highest heaven, then he came closer and hovered around" and "he revealed to his servant what he revealed, the heart did not deny what it saw"? (Q 53:7-8, 10) Is God a creature or not?[423]

Abraham's argument is that al-Basri has mistakenly given an anthropomorphic description of God. In response, Abraham asks him what would happen if God was seated on the highest heaven and slipped off and fell to his death. Al-Basri declares this is absurd, and Abraham agrees, declaring that Muslims cannot accuse Christians of anthropomorphism with regard to Christ without being liable to the same charge in their Qur'an.

In his next question, the Muslim al-Basri asks Abraham if Jesus' prayers were a sign of his servitude, since God does not pray. Abraham argues that Jesus' prayer was not a sign of servitude but mercy and model for his disciples and followers. Abraham insists that al-Basri has contradicted the Qur'an by claiming God does not pray, for it says: "God and his angels pray for the prophet. O you Believers, pray for him and offer peace" (Q 33:56). Abraham's interpretation of the Qur'an leads him to one of two conclusions:

---

[423] Ibid., 465.

either God prays offering mercy and forgiveness and so there is no argument against Jesus' prayer of mercy and forgiveness, or al-Basri is accusing the Qur'an of lying.

When the subject changes to whether Jesus is creator or created, al-Basri asks Abraham to analyze the question within the context of the Qur'an:

> Al-Basri said: "I want you to debate with me via the Qur'an. Do you acknowledge that the Qur'an is a revelation from God which he sent to our prophet Muhammad?" The monk replied: "By my life, no. I don't acknowledge any of this, and I do not acknowledge that your prophet is a prophet. He is only a king in whom God found approval, and through him he fulfilled the promise made to Abraham about Ishmael, because prophecy and revelation were taken away after the time of John the son of Zacharia. The prophet Daniel and Christ testified about this."[424]

For Abraham, the Qur'an cannot be considered divine revelation, but this does not invalidate Muhammad's role as God's instrument in salvation history. Despite his refusal to acknowledge the Qur'an as divine, he considers its insights worthy of authority in the dialogue. Abraham says that since the Qur'an acknowledges that Mary was chosen over other women and purified at the Annunciation, this affirmed Christ's status as Word of God (Q 3:42). Abraham also argues that the prophets have died and are buried in the earth, whereas Christ is in heaven as the Qur'an acknowledges (Q 4:158). Then he quotes a series of biblical testimonies concerning Jesus, but he also appends qur'anic verses to his collection. He reinterprets Q 3:39 to refer to Jesus as Word of God: "God bids you rejoice in John, confirming the Word of God." For Abraham, the Qur'an is not revelation but it carries a sense of authority for Christian doctrine and can be interpreted for confirmation of Christian theology.

In the final dialogue exchange, al-Basri and Abraham focus on Christian veneration of the cross. For Abraham, the cross is a sign

---

[424] Ibid., 485.

of victory and power for Christians. He uses an Islamic oral tradition to defend the idea that certain things are given priority over others in Islam as well:

> Muhammad had already affirmed it when he said: 'Give the Quraysh precedence and do not place yourselves in front of them. You know something of the Quraysh but you do not know it, for the opinion of a Quraysh is equal to the opinion of ten men.' So how could anyone in this situation accept what you say about Christians worshipping the cross?[425]

According to Abraham, Muslims also have the black stone as an object of veneration, although it cannot do the same things as the power of the cross. Here Abraham shows his familiarity with Islamic tradition, arguing that while Christians may make pilgrimages to the relics of the cross in Constantinople, they can pray to Christ and venerate the cross no matter their location. Most importantly, God hears and answers their prayers, Abraham says. This truth is in contrast to Muslim claims that Muhammad is a prophet, Islam is the true religion, the Qur'an is the true guide, the Ka'ba is God's house, the black stone came from paradise, the four corner points of the Ka'ba are special, as well as the house of Abraham, and Mecca as holy places, and the other things which Muslims venerate.[426]

Because of Abraham's claims, the Muslim emir 'Abd al-Rahman requires Abraham to perform a trial by poison, an exorcism, and a trial by fire using the sign of the cross to save himself. The story concludes with the conversion of those in the audience after he successfully accomplishes these tasks, their martyrdom for apostatizing from Islam, and Abraham being allowed to depart in peace.

While the dialogue between the monk Abraham of Tiberias and the Muslims at the court of 'Abd al-Rahman al-Hashimi contains aspects of hagiography, dialectic, and entertainment, it is particularly notable for its use of the Bible and reinterpretations of the

---

[425] Ibid., 505.
[426] Ibid., 511.

Qur'an from a Christian worldview. The Qur'an is quoted extensively only on rare occasions, and rarely within a historical context. Rather, the passages are interpreted through the theological framework of Christian biblical interpretation and the legacy of proof texting in dialogues with Jews. Despite the passing quotations of the Qur'an, the dialogue is remarkably comfortable with its use of qur'anic language and terminology. The dialogue also reveals Christian knowledge in the ninth century for the formation, collation, and canonization of the Qur'an. It demonstrates knowledge of the historical context and debates between Islamic communities, and how they interpreted the Qur'an and theological ideas differently. The dialogue reveals how some Christians had assimilated into the linguistic and scriptural worldview of the Muslim communities around them in the early Islamic Middle East.

THEODORE ABU QURRA AND CALIPH AL-MA'MUN

Even during the medieval period, Christian historians made references to a dialogue between Theodore Abu Qurra and Muslim scholars at the court of the caliph al-Ma'mun as a significant historical event.[427] The first reference to Theodore's dialogue is in the Syriac *Chronicle of 1234*. It records that in the year 829, al-Ma'mun journeyed from Baghdad toward Byzantine territory on a war campaign. When al-Ma'mun came to Harran, he met with the bishop of the city, Theodore Abu Qurra:

> Now Ma'mun drew near and arrived at Harran. Theodore, bishop of Harran, who was called Abu Qurra, had a conversation with Ma'mun. There was a great debate between them about the faith of the Christians. This debate is written in a special book, for anyone who wants to read it.[428]

---

[427] For an overview, see David Bertaina, "The Debate of Abu Qurra," 556-564. See an Arabic edition in Ignace Dick, *Mujadalat Abi Qurra ma'a al-mutakallimin al-muslimin fi majlis al-khalifa al-Ma'mun* (Juniyah: Matba'at al-Kathulikiyya, 1999).

[428] Jean-Baptiste Chabot, ed., *Anonymi auctoris Chronicon ad annum Christi 1234 pertinens*. For a French translation of the text, see Jean Maurice

The second significant source for the existence of Theodore's dialogue comes from Shams al-Ri'asa Abu al-Barakat, also known as Ibn Kabar (d. 1324), who was a Coptic priest in Cairo. According to his catalogue, he includes the notice: "Abu Qurra, Bishop of Harran. He has a well-known debate and treatises."[429]

Modern writers have debated back and forth about the connection between the historical event and dialogue text. Some associate the dialogue with a real historical event, concluding that the debate resembles the genuine writings of Theodore in thought and style.[430] Others have argued that the dialogue could not have been written by him because it was recorded by a third-person narrator who did not write with the same style or vocabulary of Theodore.[431] It may be that a ninth-century Arab Orthodox Melkite, who was closely connected with Theodore Abu Qurra, his writings, and his style of argumentation sought to create an Arabic literary dialogue that was based upon a real meeting, even including firsthand memories of the debate.[432] The author must have done one

---

Fiey and A. Abouna, eds., *Anonymi auctoris chronicon ad annum Christi 1234 pertinens* (Louvain: Secrétariat du CorpusSCO, 1974), 16. The name in the Syriac text is clearly Theodore and not Theodosius as translated in Fiey and Abouna.

[429] Samir Khalil Samir, *Misbah al-zulma fi idah al-khidma li-l-qass Shams al-Ri'asa Abu al-Barakat al-ma'ruf bi-Ibn Kabar* (Cairo: Maktabat al-Karuz, 1971), 301.

[430] See for instance Constantin Bacha, ed., *Un traité des oeuvres arabes de Théodore Abou-Kurra, évêque de Haran* (Tripoli: Chez l'auteur, 1905), 13; Alfred Guillaume, "Theodore Abu Qurra as apologist," *Moslem World* 15 (1925): 42-51; A. Guillaume, "A Debate between Christian and Moslem Doctors," *Journal of the Royal Asiatic Society of Great Britain and Ireland* (Centenary supplement 1924): 233-244; Ignace Dick, "La Discussion d'Abu Qurra avec les Ulémas musulmans devant le Calife al-Ma'mun," *Parole de l'Orient* 16 (1990-1991): 107-113; Wafik Nasry, *The Caliph and the Bishop*, 121-123.

[431] See Griffith, "The Qur'an in Arab Christian Texts," 214; and Griffith, "The Monk in the Emir's Majlis."

[432] There is a literary precedent for the practice of commending Theodore's controversies in the writings recorded by John the Deacon, in

of three things: either he recorded the memories provided to him by Theodore, or he paraphrased material that is found in Theodore's works, or he remembered Theodore's method of responding to Muslims in a real debate in order to compose the literary encounter.[433] Since the manuscripts of the debate are found throughout Melkite and Jacobite monasteries, it seems likely that the author was a monk and/or a scribe affiliated with Theodore Abu Qurra, who was obviously educated in Christian dialectical reasoning (*kalam*) and familiar with qur'anic citations that supported Christian claims.

The story begins without mentioning the circumstances surrounding the debate. Abu Qurra comes into the court of the Abbasid caliph al-Ma'mun. According to the text, Theodore disputed with at least five different Muslim theologians over two days.[434] After introducing the characters, the dialogue begins with a discussion between the bishop Theodore Abu Qurra and the caliph al-Ma'mun. Al-Ma'mun asks him whether the foreskin is clean or unclean. Theodore responds with a carefully constructed apologetic with qur'anic turns of phrase to demonstrate two chief points, one scriptural and the next logical. First, God created Adam and fashioned him with His own hands (Q 38:75) and had him dwell in the garden with Eve (Q 2:35; 7:19). The concept of God fashioning humans is also found in Q 15:28-29 and Q 32:9, when God forms Adam from clay and breathes into him of his Spirit. This is reminiscent of the creation account in Gen. 2:7: "Then the Lord God formed man of dust from the ground, and breathed into his nostrils the breath of life; and man became a living being." For Theodore, the implication is that humans have been created in the image of God. Second, since Theodore and the caliph agree that God

---

some of the Greek works attributed to Theodore Abu Qurra. See John Lamoreaux, transl., *Theodore Abu Qurrah*, 211.

[433] For examples of similarities with Theodore's authentic writings, see Wafik Nasry, *The Caliph and the Bishop*, 107-121.

[434] Some versions of the dialogue add more characters. On the historicity of the figures, see Wafik Nasry, "Abu Qurrah, al-Ma'mun, and Yahya ibn Aktham," *Parole de l'Orient* 32 (2007): 285-290.

would not have created something unclean, he logically concludes that the Christian resemblance to the uncircumcised Adam is clean and superior to circumcision. Third, he crafts his argument in such a way as to indicate his knowledge that the command for circumcision never appears in the Qur'an. The method of qur'anic citation and reasoning characterizes his responses throughout the dialogue.

In the next discussion, al-Ma'mun defends himself by asking why the foreskin should be considered a significant issue, to which Theodore presents the traditional argument that God created Adam in perfection, and this practice remained so until the time of Abraham and his family (Gen. 11:22-26). According to Theodore, Abraham signified a changing point since he acknowledged God and believed in him rather than worshipping idols (Gen. 11:26-12:8 and Q 6:74-75, 14:35). God prescribed circumcision for Abraham as a mark like a sheep and as an example for his people so that they would follow God (Gen. 17:1-14). But with the coming of Jesus Christ, the archetype of the perfect man created in Adam has been restored, and the new covenant established for the faithful would no longer require circumcision.

Next, al-Ma'mun asks Theodore to explain the new covenant and the concept of its fulfillment. According to Theodore, Jesus Christ provided the Gospel in place of the Torah, Baptism in place of circumcision, Sunday in place of the Sabbath, the Eucharist in place of sacrifice, and prayer toward the east in place of the Temple in Jerusalem (*qibla*). This was a traditional argument made by Christians in debate with Jews.[435] But for Theodore, this is a fulfillment

---

[435] On Christian Arabic theologians concerning Judaism, see the article by Sidney Griffith, "Jews and Muslims in Christian Syriac and Arabic Texts of the Ninth Century," *Jewish History* 3 (1988): 65-94. On the Islamic side, see Camilla Adang, *Muslim Writers on Judaism and the Hebrew Bible*; Hava Lazarus-Yafeh, *Intertwined Worlds*; Moshe Perlmann, "The Medieval Polemics between Islam and Judaism," in *Religion in a Religious Age*, ed. S. D. Goitein (Cambridge, MA: Association of Jewish Studies, 1974), 103-138. For Jewish polemics against Christianity, see Daniel Lasker, "Qissat Mujadalat al-Usquf and Nestor Ha-Komer: the earliest Arabic and Hebrew Jewish anti-Christian Polemics" and Sarah Stroumsa, "Qissat Mujadalat al-Usquf: A Case Study in Polemical Literature," in

of Judaism, not an abrogation of Judaism. The implication is clear: while Muslims claim to abrogate Judaism and Christianity, Christians do not make the same claim against Judaism; therefore they do not need to accept the argument of abrogation from Muslims.

Theodore also uses scriptural reasoning and dialectic to point out qur'anic ideas that appear inconsistent with Christian logic. Next, Muhammad ibn 'Abd Allah al-Hashimi challenges him to explain Christ the Word and Spirit of God (Q 4:171), who is allegedly only like Adam, for God created him from dust and breathed into him from his Spirit (Q 3:59 and 32:9). Theodore draws al-Hashimi into a logical fallacy:

> Abu Qurra said: "Tell me about Christ, is he created from something or not?" He replied, "Yes, from the word of God and his Spirit." Abu Qurra said, "Is the Word of God and his Spirit limited, fashioned, and described?" He said, "No, nor can it be comprehended." Abu Qurra said, "Tell me about the Word of God is it Creator or created?" Muhammad ibn 'Abd Allah bowed his head in silence, and did not return an answer for awhile. He was thinking if he said "Creator" he would be prevailed over, and it did not occur to him to say "created."[436]

Theodore concludes that based on his silence, Christ (the Word of God) cannot be like Adam, and the qur'anic verse cannot be used as an assault on Christian orthodoxy, which Abu Qurra vehemently defends.

One persistent theme in the dialogue is that Muslims follow "that which your Scripture does not speak about nor did your

---

Genizah Research after Ninety Years: The Case of Judaeo-Arabic, ed. Joshua Blau and S. C. Reif (Cambridge: Cambridge University Press, 1992), 112-118, 155-159, respectively.

[436] *Vatican Borgia arabic MS 135*, fol. 159a. See also Wafik Nasry, *The Caliph and the Bishop*, 182. Note that since Nasry's edition is a translation based on a number of manuscripts from the debate, the English translation does not always correspond with what is in the Vatican manuscript.

prophet and your messenger pronounce it."⁴³⁷ Theodore emphasizes that Muslims must listen to their prophet and Qur'an where they speak positively about Christians and their virtues. By this Theodore means that Muslim polemics against Christian belief and practice do not conform to scriptural, historical, or logical integrity when they are set in the Christian vision of authentic Islam. His constant refrain is "Do you not know that our opposition to you is based on what [the Qur'an] says to you and your community and to your people?"⁴³⁸ Or he says: "You are telling me what you have to say about the Christians from that which your messenger does not articulate and your Scripture does not speak!"⁴³⁹ This critique also requires Theodore to defend Christian faith and practice through qur'anic interpretation. Therefore, the Qur'an propels the narrative forward.

Theodore Abu Qurra sets the terms for his debate with the Muslim scholars, reminding his opponents that "you should not dispute with the People of the Book except with that which is best," (Q 29:46) and that their prophet did not castigate Christianity but proclaimed their common revelatory belief in God.⁴⁴⁰ For Theodore, these verses abrogate any polemical attempts by his adversaries to discredit Christianity, since he argues that Muslims acknowledge his community as the "People of the Book." Theodore is able to define several terms in the debate, such as the civility of his interlocutors and their prophet's commendation of Christianity according to his interpretation of the Qur'an.

Throughout the debate, Theodore seeks to employ qur'anic citations for the purpose of commending Christian orthodoxy and practices. Besides the historical fact that the Gospel did not have one consonant changed or one consonant taken out of it, according to Theodore, the Qur'an verifies the Gospel's instructions for Christians since it praises them as "a community rightly guided by

---

⁴³⁷ Ibid., fol. 159b. The words are different but the argument is the same in Nasry, *The Caliph and Bishop*, 184-185.
⁴³⁸ Ibid., fol. 162a. Similar in Nasry, *The Caliph and Bishop*, 188.
⁴³⁹ Ibid., fol. 166a. Similar in Nasry, *The Caliph and Bishop*, 192.
⁴⁴⁰ Ibid., fol. 160a. Nasry, *The Caliph and Bishop*, 184.

truth, and among them are those who do justice" (Q 7:181). Theodore reveals a remarkable knowledge of individual suras quoting Q 3:113-114, which calls the People of the Book a virtuous community who recite God's verses night and the day and believe in God and the Last Day and command the good and forbid the evil and hasten toward good things.[441] For Theodore, qur'anic verses commending Christian beliefs and practices held authoritative merit on the basis of their historical and logical implications for his fellow Christians, and they served as a defense against Islamic interpretations that tried to abrogate such verses.

The next Muslim speaker in the dialogue reminds Theodore that whoever follows a religion other than Islam, it will not be accepted by God for salvation (Q 3:85). In response, Theodore reinterprets the Islamic concept of abrogation (*naskh, mansukh*). He asserts that the verse, when read in context with Q 3:83, gives no special status to those who submit. Even animals submit to God, willing or unwilling, so God's praise is for those who believe. Submission (*islam*) is less than the act of believing (*iman*), according to the Qur'an's description of the Arabs (Q 49:14).[442] Since Theodore equates belief with believing in Jesus Christ the Word of God, he argues that Muslims cannot be the believers in the Qur'an but only those who submit. Theodore's interlocutor and the notables of the Quraysh become angry with him at this statement. This sequence of events repeats itself in the dialogue as he cites qur'anic verses to criticize his opponent and then refuses to claim responsibility for the statement since it is their Scripture.

The combination of qur'anic abrogation and approbation for faith over submission characterizes Theodore's method. The next Muslim discussion partner, Harun ibn Hashim al-Khuza'i, asks Theodore if Christians alone have faith while Muslims do not. Theodore's goal is to commend a selected qur'anic reading without denigrating Muhammad, which would be grounds for accusing him of blasphemy. His primary target becomes his Muslim discussion partners, whom he accuses of not having faithfully followed their

---

[441] Ibid., fol. 162b. Nasry, *The Caliph and Bishop*, 192.
[442] Ibid., fol. 161a. Nasry, *The Caliph and Bishop*, 187.

Scripture and prophet. Theodore never acknowledges Muhammad as a prophet, but always uses the term "your prophet." Thus he avoids condemning Muhammad while remaining polemical in his attacks on his Muslim adversaries.

Despite granting authority to parts of the Qur'an and claiming that other parts were abrogated, Theodore rejects still other parts of it as contradictory. On the basis of his knowledge of God's justice and the permanence of marriage, Theodore denies that Muslim men will receive "women with wide, lovely eyes" in Paradise (Q 52:20, 44:54). According to Theodore, since the men desire this pleasure while their wives would be grieving and distressed, it logically contradicts our understanding of Paradise. Theodore points out that the Qur'an testifies that they will encounter the fire (Q 19:71), and since Muslims submit but do not believe, God's warning is specifically for them (Q 11:119). Theodore points out that believing expressly in Christ the Word and Spirit of God is the assurance of faith. Since his Muslim opponents violate this aspect of belief in their criticisms of Christianity, they do not adhere to their prophet or their Scripture. Theodore also claims that the actions of Muslims subvert the intended meanings expressed in the texts, such as the fact that the Qur'an recognized the Gospel as a prior Scripture (Q 5:48). This allegation of a contradiction between Scripture and contemporary Muslim practice is a significant theme in the dialogue.[443]

Al-Hashimi offers no answer to Theodore Abu Qurra, and so al-Ma'mun invites Salam ibn Mu'awiya al-Hamdani to speak, but he inadvertently criticizes the caliph al-Ma'mun for being too lenient in allowing Theodore free speech. After this remark, he is cast out of the court, and the first day of the dialogue closes. The following day, Sa'sa'a ibn Khalid al-Basri enters the debate. He uses biblical reinterpretation as an effective method of debate. His opponent claims that Jesus was only human on the basis of John 20:17 where it states: "I am going to my Father and your Father, to my God and

---

[443] Ibid., fol. 162b. Nasry, *The Caliph and Bishop*, 192.

your God."⁴⁴⁴ In shifting the course of the debate toward Christian doctrine, Theodore is put on the defensive. He still manages to describe Jesus Christ's status as God's Spirit and Word sent into the pure virgin Mary (Q 4:171, John 1:1), who bore Christ, the light of God (John 1:4-9, 8:12), in order to manifest God's power and miracles. His reading of the scriptures requires that Jesus Christ became incarnate, "because human eyes cannot see the light of God and His power."⁴⁴⁵ For Theodore, both the Bible and the Qur'an confirmed that Christ had come to reveal what had previously remained veiled.

Theodore also reinterpreted passages of the Qur'an in order to alter the topics in the debate. He defends Jesus' foreknowledge and equality with God on the basis of Q 5:116, where God asks Jesus if he was to be taken with his mother as two gods. He reasons that God asked Jesus because he must not have known what Jesus thought on account of his divinity and equality with God. Ironically, Theodore runs completely counter to the typical use of this verse as an Islamic polemic against Jesus' divinity, showing how a text can be reevaluated and given new meaning within another community.

Next, Theodore employs a new tactic against al-Basri's claim that Christians are polytheist. The Qur'an calls Christians virtuous ones who are close in affection with those who believe, and lacking arrogance (Q 5:82). Therefore, they cannot be included in the statement: "Whoever associates something with God, he has gone astray in clear error" (Q 4:116). Instead, Theodore claims that we must understand the reference as a condemnation of polytheism among the pagan Arabs who were worshipping idols in Muhammad's day. Theodore asserts that according to the Qur'an, Christians are believers who are rightly guided (though this cannot be

---

⁴⁴⁴ For a discussion of Muslim biblical interpretation on this point, see Martin Accad, "The Ultimate Proof-Text: The Interpretation of John 20.17 in Muslim-Christian Dialogue (second/eighth-eighth/fourteenth centuries)."

⁴⁴⁵ *Vatican Borgia arabic MS 135*, fol. 164b. Nasry, *The Caliph and Bishop*, 199.

found in the Qur'an), and God will separate them from the polytheists on the Day of Resurrection (Q 22:17).[446]

Theodore was particularly concerned with qur'anic interpretation in relation to Jesus' character. Even when a qur'anic citation was critical of Jesus Christ as Son of God, the verse was reinterpreted or re-imagined in such a context that would support his Christology. After al-Basri declares that Christians are polytheist by claiming God has a son, Theodore replies:

> As for your statement, you call us polytheists, and [allege] that we make a son for God, while you say that no one is able to make a son for God! Do you not know that your messenger said in *surat al-Zumar*, "If God wanted to take a son for himself, then he would have chosen from those whom He had created, whomever he willed" (Q 39:4)? So you yourselves deny that God would choose His Word and His Spirit and take it as a son, but your messenger does not deny that, rather he has acknowledged [it], since it says in his Scripture, "I call witness to this son, and the begetter and what he begot" (Q 90:1, 3).[447] So who is this begetter and what did he beget? You have put mankind into deceit; I mean about the beginning.

> And in *surat al-Baqara* it says, "They said, has God, glory be to Him, taken a son? Rather to Him belongs what is in the heavens and the earth" (Q 2:116). Your messenger did not argue with this, rather he acknowledges the truth that God has taken His Word and His Spirit as offspring. Both we and you acknowledge that the Merciful One is His Word, whose name the angels called out, and David called him "Lord," and "Son" (Ps. 109/110:1). So how can you deny what is in the Psalms and the Qur'an on the matter of Christ?[448]

---

[446] Ibid., fol. 165b. Nasry, *The Caliph and Bishop*, 203.
[447] The author changed the word to "son" in the first verse.
[448] *Vatican Borgia arabic MS 135*, fols. 166a-166b. Similar in Nasry, *The Caliph and Bishop*, 206-208.

Theodore's scriptural reinterpretation defends his Christology in much the same way as in earlier works such as the anonymous Melkite Arabic treatise *On the Triune Nature of God*.[449] By utilizing verses that proved the prophecy of the coming of the Messiah and identifying the Messiah's characteristics with Jesus, he presents a coherent and progressive narrative of salvation in the unfolding of history through God's manifestations. Theodore attempts to use this method of persuasion, yet it is convoluted in that the Qur'an postdates Christianity.

For Theodore Abu Qurra, a valid argument could be made for the special status of Jesus Christ as Spirit of God on the basis of qur'anic reasoning. Making reference to Q 3:59, the Muslim al-Basri declares that Christ was like Adam before God, in that he was created by the same "Be!" which God spoke. Theodore says that if this applies to all creation, including animals, then al-Basri's status is no greater than a beast. Al-Basri responds with a quotation from Q 32:9, suggesting that God honored him in his creation by breathing His Spirit into him. Theodore insists that this act of creation cannot be applied to Christ, since al-Basri cannot raise the dead as Christ did. Al-Basri's status as a creature is like that of the animals, Theodore argues, while the Spirit of God is Christ himself, according to the Annunciation event in Q 3:45. He claims that when Muslims denigrate Jesus Christ by making him a creature, they have contradicted their Scripture, since their prophet guaranteed Paradise for Christians. If the Qur'an says they will enter Paradise and Christians believe in Christ, then Muslim criticisms of Jesus Christ will put them out of Paradise. Through this selective process of citations and reasoning, Theodore is portrayed as the master interpreter of qur'anic and prophetic intent in Islam, while offering an entertaining rhetorical defense of Christian belief in Christ and salvation.

Theodore substantiates his arguments with analogical arguments when qur'anic citations would not fit his particular needs. A

---

[449] Margaret Dunlop Gibson, ed., *An Arabic Version of the Acts of the Apostles and the Seven Catholic Epistles, with a Treatise on the Triune Nature of God* (London: C. J. Clay & Sons, 1899), 5-6 (English), 77 (Arabic).

member of the Quraysh tribe asks Theodore who was guiding heaven and earth when God's Word was in Mary's womb for nine months. For Theodore, this idea violates Christian and Islamic understandings of God's omnipresence, as well as the doctrine that nothing can detract from God. God could create something from dust (Q 3:59) and fashion it with his hands (Q 38:75) in his image (Gen. 1:26-27) without changing his divinity. So God is capable of sending the Word anywhere upon the earth in its own dignity, and the Word is inseparable from God's essence. He uses the analogy of the sun and its light as one example. On the other hand, Theodore charges his opponent with separating the oneness of God, thus denigrating God's omnipotence.

When the member of the Quraysh challenges Theodore to explain Trinitarian doctrine, he used biblical texts, Melkite theology, and analogies to respond along with the Qur'an. Theodore reminds him that their prophet declared that "God created all of His creation by means of His Word and His Spirit."[450] For Theodore, scriptural interpretation should judge prophetic intent, and Muhammad did not claim that the Word of God was created, nor did he clarify this in his Scripture. According to Theodore, the real prophetic intent was to laud the verified tradition of the Christian community, which teaches:

> The Father is the Mind, and the Son is the Word Begotten from the Mind, and the Spirit proceeds from the Mind and the Word. The Father is the Initiator, and the Son is the One Who gives growth, and the Holy Spirit is the One Who gives life. He is the One worshiped, with Three Persons and One Essence, the Eternal.[451]

After their discussion of the Trinity, the caliph al-Ma'mun asks Theodore to clarify Jesus' status. If Jesus is God, then how did he eat food, drink, and walk in the markets? Theodore replies that

---

[450] *Vatican Borgia arabic MS 135*, fol. 170b. Wafik Nasry, *The Caliph and the Bishop*, 226.

[451] Ibid., fol. 168b. This section is abbreviated in the manuscript, and the full translation is from Wafik Nasry, *The Caliph and the Bishop*, 226.

even though Jesus ate food with his body which was clothed from the Virgin Mary, he fed thousands in the countryside through the power of his divinity (Matt. 14-15); and as he walked in the flesh he also walked upon sea and its waves (Matt. 14:24-32; Matt. 8:23-27), which he stilled through the power of his divinity. Theodore's goal was to turn the language and ideas toward scripturally intelligible statements for his Muslim conversation partners.

At the conclusion of the debate, the Muslim scholars allege that Theodore deliberately confused them, talked too profusely, and gave baffling answers to their questions. They even claim that his knowledge must have come from the jinn. As for Theodore's reading of the Qur'an, the Muslim scholars warn the caliph about the effective yet hypocritical aspects of his arguments, declaring that Theodore is like a blazing fire from which Muslims should keep their distance.[452] Theodore Abu Qurra's adversaries end their discussion with this statement, and Theodore is declared the victor in the debate before Caliph al-Ma'mun, who acts as a benefactor for Christian discourse.[453]

There are several important characteristics in Theodore Abu Qurra's debate with Muslim scholars before the caliph al-Ma'mun. First, Theodore is portrayed as a theologian well-versed in the field of scriptural and theological apologetics. Theodore's task was similar to that of early Christians under the pagan Roman Empire. He cites a biblical or qur'anic passage and then employs dialectic to argue his position. Scriptural reasoning can work in three ways: first, as an argument that uses the Bible or Qur'an as a model for argumentation; second, as an argument that uses the Bible or Qur'an as a starting point for a dialectical exposition; and third, as an argument that uses the Bible or Qur'an as evidence to corroborate examples from nature. Theodore employs the latter two forms quite often during the debate. Most important for our purposes,

---

[452] Ibid., fol. 172a. It is not found in Nasry's edition.
[453] For more on al-Ma'mun and Christianity, see David Bertaina, "Melkites, *Mutakallimun* and al-Ma'mun: Depicting the Religious Other in Medieval Arabic Dialogues," *Comparative Islamic Studies* 4 (2008): 17-36; Mark Swanson, "The Christian al-Ma'mun Tradition," 63-92.

Theodore structured his critique around proof-texts of qur'anic passages that functioned as catechetical and apologetic guides for Christians. Theodore sought to use the passages from the Qur'an to demonstrate that the true religion is Christianity, its faith and practice are commendable, and that Muslims cannot make the same claims since their qur'anic interpretation is erroneous.

Second, Theodore knows the contents of the Qur'an and uses it for the basis of his argumentation. He employs citations and allusions from it in two ways. First, he makes use of the qur'anic vocabulary and expressions while constructing his case without specifically mentioning the authority of his qur'anic source; or he uses allusions in tandem with biblical citations. The Qur'an was a part of discourse in Arabic that was inseparable from common daily discussion; it determined the language and definitions in the debate.[454] Second, he utilizes direct quotations of the Qur'an as proof-texts and as rhetorical flourishes in his arguments. The Qur'an was a common source for discourse in the Islamic milieu, and it allowed Christians to participate in discussions through shared stories about the biblical narrative. He uses the Qur'an in a way that reflects his knowledge of contemporary Islamic discourse, matters of abrogation, oral traditions and commentaries. He shows his awareness of qur'anic phraseology. While the Qur'an is a flawed Scripture in Theodore's view, it is possible for him to formulate a Christian reading of the Qur'an which commends Christian belief and practice, while never acknowledging a special status to the Muslim prophet. The Qur'an functions as an authoritative source for Theodore while he simultaneously denies its revelatory character. He is also familiar with contemporary Islamic debates surrounding the interpretation of ambiguous or controversial passages in the Qur'an. For instance, he addresses ethical issues found in qur'anic commentaries (*tafsir*) concerning divorce and remarriage. In another section he critiques interpretations found in the oral traditions (*hadith*) on such matters as spouses in Paradise and the difference between submission (*islam*) and faith (*iman*). He is also aware of the discussion in Islam surrounding the status of the Qur'an as the cre-

---

[454] Griffith, "The Qur'an in Arab Christian Texts," 217.

ated or uncreated Word of God. Theodore acknowledges the internal conversations that established doctrinal consensuses in Islamic faith and practice.

Third, Theodore reinterprets older biblical argumentation in consideration of the Islamic milieu. He emphasizes testimony passages that meet the challenge of Islamic claims in light of his new context.[455] Therefore, the dialogue is representative of the changing endeavor among Christians to communicate and reason from a scripturally coherent viewpoint, even to the point of applying rational knowledge to a Christian reading of the Qur'an. Since Theodore Abu Qurra recognized that his Muslim opponents would not accept the authority of biblical passages in the dialogue, he appealed to the Qur'an as a point of common and reasonable discourse, provided it supplied persuasive ideas for his dialectic. Theodore's intentionally excludes biblical testimonies in favor of qur'anic proof-texts, since the debate was governed by Islamic vocabulary and expression.

Finally, Theodore's dialogue served as a refutation against the charges of polytheism and a defense for the identity of Jesus Christ. Appealing to caliph al-Ma'mun on the basis of qur'anic and traditional Islamic doctrine, the dialogue advocates tolerance for Christians living under Islamic rule. As for the text's implications in light of the Melkite community's internal concerns, the Abu Qurra literary dialogue functioned as a popular religious tract designed for commending the truth of Melkite orthodoxy and as a scripturally-reasoned response to day-to-day encounters with Muslims. The author presents a literary dialogue that is apologetical and polemical, topical in its application, instructive in its attempt to teach basic Christian doctrine, and novel in its employment of qur'anic cita-

---

[455] The author may have been utilizing his own qur'anic and biblical testimony collections in the composition of the literary dialogue. For examples, look at the writings in Sandra Keating, *Defending the "People of Truth" in the Early Islamic Period: The Christian Apologies of Abu Ra'itah* (Leiden: Brill, 2006), 299-333. For articles about the use of testimony collections, see David Bertaina, "The Development of Testimony Collections in Early Christian Apologetics with Islam."

tions for the defense of Christianity and criticism of Muslim scriptural interpretation.

The Abu Qurra debate text had particular significance for the Melkite Christian community and other communities that adopted the literary dialogue. It presented an entertaining story that inculcated Christian socio-cultural values and prevented conversion to Islam.[456] It engaged Islamic worldviews, and their texts and assumptions about the world, in order to furnish an exciting account. Its value as entertainment also lies with its hagiographic portrait of Abu Qurra as a strong persona for Melkite identity and as a beacon of hope for the audience. While Theodore explains his knowledge of God through premises and conclusions during the debate, one cannot ignore the underlying conviction that Orthodoxy was an authentic way of life, verified through experience, which needed to be expressed. The Melkite Christian audience was meant to believe and continue to think and express their intellectual insights through the eyes of faith.

The dialogue is particularly remarkable in its response to the challenge of Islam. While it seeks to entertain the audience, it also assumes that its audience is familiar with the Qur'an, Islamic literature, Islamic theology, and the popular culture of the early Islamic Middle East. Theodore's debate demonstrates a deep knowledge and ability to reinterpret qur'anic passages to counteract Islamic claims. He constructs a list of qur'anic testimonies to support a Christian scriptural perspective and an Orthodox Christian reading of the Qur'an. The text is a significant example of medieval Christian Arab entrance into the context of the qur'anic and Islamic worldviews. One remarkable feature of the literary dialogue is that it presupposes religious pluralism and the value of the dialogue approach as a process of identity formation. The dialogue was popular among Eastern Christians because it conveyed the sense of

---

[456] On the Melkite identity, see Sidney Griffith, "The Church of Jerusalem and the 'Melkites': The Making of an 'Arab Orthodox' Christian Identity in the World of Islam, 750-1050 CE," in *Christians and Christianity in the Holy Land: From the Origins to the Latin Kingdoms*, ed. Ora Limor and G. G. Stroumsa (Turnhout: Brepols, 2006), 173-202.

an ongoing conversation. It provided common definitions and the possibility for coming to similar conclusions on one's worldview while internalizing and engaging with the worldview of religious others. This process of crosspollination demonstrates the ways in which medieval Christians and Muslims shared in an ongoing historical, intellectual, and religious dialogue.

CONCLUSION

The three dialogues mentioned above show how Muslims and Christians asked one another whether the Bible or the Qur'an were considered inspired Scripture. Not surprisingly, both communities viewed the other's Scripture as fundamentally flawed, but not without apologetic and polemical merit. In each dialogue, we see that the figures found probative value in the other's Scripture for explaining their own doctrines within the context and language of the other community. For Christians in particular, their language was suffused with Arabic religious terminology that had qur'anic and Islamic connotations. This made the use of the Qur'an, Islamic oral traditions and commentaries, Islamic theology, and other concepts easier to adapt and convert to their own agenda. This phenomenon is not nearly as pronounced on the Islamic side, as the Arabic language and religious terminology was established as the mode of public interreligious discourse. That did not prevent some Muslims from taking an interest in the Christian scriptures and examining them through the qur'anic lens, such as in the debate between Imam al-Rida and the patriarch.

In terms of purpose, literary dialogues were likely used in monastic contexts as educational tools for the purpose of amusement and instructing students from the community who studied there. It would also have served as a rhetorical and scriptural example for those who were interested in engaging in apologetics and polemics on the popular level. Based on the broad diffusion of the dialogues mentioned above, they may have been distributed to lay persons for their own development and understanding of doctrine in comparison with the other community. Finally, the dialogues offered a reinterpretation of the Bible and Qur'an to explain their relationship to religious others. The dialogues show how Christians and Muslims re-evaluated their own scriptures. Therefore the literary dialogue had as one of its primary goals the catechesis of its readers and the commendation of orthodoxy through scriptural reinterpretation.

The literary form of dialogue encouraged the use of the Qur'an by Christians and the Bible by Muslims as a way to agree on a common discourse. Theodore Abu Qurra's use of the Qur'an was meant to add authority to his arguments. For Christians, this move was important since the Qur'an determined the religious thought and language of the wider culture. For Muslims, their holy book acknowledged Jews and Christians as People of the Book and their dialogues were meant to comprehend their own relationship to these earlier scriptures and peoples as much as to refute them.

The use of the Bible and Qur'an in dialogues by opposing religious speakers also reveals the pluralistic assumptions of the Christian and Muslim authors of the early Islamic Middle East. Despite Islamic hegemony, their truth claims were not universally accepted by Jews and Christians. The slow process of conversion meant that Muslims felt compelled to present a confident assertion of their views of the true religion using Bible proof texts. In this way, the dialogue form tied certain qur'anic verses to certain biblical verses, binding them together with an interpretive intertwining. The same process occurred for Christians, who assumed that their religious truth claims had to be made in a religiously plural society that would heed the Qur'an more than biblical testimonies.

For Christians, Muslims had misinterpreted their Scripture, and if only they would recognize the testimonies in the Bible, they could acknowledge how the Christian scriptures and theological claims fit together. For Muslims, the Christians had changed their scriptures, and if only they could see the predictions of Muhammad's prophethood and the clear denials of Jesus' divinity, they would understand the Qur'an and the Islamic worldview. Scriptural reinterpretation was one way to imagine this intellectual conversion. In sum, the use of scriptural reinterpretation in the dialogue form signified a willingness on the part of Christians and Muslims to consider their own identities in the context of the other's scriptures. These reinterpretations reflected the way that they shared in common discourses while negotiating their own identities within the context of other religious communities.

8 THE END OF DIALOGUE?

ELIAS OF NISIBIS AND GEORGE THE MONK

The ninth century was the height of production for interreligious literary dialogues in Arabic. In the following centuries leading up to the Crusades, Christians and Muslims wrote substantially fewer dialogues that focused on interreligious concerns. That is not to say that the genre disappeared. Rather, something changed in the lived practice of dialogue as conversions increased and religious attitudes shifted during the Islamic constructions of orthodoxies (Sunni and Shi'ite) at the end of the Abbasid period. The result was a diminished interest in dialogues since they no longer represented the culture of the period. There are some notable exceptions, such as the eleventh-century dialogue of the Coptic Patriarch John III with the Muslim governor 'Abd al-'Aziz al-Malik, which focuses on the crucifixion and the cross of Christ. The dialogue is supposed to have occurred in the later seventh century and it focuses primarily on intra-Christian debate, but a new study has demonstrated its later origins and interests within the medieval Egyptian Coptic milieu.[457]

During the eleventh century, Metropolitan (Archbishop) Elias Bar Shinaya of Nisibis (975-1046) was perhaps the most significant author of the East-Syrian Church of the East. Elias wrote in both

---

[457] See the forthcoming study, edition, and translation by Stephen Davis and Samuel Noble. For an argument that the dialogue dates to the eighth century, see Harald Suermann, "Anmerkungen zu alter und Funktion der Diskussion des Koptischen Patriarchen Johannes III. (677-686) vor dem Statthalter 'Abd al-'Aziz," *Parole de l'Orient* 32 (2007): 389-398; and Harald Suermann, "The Disputation of Patriarch John," 253-255.

Syriac and Arabic on a variety of scientific, religious, and philosophical topics. He published works in the fields of theology, history, grammar, and lexicography. One of his most significant works was the *Book of Sessions* (*Kitab al-Majalis*), which recounted his discussions with the Muslim vizier Abu al-Qasim al-Maghribi. The text is presented as a letter addressed to Elias' brother. His intention was to have a wider audience for the dialogue, based on the fact that he sent the text to the patriarchal secretary who was responsible for approving theological works.[458]

The dialogue is made up of seven sessions. The first session provides arguments for the unity and Trinity of God. The Muslim vizier asks for an account of Christianity that is logical, and Elias answers his objections concerning God as substance/essence (*jawhar*): In what sense can one say that God is substance? Is he substance in the sense of existing in himself? He also gives answers for other questions: In what sense do Christians affirm that God is three hypostases (*aqanim*)? How can Elias say that Jesus, a man born from Mary, is eternally Lord according to his Creed?

In the second session, they discuss the nature of the Incarnation and hypostatic union. Elias explains the unity of God (*tawhid*), how Jesus is favored over the prophets, how the will of God dwells within a man without God himself dwelling there, and why the Church of the East disagrees with the Melkites and Jacobites about Christology.

---

[458] Samir Khalil Samir has provided a critical edition of the Arabic text with a French translation of the first, sixth, and seventh (partial) dialogues. See the following articles by Samir Khalil Samir, "Le Premier Entretien d'Élie de Nisibe avec le vizir al-Maġribi sur l'Unité et la Trinité"; "Deux cultures qui s'affrontent: une controverse sur l'i'rab au XI. siècle entre Elie de Nisibe et le vizir Abu l-Qasim"; "Langue arabe, logique et théologie chez Élie de Nisibe"; "La réfutation de l'astrologie par Élie de Nisibe"; and "Iliyya al-Nasibini (975-1046 A.D.) wa-l-wazir Abu-l-Qasim al-Maghribi (981-1027 A.D.)." For the other dialogues, see Louis Cheikho, "Majalis Iliya mutran Nisibin." See the collected editions and translations in Samir Khalil Samir, *Foi et Culture en Irak au XIe siècle: Elie de Nisibe et l'Islam*.

During the third session, Elias and the vizier discuss Christian monotheism according to the Qur'an. The vizier quotes Q 5:77 claiming that Christians are polytheists. Elias responds to the contrary that Christians are monotheists according to the Qur'an. They also discuss qur'anic interpretation concerning the salvation of Christians and their status according to the Qur'an and Islamic tradition (*sunna*).

In the fourth session they discuss the truth of the Christian faith through reason and miracle. Elias explains that the true religion is discernible based on certain criteria, and that Christianity fulfills those requirements on the basis of reason and miracle. Elias concludes that his love for his faith is not from habit or custom, but because of the proof of its authenticity.

In the fifth session they discuss the profession of monotheistic faith, as elaborated by the Church of the East. Elias explains his confession, which is persuasive enough to convince al-Maghribi that it is a reasonable doctrine. For al-Maghribi, it is only the subject of the prophethood of Muhammad that makes him question the authenticity of Christianity.

In the sixth session, Elias and al-Maghribi discuss the merits of Arabic and Syriac in relation to their syntax, lexicography, writing and theology. Elias was an expert on this topic, having written both a Syriac grammar and a Syriac-Arabic dictionary. In this session, Elias asserts the superiority of the Syriac language over Arabic based on syntax, lexicography, and the written script.

The seventh session is a dialogue on the opinions of Christians concerning astrology, Muslims, and the soul. Elias refutes the claims of astrology concerning the freedom of the will, opposing astrology as a pseudo-science. In the second section, Elias states that Christians prefer Muslims above other communities for four reasons: Muslims respect the Christian religion (as the Qur'an prescribes); Muslims recognize that Christ is Word of God and that he is living in heaven; Muslim law protects Christians; and Christians are close to Muslims with the exception of their disagreement concerning Muhammad. Elias also explains the reciprocal obligations that the two communities have for one another. Christians should not disobey the caliph if he is just, but only if he orders something contrary to the law of God. He also shows how Christians can aid Muslims. Muslims should honor and respect Christian leaders; they should not judge between Christians, but leave matters to church courts. In the third section, Elias argues that Christians can call the soul a substance validly. Following these topics, the vizier asks for the monks in the region to pray for his health. Elias answers that the monks do not pray for long lives or benefits or dignity, but only that God makes one capable of accepting the will of God. Al-Maghribi died several months after their final dialogue.

Another example of a popular Christian literary dialogue appeared in the thirteenth century.[459] The debate takes place in 1217 between the monk George of Saint Simeon and three Muslim legal scholars at the court of the emir al-Malik al-Mushammar in Aleppo, Syria. George was a Melkite (or Maronite) Chalcedonian in his theology, while the three Muslims are legal experts from Baghdad, Mosul, and Aleppo. In the dialogue, George argues that Christianity and the monastic tradition represent the spiritual direction that God desires from his followers, and thus it is the true religion.

The dialogue begins with monks from the monastery of Saint Simeon visiting Aleppo. One of the elderly monks was George, who meets the emir and invokes God's blessing upon him. Following this action, the emir asks George to sit and discuss religious matters with him, including monastic life. George explains ascetic monasticism as the ideal spiritual life to the Muslim emir. During their conversation, three Muslim scholars enter the court, and ask to enter into a debate with the monk. After receiving freedom to speak about any topic without punishment, George analyzes whether Muhammad should be considered a prophet, since that criteria would require miracles, speaking in many languages, and

---

[459] There are approximately eighty-nine manuscripts still extant of the dialogue. For a survey of the dialogue, see Samir Khalil Samir, "Bibliographie du Dialogue Islamo-Chretien: Auteurs arabes chrétiens du XIIIᵉ siècle," *Islamochristiana* 7 (1981): 299-307. For an English translation of one manuscript, see Dale Johnson, ed., *Christian-Muslim Debate: A Debate between the Monk George and Muslim Theologians in the Court of Saladin (1165 AD)* (Portland, OR: New Sinai Press, 2007). The translation is also available online at: www.fordham.edu/halsall/source/christ-muslim-debate.html.

preaching to the whole world. For George, only the apostles fulfill these criteria.

The next question is whether Christians changed their books by deleting any mention of Muhammad. George replies that the texts are the same from the west and east, disproving any attempt to collaborate on deliberate corruption. The next topic discussed is the story of Muhammad and Bahira. Muhammad had doubts about his message, and Bahira helped strengthen him, George argues.

In the next thematic section, George and the Muslim scholar from Mosul focus on the Incarnation of Jesus Christ. They discuss how Christ is the Word and Spirit of God, the Incarnation of Christ according to the Qur'an, and the human and divine natures of Christ. According to the Muslim interlocutor al-Rashid, Christians must venerate the human Jesus or the divine Christ, but George uses a parable to explain the veneration. When a forgiving king writes a letter forgiving the sins of a prisoner, the letter is treated as the king's authority and is not separate from him, just as one cannot separate Jesus Christ in the manner described.

The next discussion question deals with the qur'anic understanding of divine unity and the claim that Christ could be the Son of God. George uses the parable of the sun, its light, and its heat to explain the Trinitarian relationship of the Father, Son, and Holy Spirit. The Muslim declares that the Passion of Christ contradicts his divinity, but George argues that God's mercy is more compelling than his justice, and only through the necessity of the Incarnation and Passion can God's will for salvation be accomplished. In fact, Christian veneration of the cross is a sign of faith, a sign against evil, a symbol of Christ's sacrifice, and a symbol of God's goodness and grace.

In the following section, George examines the criteria for the true religion. First, he analyzes the Sabaeans and Jews. Then he explains the sublime character of Christianity according to the Gospel. Next, he analyzes Islam in light of the criteria for the true religion. He uses a parable to explain that while there are four messages, only one is certain for salvation.

Christian practice is the focus of the next discussion, including the theology of Baptism and the coming of the Holy Spirit at Baptism. Next, they compare the miracles of Jesus Christ with the works of Muhammad. George notes that only Christ performed miracles, and to follow the Word of God is to confirm to the spiritual nature of God. The dialogue closes with the Muslims explaining the beauty of the pilgrimage to Mecca, and their invitation to the monk George to accompany him. However, George declines, and the emir allows him to depart with his community.

The dialogues belonging to Elias of Nisibis and George the Monk show that the literary form was still useful in Christian-Muslim dialogue until the time of the Crusades. In terms of literary form, for example, the works contain some characteristics of the educational style of questions-and-answers. For instance, Elias taught his Christian worldview through apologetic responses to particular questions proposed by the Muslim vizier al-Maghribi. Second, Elias and George offer stories of empowerment, miracles, and testimonials as methods to supplement their reasoning. Third, Elias constructed a communal memory of how Syriac Christianity responds to Muslim challenges. Similarly, George recorded a memory for the Chalcedonian community on the Arab Christian response to Islam. Finally, both authors present their audiences a comprehensive Christian worldview and attempt to frame their worldviews in such a manner so that their concepts are intelligible for their readers and Muslims. They did not offer this perspective to convince opponents as much as to invite others to logically and reasonably explore the truth of the Christian narrative. In this process, they entered into the Islamic frame of reference by using the Qur'an, Islamic theology, and Islamic terminology. In this crosspollination of Christian and Islamic material, the dialogues of Elias and George demonstrate the continued relevance of the literary form and the shared identities of Christians and Muslims through the time of the Crusades.

SIGNIFICANT THEMES OF CHRISTIAN DIALOGUES

The authors and audiences of Christian Arabic and Syriac dialogue literature played an important role in its development. The literary form was partly a continuation of Byzantine and Syriac theological disputation literature and partly a development from indigenous literary forms of the Middle East. The authors cultivated the literary form to meet the new cultural and linguistic needs of an Arabic-speaking world influenced by the hegemony of Islam.

The authors of these dialogues, for religious and political purposes, chose to compose their works in response to the challenges of Islamic practice and the ideas produced during the formative period of Islamic thought. In contrast to the Byzantine authors who wrote dialogues, Syriac and Arabic writers had a more cautious tone to their writings, never inciting violence. Also, they displayed remarkable knowledge of Islamic scriptures, texts, and arguments.

Among the dialogues surveyed in this book, it becomes evident that the ecclesiastical hierarchy and the monastic tradition played a distinguished role in the composition of such dialogues. The Christian speakers in the texts included patriarchs, bishops, and monks. It is clear that the clergy was largely responsible for the production and dissemination of the genre, especially learned clergy from monasteries or Christian leaders. The literary form was dependent upon the elite of Middle Eastern society during the late Umayyad and Abbasid periods.

Despite the fact that it appears that the genre is limited to a small number of educated clergy and separated from the wider Middle Eastern and Islamic milieu, a cursory examination of other works attributed to authors like Timothy and Elias, which are concerned with law, history, lexicography, and politics, highlights the fact that the literary genre reached a wide audience among its Christian adherents. The dialogues were an integral part of student and clerical formation, as shown by the fact that Timothy wrote his treatise to the headmaster of a well-known monastery-school for the purpose of instruction and wider dissemination. The number of manuscripts and recensions of several dialogues further attests to their popularity and practical use as learning tools for Christians. Many students and lay people were familiar with such encounters and stories, if only from real life experiences. For example, Theodore Abu Qurra's dialogues demonstrate that written compositions reflected the lived experiences of the wider community who participated in or listened to such debates. Literary dialogues were an idealized representation of the oral disputes that occurred in the sectarian milieu. The literary form is a textual witness to the cross-pollinating interactions between Christians and Muslims in the medieval Middle East.

The audience for such texts was primarily Christian, but authors found their inspiration in real dialogues that occurred throughout the period. In that sense, Christian authors of literary dialogues had a number of goals to achieve in order to reach their intended audience, and to engage a wider pluralistic environment. For its readers and listeners, the dialogue was first of all an attempt to promote orthodoxy and catechesis for the author's particular confession. By means of presenting their epistemological suppositions and theological messages to their readers, the authors instructed them in proper Christian knowledge, speech, and conduct. The didactic purpose of the texts enabled readers to learn biblical and qur'anic verses, sometimes in the form of testimonies, in order to answer for their faith.

A second use of literary dialogues was to provide security and empowerment for Christians challenged by Islam. As the officially sanctioned and endorsed faith of the new Islamic empire, Islamic politics, law, faith, and practice presented a number of obstacles for Christians trying to live under the ideals of a new religious worldview. Dialogues offered a response to Christian self-doubt about the sometimes perilous situation, by suggesting arguments for the intellectual superiority of the tradition and the miraculous proof of its scriptures as a verification of Christianity. The victorious Christian interlocutor held all the necessary qualities for the new hagiographical hero of the Christian community. The stories of debates offered a protector of individuals and the community. They presented a reminder of Christian values in response to morals and practices that were not always similar to their own.

A third use of literary dialogues was to dissuade conversion to Islam through apologetic techniques that were designed to maintain communal morale. Due to the processes of Arabization and Islamicization, Christian Arabic and Syriac authors responded with positive reasons for the Christian worldview by offering alternatives to Islamic communities.

A fourth goal for composers of literary dialogues was to either convince the religious opponent of their point of view or to invite their interlocutor into a sympathetic vision of the Christian worldview. Convincing adversaries was a rarely-used tool that worked in two ways: convincing the character in the dialogue or convincing a Muslim reader of the rationality of the outcome of the debate. Persuading a Muslim character in a dialogue happens occasionally, depending upon the needs and interests of the author. But the goal of convincing real religious opponents was probably not an attainable goal for the authors of literary dialogues, given their social status in the medieval Middle East.[460] Their primary audience was the Christian community, and the intent was that if a Muslim should read the dialogue, it should at least be reasonable in its portrayal of their arguments. Only then could a religious interlocutor gain some understanding of the Christian position on faith and practice.

A fifth goal, which was only used by a few authors, was to denigrate Islam or Muhammad or both and separate Muhammad from Islam or vice versa, often using the Qur'an as tool for these ends. By commending Muhammad's virtues but criticizing Islamic practice, an author could reverse the idea of Christian corruption and claim that the Muslim community was the reason for corruption in Islam. In Theodore Abu Qurra's debate, his goal was to commend Muhammad and the "authentic" parts of the Qur'an while arguing that later interpreters and the Islamic community had perverted the pristine faith which Muhammad had transmitted. In sum, each author of a literary dialogue had some of these objectives in mind for his composition, although they did not necessarily have all of these goals in mind.

The various forms of scriptural reasoning, augmented with logical methods of debate, were important in medieval Christian dialogues. Authors of literary dialogues utilized the Old and New Testaments as sources for their contentions. The Old Testament was viewed as a prophetic guarantee of Christian doctrine and the gradual unfolding of salvation history in God's Church. The New Testament scriptures served as the confirmation of Old Testament

---

[460] See for instance the work by Daniel J. Sahas, "The Art and Non-Art of Byzantine Polemics: Patterns of Refutation in Byzantine Anti-Islamic Literature," 55-73. On page 68 he notes: "Notwithstanding the nature, artistic or non-artistic style, or content of dialogue or disputation, we have no indication that any of these polemic pieces of literature achieved the goal for which they were written, if the goal of those polemic writings was to embarrass, ridicule, convince or, in the end, convert the opponent."

promises and provided a framework for disputing with Jews and Muslims about various doctrines, especially the Trinity and the divinity of Jesus Christ.

Scriptural reasoning in the medieval Middle East had a second source: the Qur'an. Christian Arabic and Syriac writers employed testimonies from the Qur'an in a theological fashion, and in conjunction with biblical citations and analogical or dialectical reasoning, in order to commend the veracity of their doctrines. Since the Qur'an had determined Christian religious language and terminology, it had probative significance because it contributed to the authority of their arguments. In this way, Christian authors helped to establish the hermeneutical possibilities of qur'anic interpretation in the Islamic world. As Sidney Griffith has pointed out, the Qur'an was viewed as a flawed Scripture but also as a testimony to the truth with a semi-Christian origin.[461]

Besides the Qur'an, Christian authors showed a remarkable knowledge of early Islamic literature. The dialogues demonstrate an awareness of early biographical stories of Muhammad as well as important traditions that were related to passages in the Qur'an. The authors were quick to employ Muslim narratives that imparted credibility to the Christian argument when they fit into their theological and literary framework.

Concomitant with scriptural reasoning was the use of dialectical reasoning by Christian Arabic and Syriac authors. The Aristotelian dialectical method, as it was transmitted through the Byzantine Hellenistic tradition, was adapted for use in Christian-Muslim disputations. They recreated the verbal exchange in a dialectical presentation between two characters in order to demonstrate the intellectual coherence of their theological system. While scriptural reasoning was primarily based on revelation, dialectical reasoning was primarily based upon definitions and terms of logic. The goal was a rigorous cross-examination of the Muslim interlocutor that utilized the powers of speech, composition and logical argumentation to stifle any response, reducing the adversary to silence. In this approach, Christian dialectical reasoning and its theological and

---

[461] Sidney Griffith, "The Qur'an in Arab Christian Texts," 214.

philosophical adaptations of the method became the standard by which to judge Muslims.

SIGNIFICANT THEMES OF MUSLIM DIALOGUES

Early Muslim dialogues attempted to connect the Qur'an with a historical grounding and used the form as a way of bridging history. Some dialogues responded to Christian apologetics by bringing the argument into Christian territory, utilizing polemical strategies to provide encouragement for Muslims, and as a challenge to Christian apologists. Others promoted the Shi'ite religious worldview and its claims about the imamate, while utilizing the dialogue method as a way of creating a historical memory that could verify the Shi'ite faith. Other dialogues endorsed certain figures, such as the imams. Through Muslim biblical apologetics and polemics, they produced hagiographical memories for the community's faithful. Some reports of dialogues commemorated real encounters that authentically described theological differences between Christians and Muslims. The literary form provided a framework for a number of Islamic theological projects during the early medieval period.

Authors and audience played an important role in the literary form. The development of the literary genre among Muslims was shaped by its historical discourse with Jews and Christians. Based on the formation of the Qur'an within a sectarian environment, Muslims continued to adapt genres such as the literary dialogue to reproduce and interpret the theological and interreligious messages in the Qur'an. The development of the genre was also dependent upon its literary antecedents among Greek, Syriac, and other early Christian disputation literature. Muslim authors were conscious and receptive to literary compositions that effectively communicated their agendas to the religious community. It may be argued that the Qur'an itself participated in these pre-Islamic literary patterns of dialogue, and thus shaped the literary form through internal modes of discourse within the Islamic community.

Muslims who participated in interreligious debates and composed literary dialogues belonged to the educated elite (*'ulama'*). These authors would have been attached to patrons of learning, and many would have participated in the court (*majlis*) of the emir or caliph or Shi'ite imam. However, Muslim students and common folk were also listeners and participants in interreligious discussions. They provided a receptive audience for apologetic and polemical dialogues that addressed the problems of Christian doctrine and attempted to provide coherent answers to questions of Islamic faith. More importantly, each author's imagined audience determined how they constructed their discourse. When the audience was perceived as a Shi'ite minority among Muslims, the dialogue took a different tact than a dialogue in debate within the Byzantine world. The authors' perceptions of their audiences governed the goals and methods by which they would construct their literary dialogues. On the whole, the production of such literary endeavors was for internal consumption. The continued interest in Christian ideas reflected the reality of Muslim and Christian interaction at a number of levels in the Islamic Middle East, and the likelihood of the dialogues as a symbol of those lived historical experiences.

Through the dialogue form, Muslim authors reflected on the significant cultural and linguistic developments within the empire and proposed new methods of interpreting Islamic worldviews. While literary dialogues from Syriac and Christian Arabic literature were on the whole apologetic, Muslim dialogues were more like their Byzantine counterparts due to the polemical approach of the authors. It also seems likely that the audience for Muslim dialogues were students being educated in a school (*madrasa*) that taught the Qur'an and how to offer apologetic suggestions to fellow Muslims. Most prominently, Muslims who studied within the fields of dialectical theology (*kalam*) and philosophy required knowledge of Socratic discourse and the ability to reproduce its literary genre as part of their education. Literary dialogues are a genuine product of those who lived, experienced, and practiced interreligious dialogue.

Understanding the goals of the authors of dialogues reveals significant information about them. Much like the Christian authors of literary dialogues, Muslim composers sought to promote their particular religious communities while offering catechesis for their readers and listeners. Muslim authors accomplished this through interpretive readings of the Qur'an, critical readings of the Bible, and historical interpretations that validated their specific community.

A second use of the literary form was to provide a sense of security and empowerment for Muslim communities, particularly for the Shi'ite community and for Muslims who felt challenged by Christian apologists. The dialogues put added religious pressure upon subject communities (*dhimma*) and reminded them of their place within the Islamic political realm. Such texts were produced to verify the religious and intellectual superiority of Islam over Christianity. At the same time, dialogues were responses to Christian interpretations of Islamic texts and ideas. Muslim dialogues tried to explain their theology systematically, contributing to the construction of Islamic orthodoxies. They also commended the memory of rhetorical champions in debates. The memories produced from such encounters sustained and supported the author's particular Islamic community.

A third strategy in using literary dialogues was to dissuade Muslims from conversion through apologetic methods. Although the potential for conversion was never a demographic problem in the Middle East and Central Asia, the apprehension toward the Christian community expressed by certain Muslim writers such as al-Jahiz and 'Abd al-Jabbar represented genuine concern in producing reliable apologetic and polemical works.

A fourth goal of Muslim literary dialogues was the attempt to invite the religious interlocutor into the Islamic worldview. In his story of Bariha's conversion, authors such as Ibn Babawayh sometimes revealed their hope that intelligent people of good faith would understand the value of a Muslim community's religious outlook.

A fifth use of the literary form was to denigrate Christian faith and/or practice by denying the divinity of Jesus Christ and by separating him from the one God. Christian practices were seen as extensions of a corrupted Gospel, and these flaws needed to be demonstrated in dialogue. In this endeavor, Muslim writers employed the Qur'an as the primary tool for interpreting Christian beliefs about the Incarnation and the Trinity.

Reasoning with the Qur'an and the Bible was a key feature of medieval Muslim dialogues with Christians. In their search for a common source of interreligious discourse, some Muslim writers used the Bible as a means to discuss theological truths with Christian interlocutors. Scriptural reasoning provided Islamic interpretations of prophetic sayings in the Old and New Testaments, which were said to refer to Muhammad and his prophethood. Scriptural reasoning was also a means to apply the doctrine of corruption to Jewish and Christian scriptures, pointing out the mutual disagreements and various inconsistencies vis-à-vis the Qur'an. The Bible had probative worth for Muslim composers because they sought to apply the Islamic vision to it as the rule of faith.

The Qur'an and the oral traditions were especially significant sources for interreligious discourse during the Abbasid period. Interestingly, Muslim authors of literary dialogues did not employ the Qur'an in the manner of a testimony collection against their religious interlocutors; they seemed aware that their works required more tact. Rather, the Qur'an and its interpretation in the traditions, often not explicitly mentioned in the dialogue but used nonetheless, provided the framework by which Muslims would conduct their discussions about Christian doctrines. Thus, the hermeneutical world of the Qur'an would determine the conduct for interlocutors, the sources for speakers, and the evaluation of every aspect of Christianity.

Dialectical reasoning had a prominent place in *kalam* texts, but also in the literary dialogue form. Muslim writers adopted the Byzantine Hellenistic tradition of argumentation and reinvented it for their own particular necessities and usages. However, dialectical methods were nearly absent from Muslim literary dialogues with characters. Because theologians sought to present their ideas in the intellectual forum rather than in the literary environment, dialectic was subservient to scriptural reasoning and other concerns in the texts studied above. The most important exception to this case is the Wasil of Damascus dialogue, which uses dialectical methods as its principal debating technique.

Identity was a key factor in the composition of dialogues. For Muslims, this identity formation with religious others often took place in debates at court. The court was the most important source and motivation for interreligious and intra-faith discourse in the early Islamic Middle East. Many of the dialogues studied in this book took place at courts of Muslim leaders. For educated Muslims, the Islamic court (*majlis*) offered a location for commending the authenticity of dialogue and a place where writers could communicate their perceptions of religious truth to their readers. It was a location for continuous conversation that supplied the perfect literary setting for the compositions of dialogues. Muslim writers would usually abide by the framework which the court provided, in its rules for the art of disputation, satisfactory methods of reasoning, acceptable methods of argumentation, and code of behavior for its participants. Muslim dialogues recaptured the oral nature of such debates in a creative manner that permitted the authors to include their own theological vision to meet contemporary needs.

The literary dialogue was also a source for the formation of memory among various Islamic communities. The literary form was a tool of empowerment for dominant or marginalized communities. Muslims adapted established traditions using the literary form in order to express their vision of the ideal Islamic community. The literary dialogues established communal memories of remarkable events in a community's history. The composition of literary dialogues gave them the opportunity to effectively respond to religious challenges and reflect upon the primacy of one's faith and practice from a historical perspective. Literary dialogues were valuable tools in forming collective memory and historically coherent narratives of the past. In the presentation of rhetorical victors, authors furnished a memorable portrait of their hagiographical heroes for the community.

The dialogue form provided Muslim writers with opportunities to portray their religious interlocutors in light of the Islamic worldview. Literary dialogues imagined an intelligible, compelling, and believable worldview in which their discussion partners would be sympathetic to their definitions and descriptions of reality. Muslim writers sought to communicate their hopes in both apologetic and polemical fashions that would commend their faith and practice to the religious other. Theologians involved in interreligious matters would find the literary dialogue genre one of the most amenable forms of conversation in the early Islamic Middle East.

FROM CREATION TO COLLATION

Literary dialogues were popular and effective presentations because they created the sense of an ongoing conversation. Unlike the essay genre, literary dialogues do not present one perspective or a single narrative. Instead, they capture the unregulated interactions via daily speech that communicate a polyphony of voices and worldviews. Within the world of Islam, the medieval court culture was the home of dialogue and the intellectual center for the educated. The court was connected with wealthy and powerful persons, such as a caliph or an emir. Learned scholars, scientists, physicians, and others would assemble around their patron, who would provide for their needs in return for their knowledge of the arts and sciences. Their work was not only a symbol of prestige for the leader; the educated elite provided a source of entertainment and debate between learned individuals. Within this context, the court was the perfect setting for dialogue in the Islamic milieu. Sarah Stroumsa has described the widespread court culture in the early Islamic Middle East as a place of learned dialecticians who followed the appropriate form, technique, and manner expected of the dialogue culture.[462]

The authors of the literary dialogue form did not reproduce the verbal exchanges exactly as such discussions occurred in the court. They sought to use these conversations as a fount for ideas. The dialogue culture, along with its art of disputation and manners (good or bad), was appropriated from the medieval Islamic court as a literary setting for dialogues. Once the form fit the cultural outlook of medieval Middle Eastern society, they used dialogues as a way to invite religious others into their worldview. Even if this did not necessarily occur in real events, the authors of dialogues attempted to conceive of a world in which their terms, definitions, and ideas might be intelligible, convincing, and persuasive. But what happened in the later medieval period?

In the subsequent centuries, Christians and Muslims continued to copy and recount stories of dialogues between their past leaders and religious others. In particular, the later medieval period was marked by an attention to collation of earlier written material and the creation of theological compendia. Numerous manuscripts attest to the interest in remembering dialogue during the early Islamic Middle East, and the copying of the manuscripts up until the early twentieth century confirms this idea. However, later medieval authors did not continue to write dialogues in the same manner. Perhaps the emphasis on collation and recounting past dialogues was a factor in their decline as a literary form. Perhaps there were other deeper reasons for the lack of Christian and Muslim dialogues in later centuries.

The decline of the dialogue form likely had much to do with the shift in court culture and patronage, the changing de-

---

[462] Sarah Stroumsa, "Ibn al-Rawandi's *su adab al-mujadala*: The Role of Bad Manners in Medieval Disputations," 66.

mographics of the Middle East, and the hardening attitudes of Muslims against religious minorities. With the transformation of medieval Islamic society, the construction of theological and legal orthodoxies, and the diminishment of the court culture that provided the lived experience for dialogues, there was no motivating factor to compose literary dialogues. They no longer appeared as realistic depictions of the culture. Instead, Christians and Islamic minorities, such as the Shi'ites, preserved their dialogues as memories of an age when religious pluralism was assumed, religious truth claims were taken seriously rather than as examples of a literary exercise, and the People of the Book were a substantial part of the fabric of Middle Eastern society. As these realities diminished over time, the literary form became something to be copied in monasteries or scriptoriums and read as a memory of a past that no longer existed. When dialogue in the lived sense died, the creative writing of literary dialogues died as well. In its place, Christians and Muslims preserved and collected dialogues, treasuring those copied memories.

BIBLIOGRAPHY

Accad, Martin. "The Ultimate Proof-Text: The Interpretation of John 20.17 in Muslim-Christian Dialogue (second/eighth-eighth/fourteenth centuries)." In *Christians at the Heart of Islamic Rule: Church Life and Scholarship in 'Abbasid Iraq*, ed. David R. Thomas, 199-215. Leiden: Brill, 2003.

———. "The Gospels in the Muslim Discourse of the Ninth to the Fourteenth Centuries: An Exegetical Inventorial Table." *Islam and Christian-Muslim Relations* 14 (2003): 67-81; 205-220; 337-352; 459-479.

Adang, Camilla. *Muslim Writers on Judaism and the Hebrew Bible: From Ibn Rabban to Ibn Hazm*. Leiden: Brill, 1996.

Albl, Martin. *'And Scripture Cannot Be Broken': The Form and Function of the Early Christian Testimonia Collections*. Leiden: Brill, 1999.

al-Hamadhani, 'Abd al-Jabbar. *Al-Mughni fi-abwab al-tawhid wa-l-'adl*. Al-firaq ghayr al-islamiyya, ed. Taha Husayn, vol. 5. Cairo: Al-Dar al-Misriyya lil-ta'lif wa al-tarjama, 1958.

al-Humaydi, Abu 'Abd Allah. *Jadhwat al-Muqtabis*. Ed. Muhammad ibn Tawit al-Tanji. Cairo: Dar al-Misriyya, 1953.

al-Kulayni, Muhammad ibn Ya'qub. *al-Kafi*. 8 vols. Ed. 'Ali Akbar Ghaffari. Tehran, 1957-1961.

al-Majlisi, Muhammad Baqir ibn Muhammad Taqi. *Bihar al-Anwar al-Jami'a li-Durar akhbar al-A'imma al-athar*. 4 vols. Beirut: Dar al-Fiqh lil-Tiba'ah wa-al-Nashr, 1421/2001.

al-Najashi. *Rijal al-Najashi*. Beirut: Dar al-Adwa', 1408/1988.

al-Qummi, Shadhan ibn Jibra'il. *Kitab al-Fada'il*. Najaf: al-Maktabat al-Haydariya, 1950.

al-Tabarsi, Ahmad ibn 'Ali. *Al-Ihtijaj*. 2 vols. Ed. Muhammad Baqir al-Khursan. Najaf: Dar al-Nu'man, 1966.

al-Tusi, Muhammad ibn al-Hasan. *Al-Fihrist al-Tusi*. Najaf: al-Matba'a al-Hadariyya, 1356/1937.

_____. *Amali al-Shaykh al-Tusi*. 2 vols. Najaf: Matbaʿat al-Nuʿman, 1964.

Bacha, Constantin, ed. *Un traité des oeuvres arabes de Théodore Abou-Kurra, évêque de Haran*: Tripoli: Chez l'auteur, 1905.

Bardy, Gustave, ed. *Les Trophées De Damas: Controverse Judéo-Chrétienne Du Viie Siècle*, Patrologia Orientalis, T. 15, Fasc. 2. Paris: Firmin-Didot, 1927.

Barsoum, Ignatius Aphram. *The Scattered Pearls: A History of Syriac Literature and Sciences*. Translated by Matti Moosa. 2nd rev. ed. Piscataway, NJ: Gorgias Press, 2003.

Baumer, Christoph. *The Church of the East: An Illustrated History of Assyrian Christianity*. London: I.B. Tauris, 2006.

Baumstark, Anton. "Das Problem eines vorislamischen christlich-kirchlichen Schrifttums in arabischer Sprache." *Islamica* 4 (1929-1931): 562-575.

Bayhom-Daou, Tamima. "'Ali al-Rida." In *The Encyclopaedia of Islam, Third Edition*, ed. Gudrun Krämer, Denis Matringe, John Nawas, and Everett Rowson, vol. 2, 69-74. Leiden: Brill, 2009.

Beaumont, Mark. *Christology in Dialogue with Muslims: A Critical Analysis of Christian Presentations of Christ for Muslims from the Ninth and Twentieth Centuries*. Carlisle: Paternoster, 2005.

_____. "'Ammar al-Basri." In *Christian-Muslim Relations: A Bibliographical History, Volume One (600–900)*, eds. David Thomas and Barbara Roggema, 604-610. Leiden: Brill, 2009.

Becker, Adam. *Fear of God and the Beginning of Wisdom: The School of Nisibis and Christian Scholastic Culture in Late Antique Mesopotamia*. Philadelphia: University of Pennsylvania Press, 2006.

_____. *Sources for the History of the School of Nisibis*. Liverpool: Liverpool University Press, 2008.

Beckmann, Jan. "Dialektik." In *Lexicon für Theologie und Kirche*, ed. Michael Buchberger and Walter Kasper, vol. 3, 188-189. Breisgau: Herder, 1995.

Bell, Richard. *The Origin of Islam in Its Christian Environment*. London: Macmillan, 1926.

Berg, Herbert. "Context: Muhammad." In *The Blackwell Companion to the Qur'an*, ed. Andrew Rippin, 187-204. Malden, MA: Blackwell, 2006.

Bertaina, David. "The Development of Testimony Collections in Early Christian Apologetics with Islam." In *The Bible in Arab Christianity*, ed. David Thomas, 151-173. Leiden: Brill, 2007.

———. "Melkites, *Mutakallimun* and al-Ma'mun: Depicting the Religious Other in Medieval Arabic Dialogues." *Comparative Islamic Studies* 4 (2008): 17-36.

———. "Safwan ibn Yahya." In *Christian-Muslim Relations: A Bibliographical History, Volume One (600–900)*, eds. David Thomas and Barbara Roggema, 535-539. Leiden: Brill, 2009.

———. "The Debate of Abu Qurra." In *Christian-Muslim Relations: A Bibliographical History, Volume One (600–900)*, eds. David Thomas and Barbara Roggema, 556-564. Leiden: Brill, 2009.

Bignami-Odier, J., and G. Levi della Vida. "Une version latine de l'Apocalypse syro-arabe de Serge-Bahira." *Mélanges d'archéologie et d'histoire* 62 (1950): 125-48.

Binggeli, A. "Anastasius of Sinai." In *Christian-Muslim Relations: A Bibliographical History, Volume One (600–900)*, eds. David Thomas and Barbara Roggema, 193-202. Leiden: Brill, 2009.

Blanchard, Monica. "The Georgian Version of the Martyrdom of Saint Michael, Monk of Mar Sabas Monastery." *ARAM* 6 (1994): 149-163.

Bobichon, Philippe, ed. *Justin Martyr, Dialogue Avec Le Tryphon: Edition Critique*. Fribourg: Academic Press Fribourg, 2003.

Boullata, Issa, ed. *Literary Structures of Religious Meaning in the Qur'an*. Richmond: Curzon Press, 2000.

Braun, Oskar. "Der Katholikos Timotheos I und seine Briefe." *Oriens Christianus* 1 (1901): 138-152.

———, ed. *Epistulae Timothei patriarchae I*, Corpus Scriptorum Christianorum Orientalium, vols. 74-75. Paris: E Typographeo Reipublicae, 1914. Reprint, Louvain: L. Durbecq, 1953.

Brock, Sebastian. "Syriac Sources for Seventh-Century History." *Byzantine and Modern Greek Studies* 2 (1976): 17-36.

———. "The Dispute Poem: From Sumer to Syriac." *Bayn al-Nahrayn* 7 (28) (1979): 417-426.

———. "Syriac Historical Writing: A Survey of the Main Sources." *Journal of the Iraqi Academy* 5 (1979/1980): 297-326.

———. "The Conversations with the Syrian Orthodox under Justinian (532)." *Orientalia Christiana Periodica* 47 (1981): 87-121.

———. "Syriac Views of Emergent Islam." In *Studies on the First Century of Islamic Society*, ed. G. H. A. Juynboll, 9-21. Carbondale: Southern Illinois University Press, 1982.

———. "Christians in the Sassanian Empire: A Case of Divided Loyalties." *Studies in Church History* 18 (1982): 1-19. Reprint, *Syriac Perspectives on Late Antiquity*. London: Variorum Reprints, 1984.

———. "Dialogue Hymns of the Syriac Churches." *Sobornost* 5:2 (1983): 35-45.

———. "Dramatic Dialogue Poems." In *IV Symposium Syriacum 1984: Literary Genres in Syriac Literature*, ed. H. J. W. Drijvers, R. Lavenant, C. Molenberg and G.J. Reinink, 135-147. Rome: Pont. Institutum Studiorum Orientalium, 1987.

———. "The Sinful Woman and Satan: Two Syriac Dialogue Poems." *Oriens Christianus* 72 (1988): 21-62.

———. "Syriac Culture in the Seventh Century." *ARAM* 1/2 (1989): 268-280.

———. "Syriac Dispute Poems: The Various Types." In *Dispute Poems and Dialogues in the Ancient and Mediaeval Near East*, ed. G.J. Reinink and H.L.J. Vanstiphout, 109-119. Louvain: Peeters, 1991.

———. "The Christology of the Church of the East in the Synods of the Fifth to Early Seventh Centuries: Preliminary Considerations and Materials," in *Studies in Syriac Christianity: History, Literature, and Theology*, Chapter XII. Aldershot, England: Ashgate Variorum, 1992.

———. "1. Syriac Poetry on Biblical Themes: 2. A Dialogue Poem on the Sacrifice of Isaac (Gen 22)." *The Harp* 7 (1994): 55-72.

———. *Bride of Light*. Kottayam, India: St. Ephrem Ecumenical Research Institute, 1994.

———. *A Brief Outline of Syriac Literature*. Kottayam, India: St. Ephrem Ecumenical Research Institute, 1997.

———. *From Ephrem to Romanos: Interactions between Syriac and Greek in Late Antiquity*. Aldershot, England: Ashgate Variorum, 1999.

———. "The Dialogue between the Two Thieves." *The Harp* 20 (2006): 151-170.

Brock, Sebastian, and Susan Ashbrook Harvey, eds. *Holy Women of the Syrian Orient*. Berkeley: University of California Press, 1987.

Brown, Peter. *Society and the Holy in Late Antiquity*. Berkeley: University of California Press, 1982.

Bukhari, *Sahih al-Bukhari*, 9 vols. Riyadh: Darussalam, 1997.

Bulliet, Richard. *Conversion to Islam in the Medieval Period: An Essay in Quantitative History*. Cambridge, MA: Harvard University Press, 1979.

Buyukkara, M. Ali. "The Schism in the Party of Musa al-Kazim and the Emergence of the Waqifa." *Arabica* 47 (2000): 78-99.

Cameron, Averil. "Disputations, Polemical Literature and the Formation of Opinion in the Early Byzantine Period." In *Dispute Poems and Dialogues in the Ancient and Mediaeval Near East*, ed. Gerrit J. Reinink and

H. L. J. Vanstiphout, 91-108. Louvain: Departement Oriëntalistiek, 1991.

———. "New Themes and Styles in Greek Literature: Seventh-Eighth Centuries." In *The Byzantine and Early Islamic Near East: Problems in the Literary Source Material*, vol. 1, ed. Averil Cameron and Lawrence Conrad, 81-105. Princeton: Darwin Press, 1992.

Caspar, Robert, et al. "Bibliographie du dialogue islamo-chrétien." *Islamochristiana* 1 (1975): 125-181; 2 (1976): 187-249; 3 (1977): 255-286; 4 (1978): 247-267; 5 (1979): 299-317; 6 (1980): 259-299; 7 (1981): 299-307.

Castelli, Elizabeth A. *Martyrdom and Memory: Early Christian Culture Making*. New York: Columbia University Press, 2004.

Chabot, Jean-Baptiste, ed. *Chronique de Michel le Syrien, Patriarche Jacobite d'Antioche (1166-1199)*. 5 vols. Paris: Ernest Leroux, 1899-1924.

———, ed. *Anonymi auctoris Chronicon ad annum Christi 1234 pertinens*, Corpus Scriptorum Christianorum Orientalium, vols. 81-82, 109. Paris: E. Typographeo Reipublicae, 1916, 1920, 1937. Reprint, Louvain: L. Durbecq, 1952.

Charon (Korolevsky), Cyril. *History of the Melkite Patriarchates*. Vol. 3/1, Institutions, Liturgy, Hierarchy, and Statistics, ed. Bishop Nicholas Samra. Fairfax, VA: Eastern Christian Publications, 2000.

Chase, Frederic, ed. *Saint John of Damascus: Writings*. Washington, DC: The Catholic University of America Press, 1958.

Cheikho, Louis. "Al-Muhawara al-diniya allati jarat bayna al-khalifa al-Mahdi wa Timotheus al-jathaliq." *al-Machriq* 19 (1921): 359-374; 408-418.

———. "Majalis Iliya mutran Nisibin." *al-Machriq* 20 (1922): 33-44, 112-122, 267-272, 366-377, 425-434.

———. *Al-Nasraniyya wa-Adabuha bayna 'Arab al-Jahiliyya*. Beirut: Dar al-Mashriq, 1989.

Clarke, Graeme W. *The Octavius of Marcus Minucius Felix*. New York: Newman Press, 1974.

Cook, David. "Christians and Christianity in Hadith Works before 900." In *Christian-Muslim Relations: A Bibliographical History, Volume One (600–900)*, eds. David Thomas and Barbara Roggema, 73-82. Leiden: Brill, 2009.

Cook, Michael. "The Origins of 'Kalam'." *Bulletin of the School of Oriental and African Studies* 43 (1980): 32-43.

Cooperson, Michael. *Classical Arabic Biography: The Heirs of the Prophet in the Age of al-Ma'mun*. Cambridge: Cambridge University Press, 2000.

Crone, Patricia. "The First-Century Concept of 'Hiǧra'." *Arabica* 41 (1994): 352-387.

Crone, Patricia, and Michael Cook. *Hagarism: The Making of the Islamic World*. Cambridge: Cambridge University Press, 1977.

Daiber, Hans. "Masa'il wa-ajwiba." In *Encyclopaedia of Islam, Second Edition*, ed. C. E. Bosworth, et al, vol. 6, 636-639. Leiden: Brill, 1991.

Daly, Robert J., ed. *Treatise on the Passover and Dialogue of Origen with Heraclides and His Fellow Bishops on the Father, the Son, and the Soul*. New York: Paulist Press, 1992.

Davids, Adelbert and Pim Valkenberg. "John of Damascus: The Heresy of the Ishmaelites." In *The Three Rings: Textual Studies in the Historical Trialogue of Judaism, Christianity, and Islam*, ed. Barbara Roggema, Marcel Poorthuis, and Pim Valkenberg, 71-90. Leuven: Peeters, 2005.

Demiri, Lejla, and Cornelia Römer, eds. *Texts from the Early Islamic Period of Egypt: Muslims and Christians at their First Encounter*. Vienna: Phoibos, 2009.

Dennett, Daniel. *Conversion and the Poll Tax in Early Islam*. Cambridge, MA: Harvard University Press, 1950.

Déroche, Vincent, and Gilbert Dagron. "Doctrina Jacobi nuper baptizati." *Travaux et mémoires (du Centre de Recherche d'Histoire et de Civilisation byzantines)* 11 (1991): 17-273.

Dick, Ignace. "Un continuateur arabe de saint Jean Damascène, Theodore Abuqurra, évêque melkite de Harran; la personne et son milieu." *Proche-Orient Chrétien* 12 (1962): 209-223; 319-332; 13 (1963): 114-129.

⸻. "La Discussion d'Abu Qurra avec les Ulémas musulmans devant le Calife al-Ma'mun." *Parole de l'Orient* 16 (1990-1991): 107-113.

⸻, ed. *Maymar fi ikram al-ayqunat; li-Thawdhurus Abi Qurrah (Théodore Abuqurra, traité du culte des icons)*, Patrimonie arabe chrétien, 10. Juniyah, Lebanon: Librarie Saint-Paul, 1986.

⸻, ed. *Mujadalat Abi Qurra ma'a al-mutakallimin al-muslimin fi majlis al-khalifa al-Ma'mun (La Discussion d'Abu Qurra avec les Ulémas Musulmans devant le Calife Al-Ma'mun)*. Juniyah: Matba'at al-Kathulikiyya, 1999.

Dodge, Bayard, ed. *The Fihrist of Al-Nadim: A Tenth-Century Survey of Muslim Culture*. New York: Columbia University Press, 1970.

Donner, Fred. *Narratives of Islamic Origins: The Beginnings of Islamic Historical Writing*. Princeton, NJ: Darwin Press, 1998.

⸻. "From Believers to Muslims: Confessional Self-Identity in the Early Islamic Community." *Al-Abhath* 50-51 (2002-2003): 9-53.

———. *Muhammad and the Believers: At the Origins of Islam.* Cambridge, MA: Belknap Press of Harvard University Press, 2010.

Drijvers, H. J. W., ed. *The Book of the Laws of Countries: Dialogue on Fate of Bardaisan of Edessa.* Piscataway, NJ: Gorgias Press, 2006.

Duval, Rubens, ed. *Iso'yahb Patriarchae III Liber epistularum,* Corpus Scriptorum Christianorum Orientalium, vols. 11-12; Scriptores Syri, t. 11-12. Louvain: Secrétariat du CorpusSCO, 1962.

Edwards, M. J., Martin Goodman, and S. R. F. Rowland Christopher Price, eds. *Apologetics in the Roman Empire: Pagans, Jews, and Christians.* Oxford: Oxford University Press, 1999.

Elders, Joseph. "The Lost Churches of the Arabian Gulf: Recent Discoveries on the Islands of Sir Bani Yas and Marawah, Abu Dhabi Emirate, United Arab Emirates." *Proceedings of the Seminar for Arabian Studies* 31 (2001): 47-58.

Ettlinger, Gérard, ed. *Theodoret, Bishop of Cyrrhus: Eranistes.* Washington, DC: Catholic University of America Press, 1975. Reprint, 2003.

Fakhry, Majid. *An Interpretation of the Qur'an, English Translation of the Meanings: A Bilingual Edition.* New York: University Press, 2002.

Farrell, Joseph P. *The Disputation with Pyrrhus of Our Father among the Saints, Maximus the Confessor.* South Canaan, PA: St. Tikhon's Seminary Press, 1990.

Fiey, Jean Maurice. *Chrétiens syriaques sous les Abbassides surtout à Bagdad, 749-1258.* Corpus Scriptorum Christianorum Orientalium, vol. 420. Louvain: Secrétariat du CorpusSCO, 1980.

Fiey, Jean Maurice, and A. Abouna, eds. *Anonymi auctoris chronicon ad annum Christi 1234 pertinens,* Corpus Scriptorum Christianorum Orientalium, vol. 354. Louvain: Secrétariat du CorpusSCO, 1974.

Finkel, Joshua. "A Risala of al-Jahiz." *Journal of the American Oriental Society* 47 (1927): 311-334.

Finster, Barbara. "Arabia in Late Antiquity: An Outline of the Cultural Situation in the Peninsula at the Time of Muhammad." In *The Qur'an in Context: Historical and Literary Investigations into the Qur'anic Milieu,* ed. Angelika Neuwirth, Nicolai Sinai, and Michael Marx, 61-114. Leiden: Brill, 2010.

Firestone, Reuven. "The Qur'an and the Bible: Some Modern Studies of Their Relationship." In *Bible and Qur'an: Essays in Scriptural Intertextuality,* ed. John Reeves, 1-22. Atlanta: Society of Biblical Literature, 2003.

Frank, Richard. *Texts and Studies on the Development and History of Kalam.* 3 vols. Aldershot, England: Ashgate Variorum, 2005-2008.

Friedmann, Yohanan. *Tolerance and Coercion in Islam: Interfaith Relations in the Muslim Tradition.* Cambridge: Cambridge University Press, 2006.

Gardet, Louis. "Al-Burhan." In *Encyclopaedia of Islam, Second Edition*, vol. 1, 1326-1327. Leiden: Brill, 1960.

———. "Iman." In *Encyclopaedia of Islam, Second Edition*, vol. 3, 1170-1174. Leiden: Brill, 1971.

Gardet, Louis, and Marshall Hodgson. "Hudjdja." In *Encyclopaedia of Islam, Second Edition*, vol. 3, 543-545. Leiden: Brill, 1971.

Gaudeul, Jean-Marie. *Encounters & Clashes: Islam and Christianity in History.* 2 vols. Rome: Pontificio istituto di studi arabi e d'islamistica, 2000.

Gaudeul, Jean-Marie, and Robert Caspar. "Textes de la Tradition Musulmane concernant le Tahrif (Falsification) des Écritures." *Islamochristiana* 6 (1980): 61-104.

Gero, Stephen. "The Legend of the Monk Bahira, the Cult of the Cross, and Iconoclasm." In *La Syrie de Byzance à l'Islam, VIIe-VIIIe siècles: Actes du colloque international Lyon-Maison de l'Orient méditerranéen, Paris-Institut du monde arabe, 11-15 septembre 1990,* ed. Pierre Canivet and Jean-Paul Rey-Coquais, 47-58. Damascus: Institut français de Damas, 1992.

Gervers, Michael, and Ramzi Jibran Bikhazi, eds. *Conversion and Continuity: Indigenous Christian Communities in Islamic Lands, Eighth to Eighteenth Centuries.* Toronto: Pontifical Institute of Mediaeval Studies, 1990.

Gibson, Margaret Dunlop, ed. *An Arabic Version of the Acts of the Apostles and the Seven Catholic Epistles, with a Treatise on the Triune Nature of God.* London: C. J. Clay & Sons, 1899.

Gilliot, Claude. "Creation of a Fixed Text." In *The Cambridge Companion to the Qur'an*, ed. Jane Dammen McAuliffe, 41-57. Cambridge: Cambridge University Press, 2006.

———. "Reconsidering the Authorship of the Qur'an: Is the Qur'an Partly the Fruit of a Progressive Work?" In *The Qur'an in its Historical Context*, ed. Gabriel Said Reynolds, 88-108. London: Routledge, 2008.

———. "Christians and Christianity in Islamic Exegesis." In *Christian-Muslim Relations: A Bibliographical History, Volume One (600–900)*, eds. David Thomas and Barbara Roggema, 31-56. Leiden: Brill, 2009.

Goddard, Hugh. *Muslim Perceptions of Christianity.* London: Grey Seal, 1996.

Gottheil, Richard J. H. "A Christian Bahira Legend." *Zeitschrift für Assyriologie* 13 (1898): 189-201, 252-268; 14 (1899): 203-268; 15 (1900): 56-102; 17 (1903): 125-166.

Graf, Georg. "Christliche Polemik gegen den Islam." *Gelbe Heft: Historisch und Politische Blätter für das Katholische Deutschland* 2 (1926): 825-842.

_____. "Christlich-arabische Texte: Zwei Disputationem zwischen Muslimen und Christen." In *Veröffentlichungen aus den badischen Papyrus-Sammlungen: Griechische, Koptische und Arabische Texte zur Religion und religiösen Literatur in Ägyptens Spätzeit*, eds. Friedrich Bilabel and Adolf Grohmann, 1-31. Heidelberg: Universitätsbibliothek Verlag, 1934.

_____. *Geschichte der Christlichen Arabischen Literatur.* 5 vols. Biblioteca apostolica vaticana. Studi e testi, 118, 133, 146-147, 172. Vatican City: Biblioteca apostolica vaticana, 1944-1953.

_____, ed. *Die Arabischen Schriften des Theodor Abû Qurra, Bischofs von Harrân (ca. 740-820): Literarhistorische Untersuchungen und Übersetzung,* Forschungen zur christlichen Litteratur- und Dogmengeschichte, Bd. 10, Hft. 3/4. Paderborn: Ferdinand Schöningh, 1910.

Griffith, Sidney. "Chapter Ten of the *Scholion*: Theodore Bar Kônî's Apology for Christianity." *Orientalia Christiana Periodica* 47 (1981): 158-188.

_____. "Theodore Bar Kônî's *Scholion*: A Nestorian *Summa Contra Gentiles* from the First Abbasid Century." In *East of Byzantium: Syria and Armenia in the Formative Period*, ed. N. G. Garsoïan, Thomas F Mathews and Robert W Thomson, 53-72. Washington DC: Dumbarton Oaks, 1982.

_____. "The Gospel in Arabic: An Inquiry into its Appearance in the First Abbasid Century." *Oriens Christianus* 69 (1985): 126-167.

_____. "Anastasios of Sinai, the Hodegos, and the Muslims." *Greek Orthodox Theological Review* 32 (1987): 341-358.

_____. "Jews and Muslims in Christian Syriac and Arabic Texts of the Ninth Century." *Jewish History* 3 (1988): 65-94.

_____. "Bashir/Beser: Boon Companion of the Byzantine Emperor Leo III; the Islamic Recension of His Story in Leiden Oriental Ms 951 (2)." *Le Muséon* 103 (1990): 293-327.

_____. "Disputes with Muslims in Syriac Christian Texts: from Patriarch John (d. 648) to Bar Hebraeus (d. 1286)." In *Religionsgespräche im Mittlealter*, ed. Bernard Lewis and Friedrich Niewöhner, Wolfenbütteler Mittelalter-Studien, vol. 4, 251-273. Wiesbaden: Otto Harrassowitz, 1992.

_____. *Theodore Abu Qurrah: the intellectual profile of an Arab Christian writer of the first Abbasid century.* Tel Aviv: Tel Aviv University, 1992.

_____. "Reflections on the biography of Theodore Abu Qurrah." *Parole de l'Orient* 18 (1993): 143-170.

_____. *Syriac Writers on Muslims and the Religious Challenge of Islam*. Moran Etho series, vol. 7. Kottayam: St. Ephrem Ecumenical Research Institute, 1995.

_____. "Muhammad and the Monk Bahira: Reflections on a Syriac and Arabic Text from Early Abbasid Times." *Oriens Christianus* 79 (1995): 146-174.

_____. "From Aramaic to Arabic: the Languages of the Monasteries of Palestine in the Byzantine and Early Islamic Periods." *Dumbarton Oaks Papers* 51 (1997): 11-31.

_____, ed. *A Treatise on the Veneration of the Holy Icons; Written in Arabic by Theodore Abu Qurrah*. Eastern Christian texts in translation, vol. 1. Louvain: Peeters, 1997.

_____. "The Monk in the Emir's Majlis: Reflections on a Popular Genre of Christian Literary Apologetics in Arabic in the Early Islamic Period." In *The Majlis*, ed. Hava Lazarus-Yafeh, et al, 13-65. Wiesbaden: Harrassowitz, 1999.

_____. "The Qur'an in Arab Christian Texts; The Development of an Apologetical Argument: Abu Qurrah in the Maǧlis of Al-Ma'mun." *Parole de l'Orient* 24 (1999): 203-233.

_____. "Disputing with Islam in Syriac: The Case of the Monk of Bet Hale and a Muslim Emir." *Hugoye: Journal of Syriac Studies* 3/1 (2000): 1-19.

_____. "Christians and Christianity." In *Encyclopaedia of the Qur'an*, ed. Jane Dammen McAuliffe, vol. 1, 307-316. Leiden: Brill, 2001.

_____. "'Melkites,' 'Jacobites,' and the Christological Controversies in Arabic in Third/Ninth-Century Syria." In *Syrian Christians under Islam: The First Thousand Years*, ed. David Thomas, 9-55. Leiden: Brill, 2001.

_____. *The Beginnings of Christian Theology in Arabic: Muslim-Christian Encounters in the Early Islamic Period*. Variorum Collected Studies Series. Aldershot, England: Ashgate Variorum, 2002.

_____. "Arguing from Scripture: The Bible in the Christian/Muslim Encounter in the Middle Ages." In *Scripture and Pluralism: Reading the Bible in the Religiously Plural Worlds of the Middle Ages and Renaissance*, ed. T.J. Heffernan & T.E. Burman, 29-58. Leiden: Brill, 2005.

_____. "The Church of Jerusalem and the 'Melkites': The Making of an 'Arab Orthodox' Christian Identity in the World of Islam, 750-1050 CE." In *Christians and Christianity in the Holy Land: From the Origins to the Latin Kingdoms*, ed. Ora Limor and G. G. Stroumsa, 173-202. Turnhout: Brepols, 2006.

_____. "*Answers for the Shaykh*: A 'Melkite' Arabic Text from Sinai and the Doctrines of the Trinity and the Incarnation in 'Arab Orthodox' Apologetics." In *The Encounter of Eastern Christianity with Early Islam*, eds. Emmanouela Grypeou, Mark Swanson and David Thomas, 277-309. Leiden: Brill, 2006.

_____. "The Syriac Letters of Patriarch Timothy I and the Birth of Christian *Kalam* in the Mu'tazilite Milieu of Baghdad and Basrah in Early Islamic Times," in *Syriac Polemics: Studies in Honour of Gerrit Jan Reinink*, ed. W. J. van Beekum, J. W. Drijvers, and A. C. Klugkist, 103-132. Leuven: Peeters, 2007.

_____. "Syriacisms in the "Arabic Qur'an": Who were "those who said 'Allah is third of three'" according to al-Ma'ida 73?." In *A Word Fitly Spoken: Studies in Mediaeval Exegesis of the Hebrew Bible and the Qur'an*, eds. Meir M. Bar-Asher, Simon Hopkins, Sarah Stroumsa, and Bruno Chiesa, 83-110. Jerusalem: Ben-Zvi Institute, 2007.

_____. "Christian Lore and the Arabic Qur'an: The 'Companions of the Cave' in *Surat al-Kahf* and in Syriac Tradition." In *The Qur'an in its Historical Context*, ed. Gabriel Said Reynolds, 109-137. London: Routledge, 2008.

_____. *The Church in the Shadow of the Mosque*. Princeton: Princeton University Press, 2008.

Grillmeier, Alois. *Christ in Christian Tradition*, 2 vols. in 4 parts. Atlanta: John Knox Press, 1975-1995.

Gruendler, Beatrice. "Arabic Script." In *Encyclopaedia of the Qur'an*, ed. Jane D. McAuliffe, vol. 1, 135-144. Leiden: Brill, 2001.

Guenther, Alan M. "The Christian Experience and Interpretation of the Early Muslim Conquest and Rule." *Islam and Christian-Muslim Relations* 10 (1999): 363-378.

Guidi, Ignazio, E. W. Brooks, and Jean Baptiste Chabot, eds. *Chronica minora*, Corpus Scriptorum Christianorum Orientalium, vols. 1-6. Paris: E Typographeo Reipublicae, 1903. Reprint, Louvain: Secrétariat du CorpusSCO, 1955-1961.

Guillaume, Alfred. "Theodore Abu Qurra as apologist." *Moslem World* 15 (1925): 42-51.

_____. "A Debate between Christian and Moslem Doctors." *Journal of the Royal Asiatic Society of Great Britain and Ireland* (Centenary supplement 1924): 233-244.

_____. *The Life of Muhammad: A Translation of Ishaq's Sirat rasul Allah*. London: Oxford University Press, 1955. Reprint, 2006.

Guillaumont, Antoine. "Justinien et l'Église de Perse." *Dumbarton Oaks Papers* 23/24 (1969-1970): 39-66.

Gutas, Dimitri. *Greek Thought, Arabic Culture: The Graeco-Arabic Translation Movement in Baghdad and Early Abbasid Society (2nd-4th/8th-10th Centuries)*. London: Routledge, 1998.

Gwynne, Rosalind Ward. *Logic, Rhetoric, and Legal Reasoning in the Qur'an: God's Arguments*. London: RoutledgeCurzon, 2004.

_____. "Sign, Analogy, and the *Via Negativa*: Approaching the Transcendent God of the Qur'an." In *Sacred Tropes: Tanakh, New Testament, and Qur'an as Literature and Culture*, ed. Roberta Sterman Sabbath, 53-63. Leiden: Brill, 2009.

Haar Romeny, Bas ter. "Question-and-Answer Collections in Syriac Literature." In *Erotapokriseis: Early Christian Question-and-Answer Literature in Context*, ed. Annelie Volgers and Claudio Zamagni, 145-163. Louvain: Peeters, 2004.

Hämenn-Anttila, Jaakko. "Christians and Christianity in the Qur'an." In *Christian-Muslim Relations: A Bibliographical History, Volume One (600–900)*, ed. David Thomas and Barbara Roggema, 21-30. Leiden: Brill, 2009.

Harun, A-S. M. *Rasa'il Al-Jahiz*. 4 vols. Cairo: Maktabat al-Khanji, 1964-1979.

Hayek, Michel. *Le Christ de l'Islam: Textes Présentés, Traduits et Annotés*. Paris: Éditions du Seuil, 1959.

_____, ed. *'Ammar al-Basri, apologie et controverses*. Beirut: Dar al-Machriq, 1977.

Hayman, Allison Peter. *The Disputation of Sergius the Stylite against a Jew*. Corpus Scriptorum Christianorum Orientalium, vols. 338-339. Louvain: Secretariat du CorpusSCO, 1973.

Heimgartner, Martin. "Timothy I." In *Christian-Muslim Relations: A Bibliographical History, Volume One (600–900)*, eds. David Thomas and Barbara Roggema, 515-519. Leiden: Brill, 2009.

Hoffmann, Manfred. *Der Dialog bei den Christlichen Schriftstellern der Ersten Vier Jahrhunderte*. Berlin: Akademie-Verlag, 1966.

Holmberg, Bo. "The Public Debate as a Literary Genre in Arabic Literature." *Orientalia Suecana* 38-39 (1989-1990): 45-58.

Hoyland, Robert. *Seeing Islam as Others saw It: A Survey and Evaluation of Christian, Jewish, and Zoroastrian Writings on Early Islam*. Princeton, NJ: Darwin Press, 1997.

_____. "Introduction." In *Muslims and Others in Early Islamic Society*, xiii-xxxiv. Aldershot, England: Ashgate Variorum, 2004.

———. "Epigraphy and the Linguistic Background to the Qur'an." In *The Qur'an in Context: Historical and Literary Investigations into the Qur'anic Milieu*, ed. Angelika Neuwirth, Nicolai Sinai, and Michael Marx, 51-69. Leiden: Brill, 2010.

———, ed. *Muslims and Others in Early Islamic Society*. Aldershot, England: Ashgate Variorum, 2004.

Hunter, Erica C. "Interfaith Dialogues: The Church of the East and the Abbasids." In *Der Christliche Orient und seine Umwelt*, ed. S.G. Vashalomidze and L. Greisiger, 289-302. Wiesbaden: Harrassowitz, 2007.

Hurst, Thomas. "Letter 40 of the Nestorian Patriarch Timothy I (727-823): An Edition and Translation." Master's Thesis, The Catholic University of America, 1981.

———. "The Syriac Letters of Timothy I (727-823): A Study in Christian-Muslim Controversy." PhD diss., The Catholic University of America, 1986.

Ibn Babawayh al-Qummi, Abu Ja'far Muhammad ibn 'Ali. *'Uyun Akhbar Al-Rida*. al-Najaf: al-Matba'a al-Haydariya, 1970.

Ibn Hisham. *Al-Sirat al-Nabawiyya*, 4 vols. Ed. Mustafa al-Saqqa et al. Beirut: al-Maktabat al-'Ilmiya, 1990.

Jeffery, Arthur. *The Foreign Vocabulary of the Qur'an*. Baroda: Oriental Institute, 1938. Reprint, Leiden: Brill, 2006.

Johnson, Dale, ed. *Christian-Muslim Debate: A Debate between the Monk George and Muslim Theologians in the Court of Saladin (1165 AD)*. Portland, OR: New Sinai Press, 2007.

Kahn, Charles. *Plato and the Socratic Dialogue: The Philosophical Use of a Literary Form*. Cambridge: Cambridge University Press, 1996.

Keating, Sandra. *Defending the "People of Truth" in the Early Islamic Period: The Christian Apologies of Abu Ra'itah*. Leiden: Brill, 2006.

Kellermann, Mechthild. "Ein pseudoaristotelischer Traktat über die Tugend: Edition und Übersetzung der arabischen Fassungen des Abu Qurra und des Ibn at-Tayyib." Ph.D. diss., Friedrich-Alexander-Universität zu Erlangen-Nürnberg, 1965.

Kennedy, Hugh. "Change and continuity in Syria and Palestine at the time of the Moslem conquest." *ARAM* 1/2 (1989): 258-267.

Khoury, Adel Théodore. *Les théologiens byzantins et l'Islam. Textes et auteurs. VIIIe-XIIIe s.* Louvain: Nauwelaerts, 1969.

Kotter, P. Bonifatius, ed. *Die Schriften des Johannes von Damaskos*, Patristiche Texte und Studien, vols. 7, 12, 17, 22, 29. Berlin and New York: de Gruyter, 1969-1988.

Kytzler, Bernhard. *M. Minuci Felicis: Octavius*. Stuttgart and Leipzig: B.G. Teubner, 1992.

Lang, David Marshall. *Lives and Legends of the Georgian Saints*. Crestwood, NY: St. Vladimir's Seminary Press, 1976. Second revised edition.

Lamoreaux, John. "The Biography of Theodore Abu Qurrah Revisited." *Dumbarton Oaks Papers* 56 (2002): 25-40.

_____, ed. and transl. *Theodore Abu Qurrah*. Chicago, IL: University of Chicago Press, 2005.

_____. "Theodore Abu Qurra." In *Christian-Muslim Relations: A Bibliographical History, Volume One (600–900)*, eds. David Thomas and Barbara Roggema, 439-491. Leiden: Brill, 2009.

Lamoreaux, John, and H. Khairallah. "The Arabic Version of the Life of John of Edessa." *Le Muséon* 113 (2000): 439-460.

Lasker, Daniel J. "Qissat Mujadalat al-Usquf and Nestor Ha-Komer: the earliest Arabic and Hebrew Jewish anti-Christian Polemics." In *Genizah Research after Ninety Years: the Case of Judaeo-Arabic*, ed. Joshua Blau and S. C. Reif, 112-118. Cambridge: Cambridge University Press, 1992.

Lawson, Todd. *The Crucifixion and the Qur'an: A Study in the History of Muslim Thought*. Oxford: Oneworld, 2009.

Lazarus-Yafeh, Hava. *Intertwined Worlds: Medieval Islam and Bible Criticism*. Princeton, NJ: Princeton University Press, 1992.

Le Boulluec, Alain, ed. *La Controverse Religieuse et ses Formes*. Paris: Cerf, 1995.

Leeming, Kate. "The Adoption of Arabic as a Liturgical Language by the Palestinian Melkites." *ARAM* 15 (2003): 239-246.

Leemhuis, Fred. "A Koranic Contest Poem in Surat As-Saffat?" In *Dispute Poems and Dialogues in the Ancient and Mediaeval Near East: Forms and Types of Literary Debates in Semitic and Related Literatures*, ed. G. J. Reinink and H. L. J. Vanstiphout, 165-177. Louvain: Department Oriëntalistiek, 1991.

Leslau, Wolf. *Comparative Dictionary of Ge'ez (Classical Ethiopic)*. Wiesbaden: Otto Harrassowitz, 1991.

Levtzion, Nehemia. "Conversion to Islam in Syria and Palestine and the Survival of Christian Communities." In *Conversion and Continuity: Indigenous Christian Communities in Islamic Lands, Eighth to Eighteenth Centuries*, ed. Michael Gervers and Ramzi Jibran Bikhazi, 289-311. Toronto: Pontifical Institute of Mediaeval Studies, 1990.

Lim, Richard. *Public Disputation, Power, and Social Order in Late Antiquity*. Berkeley: University of California Press, 1995.

Lodahl, Michael. *Claiming Abraham: Reading the Bible and the Qur'an Side by Side*. Grand Rapids, MI: Brazos Press, 2010.

Luxenberg, Christoph. *Die syro-aramäische Lesart des Koran: ein Beitrag zur Entschlüsselung der Koransprache*. Berlin: Das Arabische Buch, 2000.

———. *The Syro-Aramaic Reading of the Koran: A Contribution to the Decoding of the Language of the Koran*. Berlin: Han Schiler, 2007.

Madelung, Wilferd. "Al-Qasim ibn Ibrahim and Christian theology." *ARAM* 3 (1991): 35-44.

Madigan, Daniel. *The Qur'an's Self-Image: Writing and Authority in Islam's Scripture*. Princeton, NJ: Princeton University Press, 2001.

———. "The Limits of Self-Referentiality in the Qur'an." In *Self-Referentiality in the Qur'an*, ed. Stefan Wild, 59-69. Wiesbaden: Otto Harrassowitz, 2006.

Marcinkowski, Christoph. "A Glance on the First of Four Canonical Hadith Collections of the Twelver Shi'ites: *al-Kafi* by al-Kulayni (d. 328 or 329 A.H./940 or 941 C.E.)." *Hamdard Islamicus* 24 (2001): 13-29.

Marcuzzo, Giacinto Bulus. *Le Dialogue d'Abraham de Tibériade avec 'Abd al-Rahman al-Hashimi à Jérusalem vers 820*. Rome: Pontificia Universitas Lateranensis, 1986.

Margoliouth, David. "The Discussion between Abu Bishr Matta and Abu Sa'id al-Sirafi on the Merits of Logic and Grammar." *Journal of the Royal Asiatic Society* 37 (1905): 79-129.

Marshall, David. "Christianity in the Qur'an." In *Islamic interpretations of Christianity*, ed. Lloyd Ridgeon, 3-29. New York: St. Martin's Press, 2000.

Marx, Michael. "Glimpses of a Mariology in the Qur'an: From Hagiography to Theology via Religious-Political Debate." In *The Qur'an in Context: Historical and Literary Investigations into the Qur'anic Milieu*, ed. Angelika Neuwirth, Nicolai Sinai, and Michael Marx, 533-564. Leiden: Brill, 2010.

McAuliffe, Jane Dammen. *Qur'anic Christians: An analysis of classical and modern exegesis*. Cambridge: Cambridge University Press, 1991.

———. "'Debate with Them in the Better Way': The Construction of a Qur'anic Commonplace." In *Myths, Historical Archetypes and Symbolic Figures in Arabic Literature*, ed. B. Embaló et al., 163-188. Beirut, 1999.

———. "Debate and Disputation." In *Encyclopaedia of the Qur'an*, ed. Jane D. McAuliffe, vol. 1, 511-514. Leiden: Brill, 2001.

McAuliffe, Jane Dammen, ed. *The Encyclopaedia of the Qur'an*. 6 vols. Leiden: Brill, 2001-2006.

Meyendorff, John. *Byzantine Theology: Historical Trends & Doctrinal Themes.* New York: Fordham University Press, 1979.

———. *Imperial Unity and Christian Divisions: The Church, 450-680 A.D.* Crestwood, NY: St. Vladimir's Seminary Press, 1989.

Migne, J.-P., ed. *Patrologiæ cursus completus: Series Græca.* Paris: J.-P. Migne, 1864-1865.

Mingana, Alphonse. "The Apology of Timothy the Patriarch before the Caliph Mahdi." *Bulletin of the John Rylands Library* 12/1 (1928): 137-298.

Mir, Mustansir. "Dialogue in the Qur'an." *Religion and Literature* 24 (1992): 1-22.

———. "Dialogues." In *Encyclopaedia of the Qur'an*, ed. Jane Dammen McAuliffe, vol. 1, 531-535. Leiden: Brill, 2001.

Modarressi, Hossein. *Tradition and Survival: A Bibliographical Survey of Early Shi'ite Literature, Volume 1.* Oxford: Oneworld, 2003.

Moffett, Samuel Hugh. *A History of Christianity in Asia: Volume I.* San Francisco: Harper, 1992.

Montgomery, James M. "Islamic Crosspollinations." In *Islamic Crosspollinations: Interactions in the Medieval Middle East*, ed. Anna Akasoy, James E. Montgomery, and Peter Pormann, 148-193. Exeter: Gibb Memorial Trust, 2007.

Moosa, Matti. "A New Source on Ahmad ibn al-Tayyib al-Sarakhsi: Florentine MS Arabic 299." *Journal of the American Oriental Society* 92 (1972): 19-24.

———. *The Maronites in History.* Piscataway, NJ: Gorgias Press, 2005.

Morony, Michael. "History and Identity in the Syrian Churches." In *Redefining Christian Identity: Cultural Interaction in the Middle East since the Rise of Islam*, ed. J.J. van Ginkel, H.L. Murre-van den Berg, and T.M. van Lint, 1-33. Leuven: Peeters, 2005.

Motzki, Harald, ed. *The Biography of Muhammad: The Issue of the Sources.* Leiden: Brill, 2000.

Mourad, Suleiman. "On the Qur'anic Stories about Mary and Jesus." *Bulletin of the Royal Institute for Inter-Faith Studies* 1 (1999): 13–24.

———. "From Hellenism to Christianity and Islam: The Origin of the Palm Tree Story concerning Mary and Jesus in the Gospel of Pseudo-Matthew and the Qur'an." *Oriens Christianus* 86 (2002): 206-216.

———. "Mary in the Qur'an: A Reexamination of Her Presentation." In *The Qur'an in its Historical Context*, ed. Gabriel Said Reynolds, 163-174. London: Routledge, 2008.

_____. "Christians and Christianity in the Sira of Muhammad." In *Christian-Muslim Relations: A Bibliographical History, Volume One (600–900)*, eds. David Thomas and Barbara Roggema, 57–71. Leiden: Brill, 2009.

Musurillo, Herbert, ed. *Methodius: The Symposium, a Treatise on Chastity*. Westminster, MD: Newman Press, 1958.

Nasrallah, Joseph, ed. *Histoire du mouvement littéraire dans l'Église Melchite du Ve au XXe Siècle; contribution à l'étude de la littérature arabe chrétienne*. Louvain: Peeters, 1987.

Nasry, Wafik. *The Caliph and the Bishop: A 9th Century Muslim-Christian Debate: Al-Ma'mun and Abu Qurrah*. Beirut: CEDRAC, 2008.

_____. "Abu Qurrah, al-Ma'mun, and Yahya ibn Aktham," *Parole de l'Orient* 32 (2007): 285-290.

Nau, François. "Un colloque du patriarche Jean avec l'émir des Agaréens et faits divers des années 712 à 716 d'après le ms. du British Museum Add. 17193." *Journal Asiatique* 11/5 (1915): 225-279.

Nebes, Norbert. "The Martyrs of Najran and the End of the Himyar: On the Political History of South Arabia in the Early Sixth Century." In *The Qur'an in Context: Historical and Literary Investigations into the Qur'anic Milieu*, ed. Angelika Neuwirth, Nicolai Sinai, and Michael Marx, 27-59. Leiden: Brill, 2010.

Neuwirth, Angelika. "Structural, Linguistic and Literary Features." In *The Cambridge Companion to the Qur'an*, ed. Jane Dammen McAuliffe, 97-113. Cambridge: Cambridge University Press, 2006.

_____. "Structure and the Emergence of Community." In *The Blackwell Companion to the Qur'an*, ed. Andrew Rippin, 140-158. Malden, MA: Blackwell, 2006.

_____. "Orientalism in Oriental Studies? Qur'anic Studies as a Case in Point." *Journal of Qur'anic Studies* 9 (2007): 115-127.

_____. "The House of Abraham and the House of Amram: Genealogy, Patriarchal Authority, and Exegetical Professionalism." In *The Qur'an in Context: Historical and Literary Investigations into the Qur'anic Milieu*, ed. Angelika Neuwirth, Nicolai Sinai, and Michael Marx, 499-531. Leiden: Brill, 2010.

Neuwirth, Angelika, Nicolai Sinai, and Michael Marx, eds. *The Qur'an in Context: Historical and Literary Investigations into the Qur'anic Milieu*. Leiden: Brill, 2010.

Newman, N. A., ed. *The Early Christian-Muslim Dialogue: A Collection of Documents from the First Three Islamic Centuries, 632-900 A.D.; Translations *with Commentary*. Hatfield, PA: Interdisciplinary Biblical Research Institute, 1993.

Newsom, Carol. "The Book of Job as a Polyphonic Text." *Journal for the Study of the Old Testament* 97 (2002): 87-108.

Nöldeke, Theodor. *Geschichte des Qorans*, 3 vols. Leipzig: T. Weicher, 1909-1938. Reprint, Hildesheim: Olms, 1961.

Pahlitzsch, Johannes. "Doctrina Iacobi nuper baptizati." In *Christian-Muslim Relations: A Bibliographical History, Volume One (600–900)*, eds. David Thomas and Barbara Roggema, 117-119. Leiden: Brill, 2009.

Palmer, Andrew, Sebastian P. Brock, and Robert G. Hoyland, eds. *The Seventh Century in the West-Syrian Chronicles*. Liverpool: Liverpool University Press, 1993.

Parrinder, Geoffrey. *Jesus in the Qur'an*. New York: Barnes & Noble, 1965. Reprint, Oxford: Oneworld, 1995.

Payne Smith, J. *A Compendious Syriac Dictionary: Founded upon the Thesaurus Syriacus of R. Payne Smith*. Oxford: Oxford University Press, 1903. Reprint, Winona Lake, IN: Eisenbrauns, 1998.

Penn, Michael. "Syriac sources for the study of early Christian-Muslim relations." *Islamochristiana* 28 (2003): 87-107.

_____. "John and the Emir: A New Introduction, Edition, and Translation." *Le Muséon* 121 (2008): 65-91.

_____. "Monks, Manuscripts, and Muslims: Syriac Textual Changes in Reaction to the Rise of Islam." *Hugoye: Journal of Syriac Studies* 12 (2009): 235-257.

Perlmann, Moshe. "The Medieval Polemics between Islam and Judaism." In *Religion in a Religious Age*, ed. S. D. Goitein, 103-138. Cambridge, MA: Association of Jewish Studies, 1974.

Peters, Francis. "*Alius* or *Alter*: The Qur'anic Definition of Christians and Christianity." *Islam and Christian-Muslim Relations* 8 (1997): 165-176.

Pietruschka, Ute. "Classical Heritage and New Literary Forms: Literary Activities of Christians during the Umayyad Period." In *Ideas, Images, and Methods of Portrayal: Insights into Classical Arabic Literature and Islam*, ed. Sebastian Günther, 17-39. Leiden: Brill, 2005.

Pretty, Robert A., and G. W. Trompf, eds. *Dialogue on the True Faith in God: De Recta in Deum Fide*. Louvain: Peeters, 1997.

Putman, Hans. *L'église et l'islam sous Timothée I (780-823): étude sur l'église nestorienne au temps des premiers 'Abbasides; avec nouvelle édition et traduction du Dialogue entre Timothée et al-Mahdi*. Beirut: Dar el-Machreq [distribution, Librairie orientale], 1975.

Reed, Walter L. *Dialogues of the Word: The Bible as Literature According to Bakhtin*. New York: Oxford University Press, 1993.

Reeves, John, ed. *Bible and Qur'an: Essays in Scriptural Intertextuality*. Atlanta: Society of Biblical Literature, 2003.

Reinink, Gerrit J. "The Beginnings of Syriac Apologetic Literature in Response to Islam." *Oriens Christianus* 77 (1993): 165-187.

⸺. *Syriac Christianity under late Sasanian and early Islamic rule*. Variorum collected studies series, CS831. Aldershot, England: Ashgate Variorum, 2005.

⸺. "Following the Doctrine of the Demons: Early Christian Fear of Conversion to Islam." In *Cultures of Conversions*, ed. Jan Bremmer, Wout van Bekkum and Arie Molendijk, 127-138. Leuven: Peeters, 2006.

⸺. "Bible and Qur'an in early Syriac Christian-Islamic Disputation." In *Christians and Muslims in Dialogue in the Islamic Orient of the Middle Ages*, ed. Martin Tamcke, 57-72. Beirut: Ergon Verlag, 2007.

Reinink, Gerrit J. and H. L. J. Vanstiphout, eds. *Dispute Poems and Dialogues in the Ancient and Mediaeval Near East: Forms and Types of Literary Debates in Semitic and Related Literatures*. Louvain: Department Oriëntalistiek, 1991.

Reynolds, Gabriel Said. *A Muslim Theologian in a Sectarian Milieu: 'Abd Al-Jabbar and the Critique of Christian Origins*. Leiden: Brill, 2004.

⸺. *The Qur'an and Its Biblical Subtext*. London: Routledge, 2010.

Reynolds, Gabriel Said, ed. *The Qur'an in its Historical Context*. London: Routledge, 2008.

Reynolds, Gabriel Said and Samir Khalil Samir, eds. *'Abd al-Jabbar: Critique of Christian Origins, A Parallel English-Arabic Text*. Provo: Brigham Young University Press, 2010.

Rippin, Andrew. "Interpreting the Bible through the Qur'an." In *Approaches to the Qur'an*, ed. G. R. Hawting and Abdulkader A. Shareef, 249-259. London: Routledge, 1993.

Roberts, Alexander ed. *Sulpitius Severus, Vincent of Lerins*. Grand Rapids, MI: Eerdmans, 1982.

Robinson, Chase. "Reconstructing Early Islam: Truth and Consequences." In *Method and Theory in the Study of Islamic Origins*, ed. Herbert Berg, 101-134. Lieden: Brill, 2003.

⸺. *Islamic Historiography*. Cambridge: Cambridge University Press, 2003.

Robinson, Neal. "Jesus and Mary in the Qur'an: Some Neglected Affinities." *Religion* 20 (1990): 161-175. Reprint in *The Qur'an: Style and Con-*

tents, ed. Andrew Rippin, 21-35. Aldershot, England: Ashgate Variorum, 2001.

Roggema, Barbara. "The Legend of Sergius-Bahira: Some Remarks on its Origin in the East and its Traces in the West." In *East and West in the Crusader States*, ed. Krijna Nelly Ciggaar and Herman Teule, 107-123. Louvain: Peeters, 1999.

_____. "A Christian Reading of the Qur'an: The Legend of Sergius-Bahira and Its Use of Qur'an and Sira." In *Syrian Christians under Islam: The First Thousand Years*, ed. David Thomas, 57-73. Leiden: Brill, 2001.

_____. "The Debate between Patriarch John and an Emir of the Mhaggraye: A Reconsideration of the Earliest Christian-Muslim Debate." In *Christians and Muslims in Dialogue in the Islamic Orient of the Middle Ages*, ed. Martin Tamcke, 21-39. Beirut: Ergon Verlag, 2007.

_____. "The Confession which Ka'b al-Ahbar handed down to the Ishmaelites." In *Christian-Muslim Relations: A Bibliographical History, Volume One (600–900)*, eds. David Thomas and Barbara Roggema, 403-405. Leiden: Brill, 2009.

_____. "The Debate between Israel of Kashkar and al-Sarakhsi," in *Christian-Muslim Relations: A Bibliographical History, Volume One (600–900)*, eds. David Thomas and Barbara Roggema, 840-843. Leiden: Brill, 2009.

_____. *The Legend of Sergius Bahira: Eastern Christian Apologetics and Apocalyptic in Response to Islam*. Leiden: Brill, 2009.

Rowe, C. Kavin. *World Upside Down: Reading Acts in the Graeco-Roman Age*. Oxford: Oxford University Press, 2009.

Rubin, Uri. *The Eye of the Beholder: The Life of Muhammad as viewed by the Early Muslims*. Princeton, NJ: Darwin Press, 1995.

_____. *Between Bible and Qur'an: The Children of Israel and the Islamic Self-Image*. Princeton: Darwin Press, 1999.

_____. "Prophets and Caliphs: The Biblical Foundations of the Umayyad Authority." In *Method and Theory in the Study of Islamic Origins*, ed. Herbert Berg, 73-99. Lieden: Brill, 2003.

_____. "Prophets and Prophethood." In *Encyclopaedia of the Qur'an*, ed. Jane Dammen McAuliffe, vol. 4, 289-307. Leiden: Brill, 2004.

Rutgers, Leonard. *Making Myths: Jews in Early Christian Identity Formation*. Leuven: Peeters, 2009.

Saadi, Abdul-Massih. "The Letter of John of Sedreh: A New Perspective on Nascent Islam." *Karmo* 1/1 (1998): 18-31; 1/2 (1999): 46-64.

_____. "Nascent Islam in the Seventh Century Syriac Sources." In *The Qur'an in its Historical Context*, ed. Gabriel Said Reynolds, 217-222. London: Routledge, 2008.

Sahas, Daniel J. "The Art and Non-Art of Byzantine Polemics: Patterns of Refutation in Byzantine Anti-Islamic Literature." In *Indigenous Christian Communities in Islamic Lands, Eighth to Eighteenth Centuries*, ed. Michael Gervers and Ramzi Jibran Bikhazi, 55-73. Toronto: Pontifical Institute of Mediaeval Studies, 1990.

_____. "Sophronius, Patriarch of Jerusalem." In *Christian-Muslim Relations: A Bibliographical History, Volume One (600–900)*, eds. David Thomas and Barbara Roggema, 120-127. Leiden: Brill, 2009.

Sako, Louis. "Bibliographie du dialogue islamo-chrétien: Auteurs chrétiens de langue syriaque." *Islamochristiana* 10 (1984): 273-292.

Salah, Eid and Mark Swanson. "Masa'il wa-ajwiba 'aqliyya wa-ilahiyya." In *Christian-Muslim Relations: A Bibliographical History, Volume One (600–900)*, eds. David Thomas and Barbara Roggema, 661-663. Leiden: Brill, 2009.

Salibi, Kamal S, ed. "Muslim Perceptions of Christianity--Christian Perceptions of Islam: The historical record." *Islam and Christian-Muslim Relations* 7 (1996): 7-93.

Samir, Samir Khalil. *Misbah al-zulma fi idah al-khidma li-l-qass Shams al-Ri'asa Abu al-Barakat al-ma'ruf bi-Ibn Kabar* Cairo: Maktabat al-Karuz, 1971.

_____. "Deux cultures qui s'affrontent: une controverse sur l'i'rab au XI. siècle entre Elie de Nisibe et le vizir Abu l-Qasim." *Mélanges de l'Université Saint-Joseph* 49 (1975/1976): 619-649.

_____. "La réfutation de l'astrologie par Élie de Nisibe." *Orientalia Christiana Periodica* 43 (1977): 408-440.

_____. "Le Premier Entretien d'Élie de Nisibe avec le vizir al-Maġribi sur l'Unité et la Trinité." *Islamochristiana* 5 (1979): 31-117.

_____. "Bibliographie du Dialogue Islamo-Chretien: Auteurs arabes chrétiens du XIIIe siècle." *Islamochristiana* 7 (1981): 299-307.

_____. "Qui est l'interlocuteur musulman du patriarche syrien Jean III (631-648)?" In *IV Symposium Syriacum 1984*, ed. H.J.W. Drijvers, R. Lavenant, C. Molenberg and G.J. Reinink, Orientalia Christiana Analecta, vol. 229, 387-400. Rome: Pontifical Institute of Oriental Studies, 1987.

_____. "Langue arabe, logique et théologie chez Élie de Nisibe." *Mélanges de l'Université Saint-Joseph* 52 (1991/1992): 229-367.

_____. *Foi et Culture en Irak au XIe siècle: Elie de Nisibe et l'Islam*. Aldershot, England; Bookfield, VT: Variorum, 1996.

———. "Al-jadid fi sira Thawudurus Abi Qurra wa atharihi." *al-Machriq* 73 (1999): 417-449.

———. "Iliyya al-Nasibini (975-1046 A.D.) wa-l-wazir Abu-l-Qasim al-Maghribi (981-1027 A.D.)." *al-Machriq* 77 (2003): 83-105, 297.

———. "The Theological Christian Influence on the Qur'an: A Reflection." In *The Qur'an in its Historical Context*, ed. Gabriel Reynolds, 141-162. London: Routledge, 2008.

Samir, Samir Khalil, and Juan Pedro Monferrer-Sala, eds. *Abú Qurrah: vida, bibliografía y obras*. Córdoba: Universidad de Córdoba, 2005.

Sauter, Gerhard. "Dialogik II." In *Theologische Realenzyklopädie*, ed. Gerhard Krause and Gerhard Müller, vol. 8, 703-709. New York: Walter de Gruyter, 1981.

Schadler, Peter. "The Dialogue between a Saracen and a Christian." In *Christian-Muslim Relations: A Bibliographical History, Volume One (600–900)*, eds. David Thomas and Barbara Roggema, 367-370. Leiden: Brill, 2009.

Scher, Addai, ed. *Liber Scholiorum: Textus; Theodore bar Konai*, Corpus Scriptorum Christianorum Orientalium, vols. 55 & 59. Paris: E Typographeo Reipublicae, 1910-1912.

Scherer, Jean, ed. *Entretien d'Origèn avec Héraclide*. Paris: Cerf, 1960. Reprint, 2002.

Schmidt, P.L. "Zur Typologie Und Literarisierung Des Frühchristlichen Lateinischen Dialogs." In *Christianisme Et Formes Littéraires De L'antiquité Tardive En Occident: Huit Exposés Suivis De Discussions*, ed. Alan Cameron and Manfred Fuhrmann, 101-190. Geneva: Vandoeuvres, 1976.

Schopp, Ludwig, Denis J. Kavanagh, Robert P. Russell O.S.A., and Thomas F. Gilligan, eds. *The Happy Life, Answer to Skeptics, Divine Providence and the Problem of Evil, Soliloquies*. New York: Cima Publishing Company, 1948.

Setzer, Claudia. *Jewish Responses to Early Christians: History and Polemics, 30-150 C.E.* Minneapolis: Fortress Press, 1994.

Shahid, Irfan. *The Martyrs of Najrân: New Documents*. Subsidia hagiographica, 49. Brussels: Soc. des Bollandistes, 1971.

———. "Byzantium in South Arabia." *Dumbarton Oaks Papers* 33 (1979): 23-94.

———. *Byzantium and the Arabs in the Sixth Century*. 2 vols. Washington, DC: Dumbarton Oaks Research Library and Collection, 1995.

———. "Islam and *Oriens Christianus*: Makka 610-622 AD." In *The Encounter of Eastern Christianity with Early Islam*, eds. Emmanouela

Grypeou, Mark Swanson and David Thomas, 9-31. Leiden: Brill, 2006.

Shboul, Ahmad. "Byzantium and the Arabs: The Image of the Byzantines as Mirrored in Arabic Literature." In *Arab-Byzantine Relations in Early Islamic Times*, ed. Michael Bonner, 235-260. Aldershot, England: Ashgate Variorum, 2004.

Silverstein, Adam. *Islamic History: A Very Short Introduction.* Oxford: Oxford University Press, 2010.

Sinai, Nicolai. "Qur'anic Self-Referentiality as a Strategy of Self-Authorization." In *Self-Referentiality in the Qur'an*, ed. Stefan Wild, 103-134. Wiesbaden: Otto Harrassowitz, 2006.

––––––––. "The Qur'an as Process." In *The Qur'an in Context: Historical and Literary Investigations into the Qur'anic Milieu*, ed. Angelika Neuwirth, Nicolai Sinai, and Michael Marx, 407-439. Leiden: Brill, 2010.

Slusser, Michael, ed. *Dialogue with Trypho*, Selections from the Fathers of the Church, 3. Washington, D.C.: Catholic University of America Press, 2003.

Speight, Marston. "Christians in the Hadith Literature." In *Islamic Interpretations of Christianity*, ed. Lloyd Ridgeon, 30-53. New York: Saint Martin's Press, 2000.

Stroumsa, Sarah. "Qissat Mujadalat al-Usquf: A Case Study in Polemical Literature." In *Genizah Research after Ninety Years: the Case of Judaeo-Arabic*, ed. Joshua Blau and S. C. Reif, 155-159. Cambridge: Cambridge University Press, 1992.

––––––––. "Ibn al-Rawandi's *su adab al-mujadala*: The Role of Bad Manners in Medieval Disputations." In *The Majlis: Interreligious Encounters in Medieval Islam*, ed. Hava Lazarus-Yafeh, Mark R. Cohen, Sasson Somekh and Sidney Griffith, 66-83. Wiesbaden: Harrassowitz, 1999.

Stroumsa, Guy, and Sarah Stroumsa. "Aspects of Anti-Manichaean Polemics in Late Antiquity and under Early Islam." *Harvard Theological Review* 81 (1988): 37-58.

Suermann, Harald. "Orientalische Christen und der Islam: Christliche Texte aus der Zeit von 632-750." *Zeitschrift für Missionswissenschaft und Religionswissenschaft* 67 (1983): 120-136.

––––––––. "Une Controverse de Johannan de Litarb," *Parole de l'Orient* 15 (1988-1989): 197-213.

––––––––. "Timothy and his Concern for the School of Basos." *The Harp* 10 (1997): 51-58.

––––––––. "The Old Testament and the Jews in the Dialogue between the Jacobite Patriarch John I and 'Umayr ibn Sa'd al-Ansari." In

Eastern Crossroads: Essays on Medieval Christian Legacy, ed. Juan Pedro Monferrer-Sala, 131-141. Piscataway, NJ: Gorgias, 2007.

_____. "Anmerkungen zu alter und Funktion der Diskussion des Koptischen Patriarchen Johannes III. (677-686) vor dem Statthalter 'Abd al-'Aziz." *Parole de l'Orient* 32 (2007): 389-398.

_____. "The Disputation of Patriarch John." In *Christian-Muslim Relations: A Bibliographical History, Volume One (600–900)*, eds. David Thomas and Barbara Roggema, 253-255. Leiden: Brill, 2009.

_____. "John the Stylite of Mar Z'ura at Sarug." In *Christian-Muslim Relations: A Bibliographical History, Volume One (600–900)*, eds. David Thomas and Barbara Roggema, 314-316. Leiden: Brill, 2009.

_____. "Early Islam in the Light of Christian and Jewish Sources." In *The Qur'an in Context: Historical and Literary Investigations into the Qur'anic Milieu*, ed. Angelika Neuwirth, Nicolai Sinai, and Michael Marx, 135-148. Leiden: Brill, 2010.

Swanson, Mark. "Beyond Prooftexting: Approaches to the Qur'an in Some Early Arabic Christian Apologies." *Muslim World* 86 (1998): 297-319.

_____. "The Christian al-Ma'mun Tradition." In *Christians at the heart of Islamic Rule, Church Life and Scholarship in 'Abbasid Iraq*, ed. David Thomas. Leiden; Boston: Brill, 2003.

_____. "Apologetics, Catechesis, and the Question of Audience in 'On the Triune Nature of God' (Sinai Arabic 154) and Three Treatises of Theodore Abu Qurrah." In *Christians and Muslims in Dialogue in the Islamic Orient of the Middle Ages*, ed. Martin Tamcke, 113-134. Beirut: Ergon Verlag, 2007.

_____. "A Christian Arabic Disputation (PSR 438)." In *Christian-Muslim Relations: A Bibliographical History, Volume One (600–900)*, eds. David Thomas and Barbara Roggema, 386-387. Leiden: Brill, 2009.

_____. "Vienna, Papyrus Erzherzog Rainer – Inv. Ar. Pap. Nr. 10.000." In *Christian-Muslim Relations: A Bibliographical History, Volume One (600–900)*, eds. David Thomas and Barbara Roggema, 654-655. Leiden: Brill, 2009.

_____. "The Disputation of the Monk Ibrahim al-Tabarani." In *Christian-Muslim Relations: A Bibliographical History, Volume One (600–900)*, eds. David Thomas and Barbara Roggema, 876-881. Leiden: Brill, 2009.

Szilágyi, Krisztina. "Muhammad and the Monk: The Making of the Christian Bahira Legend." *Jerusalem Studies in Arabic and Islam* 34 (2008): 169-214.

Tajaddud, Rizza, ed. *Kitab al-Fihrist lil-Nadim*. Tehran, 1971.

Tartar, Georges, ed. *Dialogue islamo-chrétien sous le calife Al-Ma'mûn (813-834): Les épîtres d'Al-Hashimî et d'Al-Kindî*. Paris: Nouvelles Editions Latines, 1985.

Teule, Herman. "Ta'rikh: Christian Arabic Historiography." In *Encyclopaedia of Islam, Second Edition*, vol. 12, 807-809. Leiden: Brill, 2004.

Thomas, David. "Two Muslim-Christian Debates from the Early Shi'ite Tradition." *Journal of Semitic Studies* 33 (1988): 53-80.

————. "The Bible in Early Muslim Anti-Christian Polemic." *Islam and Christian-Muslim Relations* 7 (1996): 29-38.

————., ed. *Christian Doctrines in Islamic Theology*. Leiden: Brill, 2008.

Thomas, David and Barbara Roggema, eds. *Christian-Muslim Relations: A Bibliographical History, Volume One (600–900)*. Leiden: Brill, 2009.

Thomson, Robert. "Armenian Variations on the Bahira Legend." In *Eucharisterion: Essays Presented to Omeljian Pritsak*, ed. Ihor Ševčenko and Frank E. Sysyn, vol. 2, 884-895. Cambridge, MA: Ukrainian Research Institute, 1979-80.

Tien, Anton, ed. *Risalat 'Abdallah b. Isma'il al-Hashimi ila 'Abd al-Masih b. Ishaq al-Kindi yad'u-hu bi-ha ila l-Islam*. London: Society for Promoting Christian Knowledge, 1885. Reprint, 1912.

Toral-Niehoff, Isabel. "The 'Ibad of Al-Hira: An Arab Christian Community of Late Antique Iraq." In *The Qur'an in Context: Historical and Literary Investigations into the Qur'anic Milieu*, ed. Angelika Neuwirth, Nicolai Sinai, and Michael Marx, 323-347. Leiden: Brill, 2010.

Trimingham, J. Spencer. *Christianity among the Arabs in Pre-Islamic Times*. London: Longman, 1979.

Turner, Colin, ed. *The Koran: Critical Concepts in Islamic Studies, vol. 2: Themes and Doctrines: Form, Content, and Literary Structure*. London: RoutledgeCurzon, 2004.

Vajda, Georges. "Ahl Al-Kitab." In *Encyclopaedia of Islam, Second Edition*, vol. 1, 264-266. Leiden: Brill, 1960.

van Bladel, Kevin. "The *Alexander Legend* in the Qur'an 18:83-102." In *The Qur'an in its Historical Context*, ed. Gabriel Said Reynolds, 175-203. London: Routledge, 2008.

van der Toorn, Karel. "The ancient Near Eastern literary dialogue as a vehicle of critical reflection." In *Dispute Poems and Dialogues in the Ancient and Mediaeval Near East*, ed. Gerrit J. Reinink and H. L. J. Vanstiphout, 59-75. Louvain: Departement Oriëntalistiek, 1991.

van Ess, Josef. "Early Development of *Kalam*." In *Studies on the First Century of Islamic Society*, ed. G. H. A. Juynboll, 109-123. Carbondale: Southern Illinois University Press, 1982.

van Rompay, Lucas. "Past and Present Perceptions of the Syriac Literary Tradition." *Hugoye: Journal of Syriac Studies* 3 (2000): http://syrcom.cua.edu/Hugoye/Vol3No1/HV3N1VanRompay.html.

Varner, William, ed. *Ancient Jewish-Christian Dialogues: Athanasius and Zacchaeus, Simon and Theophilus, Timothy and Aquila: Introductions, Texts, and Translations*. Lewiston, NY: E. Mellen Press, 2004.

Vatican Borgia arabic MS 135.

Villagomez, Cynthia. "Christian Salvation through Muslim Domination: Divine Punishment and Syriac Apocalyptic Expectation in the Seventh and Eighth Centuries." *Medieval Encounters* 4 (1998): 203-218.

Volgers, Annelie, and Claudio Zamagni, eds. *Erotapokriseis: Early Christian Question-and-Answer Literature in Context. Proceedings of the Utrecht Colloquium, 13-14 October 2003*. Louvain: Peeters, 2004.

Vollers, Kurt. "Das Religionsgespräch von Jerusalem (Um 800 D) aus dem Arabischen Übersetzt." *Zeitschrift für Kirchengeschichte* 29 (1908): 29-71, 197-221.

Voss, Bernd Reiner. *Der Dialog in der frühchristlichen Literatur*. Munich: Wilhelm Fink Verlag, 1970.

Waardenburg, Jacques. *Muslim Perceptions of Other Religions: A Historical Survey*. New York: Oxford University Press, 1999.

_____. "Towards a Periodization of Earliest Islam According to its Relations with Other Religions." In *The Qur'an: Style and Contents*, ed. Andrew Rippin, 93-115. Aldershot: Ashgate Variorum, 2001.

Wagner, E. "Munazara." In *Encyclopaedia of Islam, Second Edition*, ed. C. E. Bosworth, et al, vol. 7, 565-568. Leiden: Brill, 1993.

Walker, Joel Thomas. *The Legend of Mar Qardagh: Narrative and Christian Heroism in Late Antique Iraq*. Berkeley: University of California Press, 2006.

Wansbrough, John E. *The Sectarian Milieu: Content and Composition of Islamic Salvation History*. London Oriental Series, vol. 34. Oxford: Oxford University Press, 1978.

Wasserstein, David. "The Majlis of al-Rida: A Religious Debate in the Court of the Caliph al-Ma'mun as Represented in a Shi'i Hagiographical Work about the Eighth Imam 'Ali ibn Musa Al-Rida." In *The Majlis: Interreligious Encounters in Medieval Islam*, ed. Hava Lazarus-

Yafeh, Mark R. Cohen, Sasson Somekh and Sidney Griffith, 108-119. Wiesbaden: Harrassowitz, 1999.

Wasserstrom, Steven. *Between Muslim and Jew: The Problem of Symbiosis under Early Islam*. Princeton: Princeton University Press, 1995.

Watt, W. Montgomery. *Muslim-Christian Encounters: Perceptions and Misperceptions*. London: Routledge, 1991.

Wild, Stefan. "Why Self-Referentiality?" In *Self-Referentiality in the Qur'an*, ed. Stefan Wild, 1-23. Wiesbaden: Otto Harrassowitz, 2006.

———. "Lost in Philology? The Virgins of Paradise and the Luxenberg Hypothesis." In *The Qur'an in Context: Historical and Literary Investigations into the Qur'anic Milieu*, ed. Angelika Neuwirth, Nicolai Sinai, and Michael Marx, 625-647. Leiden: Brill, 2010.

Wild, Stefan, ed. *The Qur'an as Text*. Leiden: Brill, 1996.

———, ed. *Self-Referentiality in the Qur'an*. Wiesbaden: Otto Harrassowitz, 2006.

Wilde, Clare "Is There Room for Corruption in the 'Books' of God?" In *The Bible in Arab Christianity*, ed. David Thomas, 225-240. Leiden: Brill, 2007.

Ye'or, Bat. *The Dhimmi: Jews and Christians under Islam*. Rutherford: Fairleigh Dickinson University Press, 1985.

———. *The Decline of Eastern Christianity under Islam: From Jihad to Dhimmitude*. 2nd ed. Teaneck, NJ: Fairleigh Dickinson University Press, 2002.

Young, M. J. L., J. D. Latham, and R. B. Serjeant, eds., *Religion, Learning, and Science in the 'Abbasid Period* (Cambridge: Cambridge University Press, 1990

Young, William. *Patriarch, Shah, and Caliph: A Study of the Relationships of the Church of the East with the Sassanid Empire and the Early Caliphates up to 820 A.D., with special reference to available translated Syriac sources*. Rawalpindi: Christian Study Centre, 1974.

Zebiri, Kate. "Towards a rhetorical criticism of the Qur'an." *Journal of Qur'anic Studies* 5 (2003): 95-120.

———. "Polemic and Polemical Language." In *Encylopaedia of the Qur'an*, ed. Jane D. McAuliffe, vol. 4, 114-125. Leiden: Brill, 2004.

———. "Argumentation." In *The Blackwell Companion to the Qur'an*, ed. Andrew Rippin, 266-281. Malden, MA: Blackwell, 2006.

Zimmerman, Odo John, ed. *Saint Gregory the Great: Dialogues*. Washington, DC: Catholic University of America Press, 1959. Reprint, 2007.

INDEX

'Abd al-Malik, Maslama ibn, 87, 138
'Abdisho, 138
'Umar ibn al-Khattab, 96, 98, 99, 100, 103, 104, 105, 106, 204
'Uthman, 96, 98, 106, 204
Abbasid, 9, 81, 109, 112, 113, 147, 214, 231
Abi Talib, 'Ali ibn, 14, 94, 95, 97, 98, 99, 101, 102, 103, 104, 105, 106, 107, 108, 123, 180, 198, 203, 204
Abo of Tiflis, 167
Abraham, 57, 62, 63, 64, 78, 90, 140, 189, 210, 211, 215
Abraham of Bet Hale, 138
Abraham of Tiberias, 199, 200, 201, 202, 203, 204, 205, 206, 207, 208, 209, 210, 211
Abu al-Barakat, Shams al-Ri'asa (Ibn Kabar), 213
Abu Bakr, 95, 96, 98, 99, 100, 101, 106, 123, 204
Abu Qurra, John, 159, 160, 162, 163, 164
Abu Qurra, Theodore, 182, 183, 184, 185, 186, 188, 190, 191, 212, 213, 214, 217, 219, 222, 224, 226, 237, 239
Abu Zayd, Nasr Hamid, 71

Adam, 189, 214, 215, 222
Against the Christian Abu Qurra, 111
Against the Magi in Nisibis, 41
Against the Outsiders, 182, 186, 190
al-'Absi, al-Manzur ibn Ghatafan, 205, 206
al-Ahbar, Ka'b, 126, 128
al-Ansari, 'Umayr Ibn Sa'd, 88
al-Bahili, 207, 208
al-Basri (Muslim pilgrim), 208, 209, 210
al-Basri, Sa'sa'a ibn Khalid, 219, 220, 221, 222
al-Bukhari, 116
Aleppo, 18, 234
Alexander Legend, 53
Alexandria, 34, 35, 186
al-Hakam, Hisham ibn, 16, 175, 177, 191
al-Hamadhani, 'Abd al-Jabbar, 243
al-Hamdani, Salam ibn Mu'awiya, 219
al-Hashimi, 'Abd al-Rahman, 199, 200, 211
al-Hashimi, Muhammad ibn 'Abd Allah, 216
al-Jahiz, 'Amr Ibn Bahr, 110, 111, 243

al-Kazim, Musa, 16, 175, 176, 178, 179, 180, 181, 182, 191
al-Khuza'i, Harun ibn Hashim, 218
al-Kindi, 'Abd al-Masih, 126
al-Ma'mun, 17, 159, 163, 164, 184, 195, 196, 212, 214, 215, 219, 223, 224, 226
al-Maghribi, Abu al-Qasim al-Husayn ibn 'Ali, 17, 232, 233, 234, 236
al-Mahdi, 15, 147, 148, 150, 152, 153, 154, 155, 156, 157, 158, 164, 198
al-Malik, 'Abd al-'Aziz, 231
al-Mushammar, al-Malik, 234
al-Rashid, 235
al-Rida, 'Ali ibn Musa, 16, 159, 195
al-Sadiq, Ja'far, 175, 176, 178
al-Sarakhsi, 168
al-Sirafi, Abu Sa'id, 135
al-Tabari, 'Ali ibn Rabban, 194
Ambrose of Milan, 147
Amphilochius of Iconium, 147
Analogical reasoning, 27, 157, 162, 189, 209
Antioch, 34, 35, 87
Apocalyptic, 53, 75, 78, 124, 125, 126, 131
Apologetic, 1, 28, 89, 94, 131, 135, 165, 178, 189, 194, 214, 224, 228, 238, 241, 243
Apostasy, 112, 169, 211
Arabia, 35, 54, 55, 104, 117, 179
Arabic, 12, 19, 34, 40, 54, 78, 79, 80, 81, 84, 95, 112, 135, 137, 147, 163, 228, 233
Arabization, 73, 238

Arabs, 76, 78, 79, 127, 139, 144, 194, 218, 220
Aramaic, 12, 19, 54
Aristotelian dialectic, 1, 32, 40, 240
Aristotle, 147
Armenia and Armenians, 35, 84, 125, 184, 186
Asia, 35, 243
Athanasius, 32, 147
Augustine, 31
Babai the Great, 35, 41
Baghdad, 111, 112, 136, 147, 163, 175, 212, 234
Baptism, 134, 144, 172, 215, 235
Bar Daysan, 39
Bar Koni, Theodore, 126, 133, 134
Baradeus, Jacob, 35
Bariha, 16, 175, 176, 177, 178, 179, 191, 243
Bashir, 169, 170, 171, 172
Basil of Caesarea, 147
Believers, 5, 56, 57, 58, 60, 61, 62, 63, 64, 69, 77, 78, 79, 80, 82, 83, 90, 96, 100, 101, 103, 107, 108, 117, 120
Bet Hale, 15, 126, 138
Bible
   1 Chronicles 1:29-31, 79
   1 Corinthians 3:2, 142
   1 Samuel 21:3-6, 26
   Acts 2:1-4, 151
   Acts 6:8-9, 29
   Acts 17:1-4, 29
   Acts 26:1-7 and 24-29, 30
   Daniel, 78, 210
   Deuteronomy 6:4, 90
   Deuteronomy 6:5, 27
   Deuteronomy 9:5, 144

Genesis, 25
Genesis 1:21-23, 149
Genesis 1:26-27, 223
Genesis 2:7, 214
Genesis 11:22-26, 215
Genesis 11:26-12:8, 215
Genesis 11:31, 183
Genesis 16:1-16, 78
Genesis 17:1-14, 215
Genesis 17:20, 79
Genesis 19:24, 92
Genesis 21:13, 79
Genesis 25:12-18, 79
Hebrews 5:12-13, 142
Isaiah 7:14, 153
Isaiah 21:7, 198
Job, 21, 23, 24
Job 1:21, 24
John 1:1, 220
John 1:4-9, 220
John 3:1-15, 28
John 3:5, 144
John 4:5-29, 28
John 6:41-59, 28
John 8:12, 220
John 14:26, 151, 198
John 15:26, 151, 198
John 16:5-8, 198
John 16:13-15, 151
John 16:14, 151
John 18:33-38, 28
John 20:17, 149, 198, 219
Leviticus 19:18, 27
Luke 1:28-36, 141
Luke 4:1-13, 26
Luke 5:17-26, 26
Luke 6:1-5, 26
Luke 10:25-37, 27
Luke 15:11-32, 144
Luke 20:1-8, 27

Luke 20:20-26, 27
Luke 22:66-71, 28
Mark 2:1-12, 26
Mark 2:23-28, 26
Mark 7:24-30, 27
Mark 10:18, 152
Mark 11:27-33, 27
Mark 12:13-17, 27
Mark 14:55-65, 27
Matthew, 25
Matthew 4:1-11, 26
Matthew 5:45, 203
Matthew 8:23-27, 224
Matthew 9:1-8, 26
Matthew 12:1-8, 26
Matthew 14:24-32, 224
Matthew 14-15, 224
Matthew 15:21-28, 27
Matthew 17:24-27, 208
Matthew 21:23-27, 27
Matthew 22:15-22, 27
Matthew 26:59-68, 27
Psalm 32/33:6, 151
Psalm 71/72:17, 153
Psalm 109/110:1, 221
Bishop, 35, 104, 111, 117, 168, 182, 184, 212, 213
Book of Sessions, 232
Byzantine Empire, 34, 69, 133, 169
Byzantine Orthodoxy, 33
Catechesis, 127, 158, 228, 238, 242
Catholic, 36
Catholicos, 148, 160
Chalcedonians, 33, 34, 36, 37, 41, 54, 86
China, 35, 36
Christian Bahira Legend, 124
Christianity, 2, 8, 32, 34, 54, 56

Christians
- Communities, 4, 7, 34, 40, 43, 54, 55, 76, 89, 92, 104, 118, 135, 147
- Decline, 73, 247
- Evangelization, 63
- Language, 80, 81, 84, 228
- Relations with Muslims, 2, 4, 6, 7, 9, 48, 49, 50, 56, 57, 58, 59, 61, 62, 63, 64, 68, 72, 73, 78, 80, 81, 83, 84, 85, 95, 107, 110, 112, 114, 116, 130, 131, 162, 194, 195, 209, 212, 217, 220, 226, 228, 229, 233, 237, 238
- Scripture and Worship, 8, 23, 25, 78, 80, 89, 108, 142, 143, 146, 153, 173, 193, 198, 206, 207, 211, 225, 229, 235

Christology, 23, 28, 34, 36, 59, 61, 67, 82, 86, 102, 118, 119, 129, 134, 140, 145, 155, 221, 222, 232

Chronicle of 1234, 212

Chrysostom, John, 25

Church of the East, 5, 7, 15, 17, 33, 35, 36, 40, 41, 43, 54, 74, 76, 82, 133, 135, 140, 145, 146, 147, 155, 163, 168, 176, 200, 231, 232, 233

Church of the Resurrection (Holy Sepulchre), 186

Circumcision, 140, 215

Commander of the Believers, 98, 99, 101, 102, 103, 104, 155, 203

Companions of the Cave, 66

Constantinople, 33, 34, 37, 38, 170, 211

Conversion, 3, 13, 14, 18, 63, 73, 74, 87, 94, 95, 97, 98, 99, 103, 104, 106, 107, 108, 113, 131, 169, 178, 179, 180, 182, 199, 211, 227, 229, 231, 238, 243

Copts and Coptic, 35, 84, 200, 213, 231

Councils, Christian Churches, 33, 34, 36, 37, 42

Court, 17, 29, 147, 164, 172, 195, 211, 212, 214, 234, 241, 244, 245, 246, 247

Creation, 25, 140, 157, 203, 214, 222, 223

Cross, 127, 140, 142, 171, 210, 211, 231, 235

Crosspollination, 4, 8, 12, 23, 43, 53, 70, 72, 228, 237

Crusades, 5, 17, 231, 236

Cyril of Alexandria, 35

Dhimma and Dhimmi (Subject peoples), 84, 242

Dialectic and dialectical reasoning (kalam), 11, 83, 114, 137, 146, 152, 155, 162, 164, 171, 172, 178, 184, 187, 188, 216, 240, 244

Dialogue of Jacob the Newly Baptized, 75

Dialogue on True Faith in God, 32

Dialogue with Heraclides, 32

Dialogue with Trypho the Jew, 31

Diodore, 147

Disputation against a Heretical Bishop, 41

Disputations against the Severians, Manichaeans, Cantaye, and Mandraye, 41
East Syrian. *See* Church of the East
Edessa, 142, 183
Education and Schools, 15, 19, 35, 36, 40, 80, 82, 99, 133, 135, 137, 145, 146, 147, 165, 185, 228, 236, 237, 242
Elias of Nisibis, 17, 231, 232, 233, 234, 236
Ephrem the Syrian, 40, 147
Eranistes, 32
Ethiopia and Ethiopians, 35, 55, 56, 89, 115, 117
Eucharist, 28, 134, 215
Eve, 149, 214
Exegesis, 13, 48, 57, 67, 71, 193, 198
Gabriel, 127, 204
George the Monk, 18, 231, 234, 235, 236
Georgia and Georgians, 35, 84, 167
Ghassanids, 55
Gospel, 25, 26, 27, 28, 54, 59, 84, 89, 92, 97, 99, 115, 178, 196, 197, 198, 207, 219
Greece and Greeks, 19, 20, 21, 31, 32, 33, 34, 35, 36, 38, 40, 41, 53, 54, 66, 80, 84, 89, 92, 112, 133, 135, 147, 183, 184, 197, 205, 241
Gregory of Nazianzus, 147
Gregory of Nyssa, 32
Gregory the Great, 31
Griffith, Sidney, 78, 126, 129, 169, 194, 240
Hagar, 78, 79

Hagarenes, 79, 89, 92, 93
Hagiography, 116, 167, 168, 179, 211
Harran, 182, 183, 184, 212, 213
Hasan, 97, 203
Hebrew, 19, 72, 125
Hellenism and Hellenistic thought, 8, 26, 81, 112, 240, 244
Heraclius, 76
Himyar and Himyarites, 117
Hippolytus of Rome, 147
Historiography, 1, 11, 117, 121, 124, 128, 130, 168, 174, 185, 191
Holy Spirit, 25, 90, 91, 141, 154, 223, 235
Hoyland, Robert, 112, 144
Husayn, 97, 203
Iblis, 205, 208
Ibn 'Alqama, Abu Haritha, 117
Ibn al-Nadim, 184
Ibn Babawayh al-Qummi, Muhammad ibn 'Ali, 243
Ibn Fayruz, Mutammim, 181
Ibn Hazm, 194
Ibn Hisham, 'Abd al-Malik, 14, 115
Ibn Ishaq, Muhammad, 14, 115, 116, 117, 118, 119, 120, 121
Ibn Nawfal, Waraqa, 116
Ibn Qurra, 159, 162, 163, 164
Ibn Sa'di, Ahmad ibn Muhammad, 136
Ibn Subayh al-Murdar, 'Isa, 111, 185
Ibn Yahya, Safwan, 160, 161, 162, 164
Ibn Yunus, Matta, 136
Icons, 142, 173, 174

Imams, 106, 167, 175, 176, 178, 181, 182, 191, 199
Incarnation, 61, 67, 69, 90, 150, 173, 205, 232, 235, 243
India and Indians, 35, 89, 180, 181
Inductive reasoning, 157, 165, 187, 190
Isaac, 62, 63, 79, 140, 177
Ishmael, 62, 63, 79, 177, 202, 203, 210
Isho'yahb III, 76
Islamicization, 73, 238
Israel, 27, 90, 197
Israel of Kashkar, 168
Jacob of Sarug, 40
Jacobites, 7, 35, 37, 41, 43, 55, 74, 77, 82, 86, 135, 155, 158, 183, 232
Jerusalem, 17, 34, 63, 75, 129, 181, 183, 185, 186, 200, 201, 215
Jesus Christ, 39, 75, 140, 142, 189, 215, 221, 222, 226, 235, 240
    Christian Christology, 8, 26, 34, 35, 36, 90, 140, 148, 150, 151, 162, 205, 215, 220, 235
    Islamic Christology, 86, 102, 118, 152, 157, 177, 208, 243
    Word and Spirit, 141, 150, 152, 155, 162, 218, 220, 222
Jews, 29, 32, 42, 49, 53, 57, 62, 63, 64, 65, 69, 89, 90, 91, 97, 122, 152, 153, 186, 193, 206, 209, 240
Jihad, 1
John III, Coptic Patriarch, 231
John of Apamea, 39
John of Damascus, 126, 143
John of Edessa, 167
John of Sedra, 87, 88, 108
Judaism, 29, 30, 63, 70, 90, 95, 216
Justin Martyr, 31, 147
Justinian, 41
Ka'ba, 211
Lakhmids, 54
Lamoreaux, John, 186
Late Antiquity, 34, 38, 70
Latin, 31, 33, 125
Leo III, 169
Liturgy, 34, 40, 80, 82, 119, 146, 147
Mandaeans, 113
Mar Sabas, 168, 185
Marcus Minucius Felix, 31
Maronites, 36
Martyrs and martyrdom, 41, 143, 167, 168, 191, 211
Mary, 39, 59, 67, 68, 90, 149, 171, 209, 210, 220
Maximus the Confessor, 37
Mecca, 53, 181, 211, 236
Medina, 53, 95, 98, 99, 104, 116, 117, 119, 178, 179, 181
Mediterranean, 19, 22, 37, 38, 41, 70
Melkites, 7, 34, 35, 42, 82, 135, 155, 158, 185, 232
Mesopotamia, 185
Messiah, 8, 28, 30, 78, 153, 196, 222
Methodius of Olympus, 32
Michael of Mar Sabas, 168
Miracles, 101, 151, 155, 197, 205, 206, 220, 234, 235

Monasticism, 59, 234
Monks, 56, 106, 121, 137, 139, 145, 177, 234, 237
Monophysites, 33, 35
Monotheism, 49, 57, 63, 119, 123, 126, 153, 233
Monothelitism, 36
Mosaic Law, 91, 150
Moses, 29, 90, 105, 117, 180, 205
Muhammad
  Bahira, 125, 126, 127, 128, 129, 142
  biography, 14, 15, 95, 115, 116, 117, 119, 120, 122, 123, 130, 131, 143, 240
  family of, 181, 182, 204
  prophecy, 114, 115, 120, 121, 122, 151, 177, 196, 197, 198, 199, 229, 233, 235, 243
  Qur'an, 53, 56, 58, 120, 206, 223
  views of, 141, 153, 161, 203, 204, 207, 210, 211, 219, 234, 239
Muslims
  Communities, 7, 8, 78, 80, 101, 116, 200, 242, 245
  Language, 80, 110
  Relations with Christians, 2, 4, 6, 7, 82, 84, 85, 86, 107, 109, 111, 112, 123, 130, 131, 158, 161, 162, 188, 195, 216, 217, 226, 228, 229, 233, 237, 244, 247
  Scripture and Worship, 85, 93, 143, 151, 193, 194, 206, 208, 211
Muslims and Others in Early Islamic Society, 112
Najran, 14, 16, 104, 115, 117, 118, 119, 120, 179, 180, 181, 182
Narsai, 35
Nazarenes, 53
Nestorians. *See* Church of the East
Nestorius, 147
Nicodemus, 28, 144
Nisibis, 40
Noah, 53
Octavius, 31
On Heresies, 126, 143
On the Triune Nature of God, 222
On the Virtues of the Soul, 184
Oral Traditions (hadith), 145, 159, 169, 198, 225, 228, 244
Origen, 32
Pahlavi, 19, 147
Palestine, 34, 54, 55
Paraclete, 151
Paul the Apostle, 25, 29, 30
Paul the Persian, 37
People of the Book, 53, 57, 58, 59, 60, 64, 84, 193, 217, 218, 229, 247
Persia and Persians, 19, 35, 37, 42, 84, 89
Peter, 208, 209
Pharisees, 26
Philoxenus of Mabbug, 35
Plato, 20
Pluralism, 1, 107, 227, 247
Poetry, 1, 40, 169
Poll tax (jizya), 209
Polyphony, 4, 72, 245
Pontius Pilate, 28

Prayer, 63, 92, 128, 139, 143, 146, 150, 151, 171, 172, 173, 201, 207, 208, 209, 211, 215
Prophethood, 116, 117, 120, 122, 123, 124, 127, 151, 153, 199, 204, 205, 233, 243
Questions-and-Answers, 134, 135, 186, 190
Qur'an
   2:34, 208
   2:35, 214
   2:80, 62
   2:88, 63
   2:91, 63
   2:105, 58
   2:109, 58
   2:111, 59, 62
   2:113, 63
   2:116, 67, 221
   2:135, 57, 64, 78
   2:135-142, 62
   2:140, 63
   2:170, 63
   3, 68, 71, 120
   3:3-4, 59
   3:24, 62
   3:39, 210
   3:42, 210
   3:43, 113, 118
   3:45, 222
   3:48, 152
   3:48-56, 56
   3:49, 209
   3:52, 202, 206, 209
   3:59, 102, 170, 216, 222, 223
   3:59-61, 60, 68
   3:61, 120
   3:64, 59
   3:67, 78, 202
   3:69, 60
   3:70 and 98, 60
   3:71-73, 60, 64
   3:78, 66
   3:83, 218
   3:85, 202, 218
   3:95, 78
   3:102, 208
   3:113-114, 218
   3:171, 60
   3:200, 203
   4:43, 207, 208
   4:49, 201
   4:116, 220
   4:125, 78
   4:157, 69, 86, 206
   4:158, 210
   4:171, 59, 141, 145, 202, 205, 209, 216, 220
   5:3, 201
   5:17, 68
   5:18, 65
   5:44, 201
   5:46, 201
   5:47, 54, 92
   5:48, 219
   5:51, 56
   5:60, 209
   5:65, 60
   5:72, 68
   5:73, 59, 118, 171
   5:77, 233
   5:82, 56, 220
   5:82-83, 56
   5:82-85, 144
   5:116, 220
   5:116-118, 46
   5:116-119, 57
   6:70, 203
   6:74-75, 215
   6:91, 65

6:100-101, 67
6:161, 78
7:19, 214
7:53, 205
7:181, 218
7:187, 62
9:29, 208
9:30, 60
10:38, 65
11:13, 65
11:35, 65
11:119, 219
14:35, 215
15:28-29, 214
16:24, 65
16:101-103, 65
16:103, 124, 163
16:120, 123, 78
16:125, 57
17:1, 129
18:9-26, 66
18:22, 66
18:54, 52
18:83-102, 53
19, 68, 71
19:21, 113, 118
19:34, 151
19:36-37, 60
19:71, 219
21:5, 65
22:17, 221
23:23-30, 53
25, 60
25:4-5, 65
25:5, 124
25:7, 206
28:48, 65
29:46, 57, 217
32:3, 65
32:9, 214, 216, 222

33:40, 202
33:56, 209
34:24, 203
34:29-31, 62
34:43, 65
37:99-111, 189
38:75, 214, 223
39:4, 221
43:81, 67
44:54, 219
46:9, 203
46:12, 201
49:13, 203
49:14, 218
52:20, 219
53:7-8, 10, 209
57:27, 59
58, 52
61:6, 196
90:1, 3, 221
98:6, 60

Reinink, Gerrit, 138, 144
Rhetoric, 9, 16, 18, 20, 86, 133, 161, 163, 165, 168, 172, 186, 190, 222, 225, 228, 243, 245
Roggema, Barbara, 123, 129, 130
Romanos the Melodist, 40
Romans, 89
Sabaeans, 235
Salman the Persian, 97, 101
Salvation, 62, 70, 90, 101, 109, 117, 140, 152, 203, 210, 218, 222, 233, 235, 239
Saracens, 75
Sasanian Empire, 41, 54
Satan, 23, 26, 152, 205
Scholion, 133, 134
Sectarian milieu, 237
Seleucia-Ctesiphon, 40, 112

Sergius-Bahira, 15, 122, 123, 125, 126, 127, 129, 130, 131, 142
Severus of Antioch, 35
Shi'ite Islam, 159, 175, 176, 179
Sinai, Nicolai, 48
Son of God, 26, 49, 57, 60, 67, 118, 134, 141, 148, 200, 206, 208, 221, 235
Sophronius, 75
Stroumsa, Sarah, 246
Sufi, 159
Sulpitius Severus, 31
Sunni, 8, 86, 94, 95, 97, 98, 99, 101, 104, 106, 108, 116, 123, 136, 159, 160, 169, 175, 177, 178, 195, 203, 204, 231
Surat Al 'Imran, 122
Surat al-Baqara, 122, 143, 221
Surat al-Zumar, 221
Symposium, or on Virginity, 32
Syria, 121, 181, 185
Testimony collections, 91, 145
Theodicy, 21, 23, 24
Theodore of Mopsuestia, 35
Theodoret of Cyrrhus, 32
Timothy I, Patriarch, 15, 145, 155, 164, 198
Torah, 59, 70, 78, 89, 90, 91, 92, 97, 116, 143, 180, 193, 197, 215
Translation movement, 112, 135
Trinitarian, 82, 145, 150, 153, 154, 168, 173, 187, 223, 235
Trinity, 49, 61, 90, 118, 141, 142, 145, 150, 151, 154, 157, 223, 232, 240, 243
van Bladel, Kevin, 53
Veneration, 127, 134, 142, 143, 172, 173, 210, 211, 235
  Islamic, 211
Waardenburg, Jacques, 86
Wansbrough, John, 115
Wasil of Damascus, 16, 169, 170, 174, 190, 244
West Syrian. *See* Jacobites
Word of God, 141, 149, 150, 152, 162, 205, 209, 210, 216, 218, 223, 226, 233, 235
Zoroastrians, 113, 136, 195

www.ingramcontent.com/pod-product-compliance
Lightning Source LLC
Chambersburg PA
CBHW031707230426
43668CB00006B/143